REDS OR RACKETS?

REDS OR RACKETS?

The Making of Radical and Conservative Unions on the Waterfront

HOWARD KIMELDORF

UNIVERSITY OF CALIFORNIA PRESS

BERKELEY   LOS ANGELES   LONDON

University of California Press
Berkeley and Los Angeles, California

University of California Press, Ltd.
London, England

© 1988 by
The Regents of the University of California

Library of Congress Cataloging-in-Publication Data

Kimeldorf, Howard.
    Reds or rackets? : the making of radical and conservative unions
on the waterfront / Howard Kimeldorf.
        p.   cm.
    Bibliography: p.
    Includes index.
    ISBN 0−520−06308−2 (alk. paper)
        1. International Longshoremen's and Warehousemen's Union—History.
2. Trade-unions—United States—Political activity—History—20th
century.   3. Trade-unions and communism—United States—History —
20th century.   4. Trade-unions and foreign policy—United States—
History—20th century.   I. Title.
HD6515.L82I575   1988
331.88'11'387164—dc19   88−40239
                                                                CIP

Printed in the United States of America
1 2 3 4 5 6 7 8 9

To Fay
and the Memory of Don

Contents

Preface

In the fall of 1985, as President Ronald Reagan was preparing for his first summit meeting with Soviet leader Mikhail Gorbachev, questions were raised from many quarters about whether the president, with his lack of diplomatic experience, was really the best person to carry out such an important mission. Coming to the president's defense, an aide replied that Reagan had been "dealing with communism" for almost four decades. He then went on to relate one of Reagan's favorite anecdotes, about the time he took a cruise ship to Hawaii, and West Coast longshoremen, denouncing him as "that anti-communist," refused to handle his baggage. That incident occurred nearly forty years ago. In 1988, radical longshoremen on the Pacific are still at it, refusing to handle military cargo destined for South Africa, Chile, and El Salvador, three of President Reagan's most loyal client states.

Longshoremen on the East Coast, particularly in New York, are committed to political action, too. But instead of targeting anti-communists, they have an equally long history of opposing leftist political initiatives here and pro-communist regimes abroad, beginning with their Cold War boycott of Soviet and Chinese shipping and continuing today in their refusal to load vessels bound for Vietnam and the Soviet Union. Had Reagan been sailing to Europe instead of Hawaii forty years ago, New York's conservative longshoremen would have been standing in line for the privilege of handling his bags.

This book attempts to explain how two groups of workers who have so much in common—they are based in the same industry, confront many of the same shipping lines, and belong to the same occupation—came to embrace such different political orientations. It is, to be sure, an intriguing problem, this contrast between West Coast and East Coast longshoremen. From the moment I encountered it, I was hooked.

Deciding that this was a worthwhile topic to write about was the easy part. Next came the process of collecting data. Having been trained as a sociologist, I assumed that it would be sufficient to read a dozen or so informative narrative accounts prepared by historians. This would constitute my data base. Then, drawing on the power of sociological theory, I would reconstruct what the historians told us into a number of more analytically rigorous formulations, perhaps even a "grand theory."

I soon discovered it was not going to be that simple. Although a great deal of historical work had already been done on the longshore industry, especially concerning the West Coast, many of the issues that I felt were most important to explore had been left unresolved. Where I sought answers based on hard evidence, I found instead hunches and speculation. Out of necessity, therefore, I began my own historical investigation, a process that placed me in direct contact with primary data. Poring over rare archival material, seldom-used documents, and other primary sources, I was able to reconstruct important parts of the historical drama as it unfolded on the waterfront. Still, the written record I was forced to rely on was in many places incomplete or, worse, subject to varying interpretations. So I began interviewing retired longshoremen as a way of "interrogating the data." And as I did, new avenues of inquiry, otherwise inaccessible, opened up for me. It became possible not only to reconstruct history but to do so from the standpoint of those who actually lived it.

The resulting product is intended as a work of sociological synthesis. Intertwining normally diverse intellectual strands, this study weaves together historical methods, phenomenological concerns, and structural analysis into what I hope is a single, richly textured tapestry.

Acknowledgments

It is a pleasure to acknowledge the assistance I received in the course of researching and writing this manuscript. To the many maritime workers who allowed me to enter their lives and who shared with me their personal histories and reflections, I am forever grateful. Without their participation, along with the guidance I received from countless others whose names do not appear in the text, this study would not have been possible. Among the many longshoremen who helped in arranging interviews, Gordon Giblin and Herb Mills must be singled out.

Several individuals invested considerable time on my behalf tracking down historical documents. I would like to publicly acknowledge Ken Hall, archivist with the Industrial and Social Branch of the National Archives; Terry Lane, then corporate secretary of the Pacific Maritime Association; Dione Miles, reference archivist with the Archives of Labor and Urban Affairs housed at Wayne State University; Barry Silverman, ILWU research director; and Carol Schwartz, then ILWU librarian, whose cooperation and expertise made my frequent visits to the library both enjoyable and productive.

Drafts of individual chapters were read and ably commented on by Sam Darcy, Rod Harrison, Misagh Parsa, Bill Regensburger, Judy Stepan-Norris, and Stan Weir. Their suggestions and advice have been incorporated throughout. I am even more deeply indebted to those who read the entire manuscript: Lincoln Fairley, Bruce Nelson, Jeff Paige, Harvey Schwartz, Bill Sewell, Chuck Tilly, David Wellman, Julia Wrigley, and Bob Zieger. Listing their names in this fashion does not begin to convey my appreciation for the time and effort each gave to this study, but it will have to do. Two other readers, both original members of the dissertation committee supervising the work out of which this study evolved, deserve special thanks: John Laslett, who, as the lone historian on the committee, kept me close to the data while giving free rein to my historical imagination; and Maurice Zeitlin, who, as chair, poured a good deal of himself into this project. It is to Maurice that I owe my greatest intellectual debt, not only for showing me the ropes of historical sociology but also for instilling in me the habits of critical scholarship that have inspired this work.

I am grateful to Eloise Foster-Lavin for typing various drafts of the manuscript, and to the editorial staff at the University of California Press, particularly Naomi Schneider and Mary Renaud.

Finally, I wish to thank my wife, Robin, for her incredible patience and support. Even if she were not a former ILWU member, she would still be the most important person in my life.

* * *

Funding for this study was generously provided by the National Science Foundation, supplemented by grants from the Graduate Division, University of California, Los Angeles, and the Faculty Assistance Fund, University of Michigan.

Grateful acknowledgment is made to the journal *Social Forces* and to the Institute of Industrial Relations, University of California, Los Angeles, for permission to reproduce copyrighted material. Earlier versions of several sections of this book appeared in my articles "Working-Class Culture, Occupational Recruitment, and Union Politics," *Social Forces* 64 (December 1985): 359–376; "The Social Origins of Radical and Conservative Unionism," in *How Mighty a Force? Studies of Workers' Consciousness and Organization in the United States*, ed. Maurice Zeitlin (Los Angeles: Institute of Industrial Relations, 1985), pp. 307–369; and "Sources of Working-Class Insurgency: Politics and Longshore Unionism During the 1930s," in *Insurgent Workers: Studies of the Origins of Industrial Unionism on the East and West Coast Docks and in the South During the 1930s*, ed. Maurice Zeitlin (Los Angeles: Institute of Industrial Relations, 1987), pp. 7–70.

Chapter One

Introduction: Workers, Unions, and Politics

"The more developed a society," Karl Marx wrote in reference to the United States, "the more glaringly does the social question emerge." Uncontaminated by European "backwardness" or residual feudal classes, late nineteenth-century America represented the purest example of a developing bourgeois society. "On such soil, where the worker dominates," Marx confidently predicted, a revolutionary working-class movement "is bound to strike strong roots."[1]

For a time, the American proletariat seemed destined to fulfill Marx's vision—even if Marx, who died in 1883, would not be present to witness it. In 1884 the demand for a universal eight-hour working day was picked up by local labor councils from coast to coast. For the next two years hundreds of thousands of workers, possessed by what the newspapers called "eight-hour madness," were drawn into an ever-widening struggle that, in calling for a general reduction in hours, challenged the central mechanism of exploitation on which the capitalist system itself rested. From New York to San Francisco, from Chicago to St. Louis, workers organized, marched, protested, and engaged in political activity on a scale never before seen in this country. This "Great Upheaval," as historians now refer to the period, culminated in the spring of 1886 when close to half a million workers downed tools as part of a national campaign to shorten the length of the working day.[2]

American labor had finally come of age, or so it appeared to many of Europe's hopeful revolutionaries. Friedrich Engels, ob-

serving from across the Atlantic, saw the sharpening conflict overseas as a clear sign that "the last Bourgeois Paradise on earth is fast
changing into a Purgatoria." The awakening of the American proletariat, he wrote in June of 1886, "is quite extraordinary: Six
months ago nobody suspected anything, and now they appear all
of a sudden in such organized masses as to strike terror into the
whole capitalist class. I only wish Marx could have lived to see it." [3]

What Engels himself lived to see, however, was hardly reassur-
ing. Later that summer the eight-hour movement collapsed under
the weight of increasing state and employer repression. By the fall,
the largest labor organization in the country, the visionary Knights
of Labor, was on the verge of collapse. In its place arose the more
pragmatic American Federation of Labor. Unlike the Knights,
whose program called for abolishing the wage system, the AFL accepted capital's preeminent place in the industrial environment. In
time, the new unions became gravediggers not of capitalism, as
Marx had predicted, but of socialism: in 1894, delegates attending
the AFL's ninth annual convention narrowly defeated a resolution
endorsing collective ownership of the means of production. [4]

In rejecting socialist doctrines, American labor at the turn of
the century found itself moving against the main currents of trade
union development in the West. The United States, in fact, was the
only industrializing democracy whose labor movement was not
explicitly committed to a socialist transformation of the existing
order. Why the United States should be so different, why its organized working class—alone among advanced capitalist countries—
turned away from socialism at this crucial historical moment, became the subject of Werner Sombart's provocatively titled essay
"Why Is There No Socialism in the United States?" Sombart's answer, originally appearing in 1905 as a series of articles, focused
on what he believed were the distinctive features of the class experience in the United States: the relatively high standard of living
enjoyed by lower classes; the opportunities for upward mobility;
western expansion as a safety valve for urban discontent; the
democratic tenor of daily life; and early manhood suffrage, which,
together with the two-party monopoly, facilitated the political incorporation of the working class. [5] In short, America was portrayed
as a land uniquely insulated from radicalism, where both history
and social structure conspired against the emergence of a working-
class-based socialist movement.

Succeeding generations of scholars and political activists have kept Sombart's project very much alive, readily finding additional explanations for the failure of socialism wherever they happened to look. Those with a more panoramic view of the problem have tended to emphasize either the unusual economic success of American capitalism or the strength of liberal traditions, whereas others, focusing more narrowly on the workplace, have stressed the essentially "unformed" character of the working class, its economism, or the quality of union leadership. Still others have turned to more explicitly political factors having to do with the system of federalism, the structure of politics, and the role of the state.[6]

Given the many obstacles confronting socialists in America, perhaps the most arresting fact is that they were able to make any headway at all. Indeed, asking why socialists met with even limited success—or, as Wilbert Moore posed the problem some time ago, "Why are there *any* socialists in the United States?"—would seem to be the more interesting and significant question.[7]

The rationale for Moore's question is not unlike that which prompted Sombart's original query. Though the two questions aim in different directions, both target the "deviant case" in order to explain the failure of socialism.[8] For Sombart as well as for practically all students of "American exceptionalism," the problem is to understand why the labor movement in this country deviated from the socialist path followed by most of its European counterparts,[9] whereas Moore, looking only at the United States, chooses to examine the same problem by asking why a small minority of the population deviated from the national consensus and found socialism attractive. The first of these questions has received considerable attention, but the second has scarcely been addressed.

This study takes up the neglected question: Why some socialism? In doing so, it approaches the perennial problem of exceptionalism from a fresh perspective. Instead of asking why the American left failed, for the most part, to convert the labor movement to socialism, I begin by asking why radicals, particularly Communists and their closest allies, attained positions of prominence within the industrial union movement spawned by the Great Depression. For more than two decades the Communist Party wielded significant power in some of the nation's most vital and strategic industries, including auto, electronics, metal mining, machinery, maritime, and public transportation. With nearly one of every three organized industrial workers enrolled in unions that were euphemistically characterized as left-wing or progressive, radicals of one stripe or another controlled a larger portion of the American labor movement by the end of World War II than at any time since the founding of the AFL.[10]

What accounts for the left's surprising—most specialists would say totally unpredicted—success? Was it largely a result of "historical accident," of simply being in the right place at the right time? Or were deeper sociological processes at work, such as the history and structure of certain industries, the characteristics of their workers, and the nature of the struggles these workers engaged in? And what of the radical unions themselves? What does their existence suggest not only about the historical possibilities of working-class insurgency during the New Deal and beyond, but also, more generally, about the socialist potential of organized labor? Conversely, what do these radical enclaves suggest about the alleged conservatism of American workers? Or, put differently, what can the limited *presence* of labor radicalism in the United States teach us about the wide range of theories that purport to explain its *absence*?

I explore these questions through a deviant case analysis of the West Coast International Longshoremen's and Warehousemen's Union (ILWU), one of the most radical labor organizations created by the mass working-class insurgency of the 1930s. Formed in 1937 when the Pacific Coast district of the International Longshoremen's Association (ILA) bolted the AFL, changed its name, and affiliated with the Congress of Industrial Organizations (CIO), the ILWU was a hotbed of labor militancy. In the first few years of its existence, the ILWU conducted literally hundreds of job actions, or "quickie strikes," that progressively eroded employer control over the labor process. By wedding direct action tactics to vigorous contract enforcement, the longshoremen won some of the most restrictive work rules of any industry, rivaling those of the more established printing and railroad trades.[11]

But what was perhaps most distinctive about the ILWU was its refusal to separate politics from "pork chops." Unlike the rest of the labor movement, including most other left-wing unions, the ILWU committed its considerable economic muscle to efforts aimed at realizing larger political objectives.[12] During the late

1930s, for example, with fascism menacing Europe, the ILWU imposed a boycott on all German, Italian, and Japanese shipping to protest the militarization of the emerging Axis powers. In later years, the ILWU consistently sided with the left, from its early opposition to the Cold War through its support for the 1948 Progressive Party candidacy of Henry Wallace, to its protracted fight for the rights of Communists to participate in unions.[13]

Combining militancy and radical politics, the ILWU was widely recognized as the strongest bastion of Communist unionism on the West Coast, if not in the entire country. Over the years, scores of rank-and-file dockworkers passed through the "revolving doors" of the Communist Party, with the number of dues-paying members averaging around two hundred. Surrounding this critical mass was a much larger circle of "fellow travelers," including the nearly five hundred West Coast longshoremen who subscribed to the Communist Party newspaper, the *Daily Worker*. Reviewing the party's accomplishments on the docks, Nathan Glazer, in his authoritative study on American communism, concluded that the ILWU was "one of the great successes of the Communist Party in establishing a native working-class base . . . approximat[ing] the Leninist image." On that point there is a remarkable consensus, cutting across contending theoretical perspectives and political positions. Indeed, if students of American labor agree on little else, most would describe the ILWU as the most radical union in the country, except for possibly the International Fur and Leather Workers Union.[14]

Despite its extreme radicalism, the ILWU was the union most impregnable in the face of red-baiting, remaining so even at the height of the Cold War. The real test of strength for the left came in 1950 when the national CIO, facing growing pressure from the right, expelled eleven of its affiliates, including the ILWU, for "following the Communist Party line." Expulsion dealt a severe blow to the newly independent unions, few of which were strong enough to survive on their own. Stripped of the jurisdictional protection they had enjoyed as members of the CIO, they became sitting ducks for rival CIO affiliates who raided their memberships with impunity. Only three industrial unions—the United Electrical, Radio and Machine Workers Union (UE); the International Mine, Mill and Smelter Workers Union; and the ILWU—rallied behind their embattled left-wing leaders. But neither the UE nor the Mine,

Mill workers were able to hold out for long. Within a few years the UE lost more than half its members to the anti-communist International Union of Electrical Workers, while the Mine, Mill and Smelter Workers Union, following a string of piecemeal losses to rival CIO unions, was itself eventually swallowed up by the United Steel Workers of America. Again the ILWU was the exception. Fending off repeated raids by CIO organizers, the Sailors Union of the Pacific, the Transport Workers Union, and even the powerful Teamsters, the ILWU emerged from the Cold War with its basic longshore division wholly intact and growing.[15]

The intense and enduring quality of radicalism that distinguished the ILWU from the rest of the left was embodied in its international president, former Australian seaman Harry Bridges, who led the ILWU from its founding in 1937 until his retirement in 1977 at the age of seventy-five. As a past member of the revolutionary syndicalist Industrial Workers of the World, as well as a long-time ally of the Communist Party, Bridges was "far to the left of any other American labor leader ever to attain equal prominence," observed labor reporter Richard Neuberger in 1939. "Bridges," he wrote, "epitomizes labor revolt and extremism. . . . He is . . . a symbol within our country of revolutionary tendencies and dangerous ideas. His name, far more than that of Earl Browder, the General Secretary of the Communist Party of the United States, is practically synonymous with radicalism."[16]

Class struggle was the touchstone of Bridges's trade union philosophy. When a student at the University of Washington in the mid-1930s asked him to summarize his views, Bridges replied with characteristic candor: "We take the stand that we as workers have nothing in common with the employers. We are in a class struggle, and we subscribe to the belief that if the employer is not in business his products will still be necessary and we still will be providing them when there is no employing class. We frankly believe that day is coming."[17]

Such outspokenness did little to endear "Red Harry" to more privileged groups in society. To West Coast shipowners he was "a very dangerous man" whose views "simply don't fit into the American scheme of doing things." Federal authorities agreed, attempting on five separate occasions to deport Bridges as an "undesirable alien," based on his close and intimate association with the Communist Party. Though Bridges denied ever being a member of the party, he never retreated—in court, in the media, or before his own union membership—from his commitment to socialism. It was simply not Bridges's style to hide his politics, as a reporter for *Time* magazine learned in covering the first deportation trial in 1939. "Defendant Bridges," the journalist wrote, "painted himself Red" as he expounded on the evils of capitalism, the inevitability of class war, the desirability of socialism, and the solid contribution of Communists to the labor movement. After hearing Bridges's testimony, a Seattle banker fumed: "He's the most radical labor leader in the country. Yet those longshoremen would follow him into a fiery furnace."[18] The question remains, why? Why did Bridges, one of the most radical men ever to lead an American union, command such loyalty from the rank and file?

The pat answer is that Bridges was supported because he looked after the immediate economic interests of his members. In the language of business unionism, he delivered the goods. His personal political views simply did not matter one way or the other. Thus historian David Shannon claims that Bridges was supported "despite, rather than because of, his politics" and because he "runs a union that 'delivers' in the Gompers's bread and butter sense." Other students of the ILWU offer a similar interpretation, arguing that Bridges was able to survive the Cold War because, as a *Business Week* reporter sardonically put it in 1950, "it mattered little to the members that Bridges's left hand was steeped in the waters of Communism so long as the right hand kept wringing concessions out of their bosses."[19]

To be sure, Bridges would not have remained in office for long without wringing concessions from the employers. But while a tough bargaining stance may have contributed to his popularity, Bridges's actual measure of success as a negotiator depended ultimately on the resolve of the rank and file, particularly their willingness to back him up at the bargaining table. The mere fact that he ran "a union that delivers" is almost beside the point, for his ability to deliver was more a consequence than a cause of his popular support, having less to do with Bridges's own skills as a negotiator than with the militancy of the longshoremen themselves.

The impact of the rank and file on the collective bargaining process can be seen by comparing the negotiating strategies pursued by the ILWU's longshore and warehouse divisions. Although experienced left-wingers headed both divisions, employer relations with the warehouse local were "not significantly different from the customary . . . pattern of business unionism," according to Paul Eliel, a labor relations specialist and former representative for the waterfront employers. In sharp contrast, relations with the longshore locals were "among the most troubled" of any industry in the country. The difference resulted not only from the strategic advantages enjoyed by the longshoremen, as Eliel contended,[20] but also from the more violent history of conflict on the docks and the resulting traditions of occupational solidarity and militancy that enabled longshore negotiators to take a more aggressive posture at the table and eventually walk away with better contracts. To conclude from this that Bridges remained popular with the longshoremen because he delivered the goods ignores the underlying sociological forces at work that allowed him to do so. The capacity to deliver, then, rather than explaining leadership durability, is precisely what needs to be explained.

At the same time it is clear that success at the bargaining table is only part of the answer. After all, the history of American labor includes scores of radical union leaders who, like Bridges, delivered the goods but who nonetheless failed to retain support among the rank and file. What little evidence there is strongly suggests that many of the unions led by socialists around the turn of the century were every bit as effective as the AFL in protecting the job territory and immediate economic interests of their members. Nevertheless, socialist leadership had all but disappeared by the end of World War I whereas rival craft unions flourished for many years to come—a difference that cannot be attributed to the relative efficacy of either group at the bargaining table. Much the same was true for the next generation of radicals who helped to organize the CIO. During the initial organizing drives of the 1930s, Communists and their supporters were widely regarded as among the toughest, most militant bargainers. And yet, despite delivering the goods, most "fellow travelers" were later swept aside by anti-communist challengers who were certainly no better, and in some cases much worse, at delivering the goods.[21]

As this suggests, leadership dynamics within trade unions cannot be reduced to what takes place at the bargaining table. If the traditional emphasis on economic performance is read as an argument that leaders who deliver are more likely to remain in office, then it is little more than a meaningless tautology; if, more ambitiously, it is intended as an argument that delivering the goods is a guarantee of job security, then it is simply wrong. Either way, economic interpretations of trade union loyalty are at a loss to explain why, among equally efficacious leaders, some are more resilient than others. Perhaps all that can be said with any certainty is that success at the bargaining table, while necessary, is not a sufficient condition for remaining in office.[22]

For Communists, it has been argued, the key to remaining in office was their "indisputable organizational adroitness." In this view, which gained currency during the Cold War, Communists did not so much win union posts as capture them; they did not lead unions but rather dominated them; and because their radical political philosophy was never embraced by the rank and file, they were forced to operate in secrecy, often in violation of union democracy. Relying primarily on "their mastery of the techniques of group organization and manipulation" and the strategic placement of party cadre in "key union posts," and then "reinforced by clever tactics," Communists managed to infiltrate the highest command posts of the CIO.[23]

This portrayal of the omnipotent "red machine" is a caricature. At the very least it grossly exaggerates the party's ability to organizationally manipulate its environment. To suppose that a relative handful of party functionaries, numbering in the tens or hundreds in most industries, became leaders of the industrial working class as a result of their alleged organizational adroitness is to fall back on an inflated view of the party—shared by red-baiters and Communists alike—as possessing, in John Laslett's words, "superhuman powers of organization and control."[24] Even considering all that we now know about the importance of "mobilizing agents" in building social movements, it is inconceivable that a few thousand militants, isolated in tiny cells and scattered across the country, could have captured some of the largest industrial unions without substantial rank-and-file support.

That such support was frequently based on the Communists' ability to outorganize their opposition did not mean that they were therefore more manipulative, diabolical, or underhanded. It did mean that they were usually more effective organizers, as even their harshest critics were forced to admit. Robert Ozanne, for example, in his otherwise critical study of Communist trade union leadership, reluctantly conceded that party membership was "a real asset" in organizing the CIO. "Let us 'give the devil his due,'" he wrote in 1954 in the midst of the Cold War:

> Communists were more willing than the average worker to face gross employer discrimination and even violence. In the labor relations climate of employer espionage, discrimination and violence . . . such qualities as indifference to being fired, willingness to work night and day and courage to face threats of physical violence were prerequisites for successful organizers. These qualities the Communists possessed.

Ozanne is equally candid in discussing the issue of Communist organizational domination. He acknowledges that "most organizations . . . are controlled by a small group of activists" who "meet or caucus in advance of rank and file meetings to plan strategy. Non-Communist unions have long practiced this policy." Yet Ozanne ends up attacking Communists for using this same method because, he claims, in their disciplined hands it "produces results far beyond that of the ordinary union clique of ambitious, rising leaders."[25] Of course, this still begs the question of why Communist leaders were able to produce such results. The obvious answer is that they were better organizers—a claim rejected out of hand by most Cold War analysts. Their answer, for which the evidence was far less compelling but the political climate more favorable, was that Communists, armed with what Philip Selznick once described as the "organizational weapon" of bolshevism, were able to worm their way into power through a deliberate strategy of factionalism, disruption, and manipulation.

However accurate this Cold War scenario may have been in the case of other left-wing unions, it scarcely applies to the ILWU, where Communist-supported insurgents rose to power by winning over the rank and file to their trade union program. Once in office, one of their first acts was to replace the old ILA constitution, which centralized power at the top of the union, with a more open and democratic set of procedures designed to guard against the kinds of organizational abuse that Communists were normally accused of practicing. The terms of all local officers were reduced to one year, reviving an old syndicalist tradition. In addition, most locals established a limit of two consecutive terms for each office, after which incumbents either "returned to the beach" as working longshoremen or sought some other elective position. Between elections, accountability was maintained by a simplified recall procedure: under provisions of the new constitution, recall proceedings could be initiated against any elected official on the basis of a petition bearing signatures from as few as 15 percent of the members. In a final assault on the privileges of leadership, salaries for all elected union officers were capped at no more than 10 percent above the earnings of the highest paid workers, thereby diminishing any purely economic incentive for seeking and remaining in office.[26]

The relationship between these formal procedures and the actual degree of union democracy is more problematic. Indeed, the two most detailed case studies of the ILWU's internal political process reached rather different conclusions. The first, a master's thesis written in 1949 by Wayne Hield, argued that despite the ILWU's formally democratic structure, union governance was effectively confined to a "distinct oligarchic group" of circulating elites. Hield's conclusion was challenged in 1963 by Jay Goodman, whose master's thesis contended that the ILWU was highly democratic and that it represented an exception to the rule of trade union bureaucracy. In support of Goodman's interpretation, Lipset, Trow, and Coleman, in their classic study *Union Democracy*, singled out the ILWU as "very democratic" and favorably compared its internal political process to that of the International Typographical Union, their model of union democracy.[27]

This is not to say that the ILWU was at all times a paragon of democracy. More than once, Bridges himself spoke out against the excesses of "rank-and-file-ism." In the most celebrated such case, he argued at the ILWU's 1947 convention against running competing slates of candidates on the grounds that for the union to be effective it had to operate as a "totalitarian government" with a single, unified will.[28] It would be ridiculous to think that Bridges never violated the spirit of union democracy during his forty years in office. But when he did so it was more out of simple expediency than political necessity; no one, not even his strongest critics, ever argued that his continuity in office depended on violating democratic procedures.[29] In truth, it is more accurate to say that Bridges held on as long as he did despite his infrequent transgressions, not because of them.

But truth had little if any relevance by the time the national CIO brought the ILWU up on charges of violating union democracy by "following the Communist Party line." In a classic example of Cold War reasoning, the union's support for the party line was adduced as prima facie evidence that the interests of the rank and file had been systematically ignored. Bridges bristled at the accusation. "The Union that I speak for," he declared in 1949 at the national CIO convention, "takes second place to no organization in the CIO or anywhere else in the matters of trade union democracy." He then proceeded to tick off a long list of democratic practices. His presentation was apparently convincing, so much so that National Maritime Union President Joseph Curran, by then a staunch opponent of Bridges and the left, admitted that the ILWU was, in his words, "a democratic union."[30] The three-man trial committee that heard the case the following spring saw it differently, however, and ruled that the ILWU should be expelled from the CIO. The verdict was hardly a surprise. Paul Jacobs, an ex-Trotskyist who prepared the case against the ILWU, later wrote that "the committee's decision to recommend expulsion was so certain that I began to work on the writing of it while the trial was still in progress."[31]

National CIO leaders saw the expulsion of the ILWU and ten other "Communist-dominated" unions as the first step toward freeing the industrial working class from the party's clutches. But when the moment of liberation arrived, few workers actively sought refuge from Communist domination. Congressional aide Max Kampelman, who helped orchestrate the purge, was confounded. "The power of nationalism and patriotism is great," he wrote in 1957, "and their hold on American citizens has been a potent fact in our history. Yet many thousands of American citizens have supported Communists as their union leaders, and even today continue to vote for those leaders in secret elections under government supervision."[32] Clearly, something other than Communist trickery was at work.

The competitiveness of left-wing leaders in open union elections, coupled with the resurgence of communist influence in the

French, Italian, and British labor movements after World War II, called into question the view that political radicalism was foreign, if not actually hostile, to the values of contemporary blue-collar workers. Accumulating survey data pointed to the saliency of class position in determining voting behavior and attitudes. But as social scientists began exploring the correlates of working-class leftism they discovered significant internal variations seemingly rooted in industry.[33]

This was the context in which Lipset advanced his now famous theory of the "isolated occupational mass." Drawing on Clark Kerr and Abraham Siegel's earlier work on the interindustry propensity to strike, Lipset argued that certain industrial settings, because of their isolation, serve as breeding grounds of radicalism. Where workers reside in occupationally homogeneous communities that are cut off by geography or deviant work schedules from conservatizing middle-class influences, and where as a result of their isolation they are bound together by a tight network of intraclass communication, left-wing political parties have normally enjoyed their greatest mass support. The militancy and political radicalism so often displayed by miners, seamen, loggers, commercial fishermen, and dockworkers was thus attributed to a lack of contact "with the world outside their own group."[34]

This argument rests on the assumption that isolation removes workers from the conservative values of the surrounding society. Sometimes it does; but at other times it may insulate them from left-wing political groups instead—in which case isolation can become an *obstacle* to radicalism.[35] In short, the mere fact that a group of workers is isolated tells us next to nothing about the *content* of their politics. Whether isolation makes them radical or conservative depends ultimately on whether the values being screened out are of a "proletarian" or a "bourgeois" nature.

On the waterfront, in fact, isolation was inversely related to radicalism. Consider the contrast between the two principal California ports. In San Francisco, dockworkers were not at all isolated from the general population. Rather than being territorially confined to the flophouses, bars, and cafés that hugged the waterfront, they freely roamed the city, congregating especially in the nearby North Beach district, home to many bohemians and political activists during the 1930s. Partly as a result of their integration into the vibrant intellectual life of North Beach, San Francisco's longshoremen were recruited to radicalism in far greater numbers than anywhere else on the coast. In contrast, San Pedro was perhaps the most isolated port. Located some twenty-five miles south of metropolitan Los Angeles, ringed by mountains, and lacking many connecting roads or rail lines to neighboring cities, San Pedro closely resembled the classic isolated working-class community. Cut off from any kind of intellectual or radical influences, longshoremen in San Pedro, while militant on the job, were much less responsive to radical politics.[36]

The conservatizing impact of isolation is most clearly revealed, however, in the political development of longshore unionism in the Port of New York. For unique historical and geographical reasons, the city's longshoremen tended to live and work together in many of the same dockside neighborhoods. As much as is possible in an urban milieu, theirs was a largely self-contained world, insulated from the outside by the peculiar rhythm of casual employment and held together by a strong and enduring sense of community. Yet New York's isolated dockworkers belonged to one of the most conservative unions in the country. If they were "radical" at all it was only in their intense hostility to communism.[37]

Indeed, the union representing dockworkers on the East and Gulf coasts, the old ILA, was as conservative as its West Coast descendant, the ILWU, was radical. The ILA's international president, Joseph Ryan, was a fanatical anti-communist. Ryan began his lifelong crusade against communism in the early 1920s when, as the ILA's youthful vice-president, he served on an AFL labor committee assigned to investigate "Soviet infiltration" of the New York City labor movement. From that point on he never looked back. A decade later Ryan was sharing his convention platforms with some of America's staunchest supporters of Hitler and Mussolini—at the same time that dockworkers on the West Coast were boycotting German and Italian shipping. As Ryan's "patriotic" fervor peaked, he began soliciting contributions for a secret "anti-communist fund." Over the years, thousands of dollars were collected under the table from East Coast shipowners, with much of the money ending up in Ryan's personal bank account. Not that he was insincere or only in it for the money, for, as Harry Lundberg, president of the Sailors Union of the Pacific, observed in 1951, "no

official in the maritime field or the American trade union movement . . . has fought the Commies any better, any harder than Joe
Ryan."[38]

Ryan's conservative values also spilled over into the collective
bargaining arena, where the ILA distinguished itself as one of the
least effective unions in the country. Judged by even the minimal
standards of business unionism, the ILA was an abject failure: it
restricted neither the number of jobs nor the size of the labor force;
it never established any system for equalizing or distributing employment opportunities; it tolerated cutthroat competition and
conditions of chronic job insecurity. In sum, the ILA violated practically every tenet of job control unionism.[39]

Industrial conflict was completely foreign to Ryan's trade union
philosophy. Beginning in 1927 when he was first elected to the
presidency of the ILA, and continuing until 1942 when his position was ceremonially extended for life, there was not a single
union-authorized strike in the Port of New York. During his long
reign, "King Joe's" relationship with the waterfront employers was
characterized as "exceedingly close and friendly," though collaborative would be a more accurate description. Facing an increasingly restive rank and file after World War II, East Coast shipowners literally bought labor peace. From 1947 to 1951 a total of
forty-three shipping and stevedoring companies paid out more
than $180,000 in bribes to 101 officials of the ILA in New York.
Disclosures of this sort, together with evidence of extensive underworld connections, led to the ILA's expulsion from the AFL in
1953.[40]

By the early 1950s, then, both longshore unions had been expelled from their respective labor federations: the ILWU for following the Communist Party; the ILA for collaborating with the
shipowners. It would be difficult to imagine a sharper political
contrast, particularly within the same industry, or one that more
clearly demonstrates there is no necessary connection between the
structural characteristics of certain industries and the political orientations of their workers.[41]

This contrast between the two coasts allows us to situate our
deviant case analysis of the ILWU within a comparative framework that, in effect, "holds constant" certain key aspects of the industrial environment as possible sources of radical leadership. By

introducing the ILA as a control variable, we can examine systematically a host of nonindustry factors that are rarely considered in studies of union politics. The resulting blend of deviant case and comparative methods thus provides a unique opportunity to conduct a partially controlled social experiment concerning the conditions under which, given a similar industrial setting, radical or conservative union leadership is likely to take root and flourish.

To highlight the political differences between the two coasts, analysis of the ILA is limited to the Port of New York, where Ryan's base of support was strongest and, consequently, the union's conservatism most pronounced. For similar reasons, the time frame of this study is confined to the period of greatest political contrast, beginning around World War I with the first signs of regional differentiation and ending in the early 1950s with the expulsion of both unions from the mainstream of American labor.[42]

Neither the success of the left in the West nor its failure in the East can be adequately explained by any of the standard theories of union politics: good contracts in the West no more made Bridges than bad ones in the East made Ryan; organizational manipulation in the West no more led to Communist domination there than the much more blatant lack of democracy in the East led to racketeer control in New York; social isolation in the West no more gave us the radicalism of the ILWU than the same conditions gave us the conservatism of the ILA. In short, the contrast between West and East coasts, between reds and rackets, was not in any simple way the result of business unionists delivering the goods, or tiny bands of conspirators manipulating large organizational processes, or even the impersonal forces of industry itself.

The line of inquiry developed here proceeds with a deeper appreciation of history and the role of human agency. Without neglecting the major institutional developments affecting both unions, the following analysis draws its inspiration from the "new social history" in attempting to recreate the essential richness of working-class experience. Intended as a work of emerging theoretical synthesis, it brings together an attention to culture within an overall analytic focus on the world of production, thereby bridging the gap between "culturalist" and "syndicalist" problematics as represented so eloquently in the writings of American labor historians Herbert Gutman and David Montgomery, respectively.[43]

Although the subject matter deals with history, the questions posed are sociological. Indeed, a recurring theme is to understand not merely what happened but *why* certain things happened and not others. History holds part of the answer—but only a part, for while it is true that particular outcomes were not in any strong sense of the word "determined," they were clearly foreshadowed by structural forces. And here sociology has something valuable to contribute to history. Building on the strengths of both disciplines, this study combines a classical narrative approach in emphasizing the importance of timing, unique events, and conscious choice with a more sociologically focused analysis of how such historical particularities were played out within the limits and possibilities established by existing social structural arrangements. This, at any rate, is what I see as the real promise of historical sociological analysis, and it is what this book is all about.

The analysis begins by locating the origins of dual unionism in the deep penetration of syndicalist agitators on the West Coast immediately following World War I. Chapter 2 traces this variation to the different ideological communities from which dockworkers were originally recruited on both coasts. The resulting structure of the labor force, reflecting distinct regional patterns of occupational recruitment and amplified by labor market and ecological differences, gave rise to a radical working-class culture in the West and a more conservative culture in New York.

These emerging cultures were then solidified by the way waterfront employers responded to unionization. Chapter 3 argues that employer responses were powerfully determined by the structure of industry on each coast. The higher concentration of shipping capital in the West, together with a low degree of economic fragmentation, enhanced the "class capacity" of local shipowners, enabling them to organize militant, coastwide opposition to the union. By thus legitimating the class conflict premises of syndicalism, employer intransigence strengthened the existing radicalized culture on the docks. In New York, where shipping was both less concentrated and more highly fragmented, industry structure had the opposite effect of intensifying competition and creating employer disunity, thereby precluding any unified challenge to unionism. Unable to resist effectively, the shipowners assumed a more conciliatory posture, which reaffirmed the already conservative political culture in New York.

With these two contrasting political cultures providing differing structures of opportunity for radical insurgency, we turn next to analyze how these opportunity structures were "brought to life" by human agency in the early years of the Depression. Chapter 4 begins this inquiry by closely examining the particular organizing strategies pursued by Communist activists on both coasts. Embracing a less sectarian approach in the West, radical insurgents were able to build a large following on the docks during the crucial period leading up to the 1934 maritime strike.

The walkout that year was a turning point for organized labor and longshore unionism in particular. Chapter 5 employs the concept of "political generations" to understand the impact of the 1934 strike and its aftermath. The extremely violent nature of the walkout welded its participants into a distinct generation of "'34 men" whose loyalty to one another, as well as to their radical leaders, was reinforced in later years by their collective efforts to transform class relations at the point of production. In New York, in contrast, the generation that came of age during the Depression held firmly to a more conservative worldview, reflecting their own very different set of politically relevant experiences.

With the outbreak of World War II, the generations thus formed were tested once again in battle. Wartime conditions disrupted established work groups, as veteran unionists, many of them entering the armed services, were replaced by younger, less experienced workers. Already on the defensive, the left was forced to choose between its patriotic obligation to "keep the ships sailing" and, as the war dragged on, the growing restiveness of the rank and file. Chapter 6 explores both of these developments, arguing that the different nature of the demographic and political challenges confronting the ILA and the ILWU deepened the already vast chasm separating the unions, driving them further apart as the Cold War descended on the waterfront. Chapter 7 draws the various arguments together, assembling them into a more general model of historical explanation that is predicated on the inseparability of structural and conjunctural modes of analysis. The chapter concludes with a discussion of the ILWU's success and what it implies for understanding the wider failure of socialism within the American working class.

Chapter Two

Social Foundations of Unionism

"Whoever reaches . . . unorganized masses first," labor historian David Saposs long ago observed, "generally holds their confidence permanently."[1] In the drive to organize basic industry during the 1930s, leftist insurgents were indeed most durable when they were in on the ground floor of unionization efforts, either as "union pioneers" in traditionally unorganized fields or as second-generation radicals building on an existing foundation. In fact, of the eleven left-wing unions expelled from the CIO in 1950, six were based in industries with little or no history of unionism before the appearance of Communist organizers, and the remaining five had all been founded by radicals of one stripe or another.[2] The question of leadership sequence, or, as Richard Hamilton put it, "who got there first," thus emerges as a key consideration in any study of working-class politics.[3]

But the question of who got there first, if taken literally, is scarcely helpful in explaining the emergence of radical and conservative working-class cultures on the docks after World War I. On both coasts, dockworkers were approached at nearly the same time by the Industrial Workers of the World (IWW), an anarcho-syndicalist organization that was especially active in the maritime industry. Between 1919 and 1923 IWW activists enjoyed considerable success on the West Coast, enrolling several hundred longshoremen from Seattle to San Pedro in their revolutionary Marine Transport Workers' Industrial Union (MTW)[4] and leading thousands more in mass strikes and work stoppages. In New York, however, the IWW tried but was unable to make any headway at all on the docks.

In the longshore industry, then, the question of who got there first is not one of strict chronological order but rather is a question of historical significance, concerned less with matters of timing than with the receptivity of the workers. Given the simultaneous appearance of syndicalist agitators on both coasts, we are compelled to push the analysis back a step, asking not who was first but why those who were, namely, the Wobblies, were able to penetrate one coast and not the other. The critical question of who got there first can be answered only by exploring the sociological preconditions for radicalization on the docks. This chapter examines the character of the preexisting labor force, focusing on the differing patterns of occupational recruitment on both coasts and how the resulting composition of the dockside labor force influenced the longshoremen's response to radical leadership, their organizational capabilities, and the kinds of struggles they engaged in during the crucial formative years of unionization.

Occupational Recruitment
on the West Coast

The Wobblies' success in the West can be traced to the region's distinctive sources of occupational recruitment. During the first quarter of the twentieth century, the dockside labor force on the Pacific was disproportionately recruited from two groups of workers—former seamen and loggers—whose earlier job-related experiences and lifestyles left them relatively open to radical, particularly syndicalist, conceptions and practices.

The radical propensities of seamen and loggers were partly an outgrowth of their extraordinary geographic mobility. Constant shuffling and reshuffling of work crews, whether aboard ship or in logging camps, generated a dense network of social contacts, exposing both groups to a correspondingly wide range of ideas. This was especially true for seamen, arguably the most cosmopolitan body of workers in the world. Their greatly expanded opportunities for communication with other people and their frequent contact with foreign cultures familiarized them with the breadth of socially structured inequality. Witnessing poverty on a worldwide scale led many highly impressionable young sailors to "start asking questions." As Bill Bailey, a veteran marine worker and Communist activist, recalls:

> I was beginning to see the poverty of people no matter where you went, no matter what port. I was only used to the poverty of Hell's Kitchen, or my own poverty in Hoboken or Jersey City. You didn't think the whole world was full of that until you got to visit it and found it no matter where you went. . . . So then you figure, what the hell is going on here? And these are the type of things you wonder about, and you start asking yourself questions.[5]

Simply asking questions did not always elicit a radical answer. But it did predispose seamen toward a more structuralist understanding of the causes of social inequality and unrest. In traversing the globe, American sailors encountered a way of life not so different from their own: the squalor, hunger, and human misery they saw overseas resonated all too clearly with their own personal experiences, both past and present. They were impressed by the ubiquity of social inequality and by the realization, especially painful for many younger men, that there was little chance of ever escaping the lower class—that, as far as they could see, every society had its "sea dogs," its "untouchables." If, as a result, seamen were able to perceive with great clarity what Max Weber referred to as "the transparency of the causes and consequences of their class situation,"[6] it was partly because of their uniquely cosmopolitan frame of reference.

Personal contact with exotic non-Western societies also compelled many American seamen to critically reexamine their most basic political beliefs. During layovers in foreign ports, they often confronted a reality at odds with the world depicted by the dominant ideology. Finding colonialism, dictatorship, and oppression overseas, numerous sailors were jolted out of a political complacency bred of ignorance. Harry Bridges, whose family had originally emigrated from Britain to Australia, remembers being shocked by his first visit "home" as a young seaman:

> I took a trip that gave me a look at India and another at Suez, and what I saw there didn't line up with what my father had told me about the dear old British. Then I got "home" and saw London. It

was the filthiest, most unhealthy place I ever had seen. And the
people in the slums were worse than the natives in India and Port
Said—dirty, nasty, no good. So this, I say, is British democracy. . . .
So I kept traveling around, and the more I saw the more I knew that
there was something wrong with the system.[7]

Only a minority of seamen may have been self-consciously radicalized in this way, but countless others grew more receptive to alternative interpretations of the world through such encounters.

Loggers in the Pacific Northwest embraced a similarly itinerant
lifestyle, although their nomadic wanderings were confined to a
small corner of North America, unlike the wide-ranging voyages of
the seamen. A survey conducted in 1913 among California's large
casual labor force indicated that the average length of employment
in the state's lumber camps was between fifteen and thirty days,
compared to thirty days for the seasonal canning industry and
sixty days for mining. Of the industries surveyed, only agricultural
and construction jobs were of shorter average duration. This brief
job tenure reflected an extremely high rate of labor mobility among
loggers. During World War I, the annual rate of labor turnover in
lumber camps throughout the Northwest reached an estimated
600 percent before "stabilizing" at more than 200 percent in the
immediate postwar period.[8]

These nomadic loggers were sparkplugs of labor unrest and
radicalism. Like Britain's nineteenth-century "tramping artisans,"
they served as a "walking encyclopedia of comparative trade union
knowledge," passing on information about prevailing wage rates,
working conditions, and organizing strategies. Compared to more
stably employed sawmill workers, the Northwest's hobo loggers
constituted a far more "dangerous element in the labor problem."
A 1923 government study claimed that these "foot-loose rebels no
longer recognize the ordinary conventions of modern society but
challenge the whole industrial system of which the relation of the
employer and employee forms a part."[9]

The migratory habits of West Coast loggers thus produced a noticeable shift in consciousness. Rapid labor turnover in the woods
not only removed any basis for identifying with individual employers but also rendered loggers less dependent on any one company
for their livelihood. Footloose and economically independent, they

were exposed to an unusually wide range of job-related experiences, social contacts, and ideas. Their itinerant lifestyle cultivated a more inclusive, worldly outlook—one that to some extent inverted the inwardly focused and fragmented "job consciousness" characteristic of more settled workers.[10]

As "drifters," living outside the major integrative institutions of society, loggers and seamen were most at home within their own densely organized occupational communities. From the moment a sailor joined his ship until it was once again tied up in port, crew members were placed in almost continuous contact with one another. The cramped fo'c'sle, where the men spent their nonworking hours, obliterated any spatial distinctions between living, sleeping, and eating quarters. By dissolving the boundary between work and leisure—between public and private spheres of existence—the shipboard environment generated a strong sense of solidarity and occupational camaraderie that persisted, if in somewhat diminished form, long after the voyage was completed.[11]

The ship's crew, isolated from conservative cross-pressures while at sea, functioned as a floating microcosm of society, its members relying on one another to collectively process and validate their individual perceptions. Lacking access to conventional sources of information, the seaman's view of the world and his place in it was largely shaped by what he experienced, either directly through personal exposure to alternative ways of life or vicariously through endless hours of conversation and reading. In both cases, these shared experiences fostered an independent set of values and beliefs with which to challenge the dominant political culture.[12]

Life in most logging camps was organized in a similarly communal fashion. As aboard ship, there was considerable overlap between work and leisure. The close integration of public and private realms contributed to the loggers' sociability—what the Wobblies regarded as the "timberbeasts'" strong "social instinct." "Loggers live and work in groups," noted a veteran IWW activist. "Theirs is essentially a group life both on the job, at meals and at rest. Every factor for an early development of the social instinct is present and naturally loggers took the social philosophy of the IWW to themselves."[13]

Much like a ship at sea, the typical logging camp, located in thinly settled forested regions, operated as a self-contained community. Sharply polarized along class lines, the Western lumber camp was described not too inaccurately as a "mixture of capitalism and feudalism, civilization and barbarism."[14] Radicalism flourished in this setting. Leisure time was spent huddled around the camp fire or in the bunkhouse, playing cards or conversing on topics from sports or scandal to abstruse discussions of economic theory. These informal "bull sessions," observed an official with the Department of Labor, laid a "psychological foundation for revolt" among loggers:

> Here they have the time to think and talk over their grievances and the differences between their social and economic conditions and those of other elements of the population. It is in these discussions that the opinions of loggers are formed, and here nearly everything combines to make them radical. There is little that is attractive in the lives they lead, they resent the social organization which makes that kind of life necessary.[15]

In sum, the social organization of life in the woods as well as at sea provided considerable autonomy from the dominant political culture. Isolation from cross-cutting ideological pressures was a critical feature of this lifestyle. But what most distinguished West Coast loggers and seamen from equally isolated and more conservative workers was the cosmopolitan and communal character of their work experiences. Geographic mobility simultaneously broadened and politicized their personal horizons while the intensity of interaction on the job generated a dense network of mutual support. This unique working-class culture—combining elements of rugged individualism, union militancy, and syndicalism in a highly volatile mix—was introduced onto the West Coast docks through the selective occupational recruitment of former seamen and loggers.

Seamen, loggers, and longshoremen came together in the Pacific Northwest through their involvement in some phase of logging operations. In the early days of the lumber industry, trees felled by loggers were floated downstream to the docks where longshoremen loaded them aboard steam schooners for seamen to lash in place on deck. With this vertical integration, occupational boundaries became highly fluid; many men actually followed the movement of logs from forest to dock to ship and back again. The blurring of occupational lines became so acute that seamen and longshoremen were constantly embroiled in union jurisdictional disputes over the rights to handle lumber at different stages during loading and unloading.

The Northwest's itinerant loggers moved freely between the inland forests and the waterfront. Whenever inclement winter weather at the higher elevations or hazardous fire conditions during the summer interrupted logging operations, thousands of unemployed loggers headed for the coastal communities of northern California, Oregon, and Washington, where many obtained temporary work on the docks in lumber-handling gangs. Seattle alone absorbed between five thousand and seven thousand displaced lumberjacks, construction workers, and field hands during the slack winter season. In the fall of 1917, after an unsuccessful lumber strike initiated by the IWW, more than nine thousand loggers followed their blacklisted Wobbly leaders into Seattle. Alarmed by this "seditious invasion," agents from the Office of Naval Intelligence swarmed onto the Puget Sound waterfront and promptly arrested 129 Wobblies, among whom were undoubtedly many loggers.[16]

In Portland, where loggers had been hired as "extra men" in lumber gangs for several years, they made up an even larger proportion of the labor force. A survey of occupational genealogies for Portland's active longshoremen in 1967 revealed that the most common occupation among their fathers had been longshoring, followed in order by logging and farming. Among grandfathers, the pattern was reversed: farming had been the most common occupation, followed closely by logging and longshoring. In support of these findings, several old-timers from Portland estimated that former loggers represented between one-fourth and one-third of the port's labor force during the 1920s.[17]

The other major source of occupational recruitment for the West Coast docks was the offshore maritime industry. Shipping out of the busy lumber ports of Oregon and Washington, many sailors became proficient at handling and stowing various wood products. Whenever they missed their ship or just needed a little extra cash while ashore, they could always "catch a job" on the docks, working for weeks or even months at a time in a lumber-handling gang. These experienced steam schooner men were the "biggest driving force" behind dockside organization after World War I, according to Rosco Craycraft, a former Wobbly lumber worker and ILWU leader. "In those early days," he recalled, "sailors done longshore work on the ships. . . . Most of your leaders, like gang leaders, they were ex-mates . . . coming off the old steam schooners. They really knew how to stow." [18]

Shipping was also the main feeder industry for California's longshoremen. The route from sea to shore was a well-traveled one, as countless seamen were lured ashore by marriage at some point in their lives. Reluctant to give up the waterfront ambience to which they had grown accustomed, many "old salts" naturally drifted into longshoring. Besides promising a continuing association with the maritime industry, cargo handling was one of the few trades in which an experienced sailor could utilize his specialized skills of rigging and stowing.

There are no exact figures on the percentage of California longshoremen with seafaring backgrounds, but the available evidence suggests that their numbers were considerable. Thomas Plant, who had been a corporate officer with the American-Hawaiian Steamship Company since 1907, recalled his earliest impressions of San Francisco's longshoremen as "mostly all steam schooner sailors. . . . Men who had been to sea, thorough sailors, good citizens, nearly all married. And when they married, they wanted to come to shore. So they came ashore and became longshoremen." [19]

Seamen had an even greater impact on the labor force in San Pedro. The city's invitingly warm climate made it an ideal place for winter layovers, and every year hundreds of maritime workers migrated to southern California, seeking refuge from freezing temperatures and icy conditions that paralyzed shipping operations in more northerly ports. Whether working together on the docks or socializing in neighborhood bars, seamen and longshoremen came in regular contact with one another, giving them ample opportunities to exchange information, ideas, and political philosophies. [20]

Wobblies involved in the coastwide lumber trade also left their imprint on San Pedro's maritime community. The postwar housing boom in southern California led to a growing demand for lumber from the Northwest. In 1922, the first year in which port tonnage statistics were tabulated by commodities, more than fifty thousand long tons of lumber were unloaded at San Pedro, accounting for

36 percent of all imports that year.[21] As an integral part of the coast-wide lumber trade, the port's longshoremen were placed in frequent contact with Wobbly seamen who manned the lumber schooners sailing out of the Northwest. "Every time a steam schooner comes in from Eureka," complained a West Coast shipowner in 1923, "a flood of IWW literature descends upon San Pedro." The large number of Wobblies shipping into the port every year prompted another employer to remark that "seamen of radical tendencies in the Northwest . . . have made San Pedro their Mecca."[22]

The steady influx of radicalized seamen and loggers onto the docks and their close intermingling with the longshoremen created a strong, if still largely ill defined, syndicalist mood along the waterfront. IWW organizers focused this diffuse consciousness around popular notions of workers' control, which animated the struggles of dockworkers in each of the major West Coast ports after World War I.

Wobblies on the West Coast: The Struggle for Workers' Control

For many American workers, particularly those swept up by the increasingly radical attacks on capitalism before World War I, the "new unionism" of workers' control and direct action offered an attractive alternative to the more staid electoral strategies advocated by the Socialist Party. Beginning around 1909 with the growing resistance of skilled craftsmen to the introduction of scientific management, syndicalist practices, as David Montgomery argues, "were to remain the outstanding characteristics of American labor struggles, not episodically but continuously for the next dozen years."[23]

Loosely tied, if at all, to any particular doctrine, the "syndicalist tendencies" that Montgomery and others have identified were embodied in such practices as direct action, labor solidarity, challenges to managerial authority, and, surprisingly often, demands for workers' control. The Wobblies made a name for themselves by agitating around these and other issues, but they were not alone. Joining them were some of the leading "labor aristocrats" of their day, such as the Bridgeport, Connecticut, machinists who circulated petitions calling for "co-operative ownership and democratic management of industry." Contempt for AFL policy also reached new heights. Between April 1917 and November 1918, while the federation's no-strike pledge was still in effect, more than six thousand work stoppages were recorded. When wartime restrictions were lifted, workers in Seattle took matters into their own hands, effectively running the city for five days in February 1919 as part of a highly successful general strike. The following year, more than four million workers, representing almost one-fourth of the nation's labor force, participated in work stoppages, many of which were explicitly aimed at challenging various forms of managerial authority.[24]

On the docks, such syndicalist impulses grew naturally out of the men's experience at the point of production. Employer control over hiring, leading to chronically high levels of unemployment, economic insecurity, and speed-up on the job, made practicing syndicalists out of a great many dockworkers. In Portland, for example, longshoremen took over the hiring of "steady men" in 1901—long before the first Wobbly organizer ever set foot on the docks. Following several years of effective job actions, the local union increased its power sufficiently to assume complete control over all hiring by 1908.[25]

Direct action tactics were also encouraged by the economics of marine transportation. Given the industry's proportionately high level of capital investment and fairly uniform labor costs, profit margins were largely determined by efficiency in stevedoring operations. The length of time a ship was in port, earning no revenues while costly dock charges piled up, had to be minimized. A fast "turnaround" in discharging and loading cargo was therefore essential to economic survival. Time, that most precious of commodities under capitalism, became an effective ally of the longshoremen. By simply slowing down on the job—a tactic the Wobblies later worked to perfection—dockworkers were often able to extract significant concessions from time-conscious shippers.[26]

Such syndicalist practices flourished on their own in the hothouse atmosphere of the waterfront. But it was the Wobblies who cultivated and brought to life the mass movement on the docks.[27] Resuming their agitational activities after the war, they mobilized hundreds of West Coast longshoremen, articulating their common demands in the language of workers' control. Guided by the Wobblies' vision of a worker-run society, dockworkers in each of the major ports succeeded in temporarily establishing their own systems of hiring. These popular experiments in workers' control, however brief, left their mark on the waterfront, reaffirming as well as strengthening the syndicalist components of the dockside subculture.

The casual nature of longshore employment posed the question of control in the sharpest possible terms, for whoever controlled the hiring process quite literally ran the waterfront—deciding who would work, for how long, and under what conditions. Under the employer-dominated system of hiring that prevailed on the West Coast, work assignments were capriciously offered or withheld based on an individual's level of productivity from one day to the next, even one hour to the next. With underemployed and desperate longshoremen locked in fierce competition for steady work, the intensification of the labor process was limited only by the upper level of human endurance. The resulting speed-up, unsafe working conditions, and unequal distribution of earnings all hinged on the employer's undisputed control over hiring.

Employer control was most vigorously contested in the Pacific Northwest where the IWW had sunk its deepest roots. Longshoremen and shipowners first squared off in Seattle in the spring of 1919 when the local Chamber of Commerce, stung by the recent citywide general strike, began an aggressive open-shop drive, targeting many of Seattle's most powerful unions, including the three-thousand-member ILA local.[28] In May, the waterfront employers invoked a recently enacted anti-picketing ordinance in an effort to break the union's grip on the docks. The response from the longshoremen was as imaginative as it was effective. Whenever a collective show of force was called for, they temporarily relocated their union "headquarters" in the vicinity of those docks designated for strike action. As men reported to the hiring hall for work assignments in the morning, the crowd of loyal unionists milling around the "struck" docks rapidly swelled to several hundred illegal but no less effective pickets. Through direct action tactics of this sort the longshoremen not only retained their union shop but also went on to win rotational hiring in their next contract.[29]

Rotational hiring insulated the longshoremen from most forms of employer discipline. Under this method of hiring, job assignments were drawn from a rotating list of union members. When a job vacancy appeared it was automatically filled by the next man on the list, regardless of his productivity. Being dependent on the union for employment, the men proceeded to work at "a respectable union pace" rather than the accelerated tempo previously dictated by the gang boss.

Waterfront employers charged that the list system gave "the radical or inefficient worker equal opportunity for employment with the conservative or steady man."[30] That, of course, was the union's immediate objective—to equalize employment opportunities and earnings. Much more than simply a means for achieving equity, however, rotational hiring tilted the balance of power on the waterfront toward the union. Having seized control over hiring, the men could now slow down on the job or take direct action, knowing that the employers were no longer in a position to retaliate.

Flexing their newfound economic muscle at the point of production, Seattle's dockworkers in 1919 refused to handle weapons destined for Admiral Kolchak's counterrevolutionary White forces in Siberia, thus honoring a pledge, issued six months earlier in a telegram to President Woodrow Wilson, that they would never load arms against the fledgling Soviet republic. After interminable delays in loading the disputed cargo, special police had to be brought in to finish the job. Setting sail from Seattle several weeks after its scheduled departure, the "death ship" finally reached the Russian seaport of Vladivostok in the fall, where its eight-hundred-ton shipment of arms was gratefully received not by Kolchak's forces but by the Red Army, which had recently occupied the city. This compelling lesson in the efficacy of direct political action brought an estimated seven hundred new members into the rapidly growing Seattle branch of the MTW. A leader of the ILA confided that a large majority of the longshoremen were carrying the Wobbly red card.[31]

In Portland, meanwhile, longshoremen were enjoying the fruits of one of the most effective systems of job control on the West Coast. Defying a statewide open-shop initiative passed in 1916, union longshoremen retained de facto control over hiring and implemented a plan for equalizing earnings. Local waterfront employers complained that the union's "dictatorial control" of hiring was driving up shipping rates, placing the port at a competitive disadvantage with the rest of the West Coast. But as in Seattle the real issue was job control; as one shipowner later put it, "the men had begun to boss the job."[32]

Maritime employers struck back in 1920. Beginning in Seattle, they launched a coordinated drive to break the power of longshore unionism on the West Coast by reasserting their traditional prerogatives over hiring. After the first of the year Seattle's employers unilaterally drew up a new contract abolishing rotational hiring. But before it could be put into effect as scheduled on April 12, they began hiring directly off the piers. Union leaders, claiming that this practice discriminated against their members and that it led to an unequal distribution of work, restored the system of rotational hiring. Port activity ground to a halt after the shipowners refused to hire any additional men through the union hall.[33]

The employers then publicly embraced the open-shop "American Plan," sending out a call for two thousand strikebreakers. Union leaders countered that they were in the process of finalizing plans to take over the port's stevedoring operations. In announcing formation of the worker-run Longshoremen's Cooperative Association of Washington, the Co-op's business manager proclaimed: "It's time for labor to make a beginning on real cooperation and industrial democracy. Longshoremen do all the loading and unloading of cargoes passing through Seattle, and there is no reason why longshoremen should not have a direct voice in the management of the industry in which they do all the work."[34]

The Co-op also received the stamp of approval from the head of Seattle's Central Labor Council. "Cooperation," he told a mass meeting of longshoremen, "is the most revolutionary proposal yet advanced for the elimination of capitalism," adding that collective ownership represented an important first step on the road to workers' control. "Do it now," he implored. "You will have to run industry some day, why not begin now?" For their part, the Wobblies parlayed this explosion of syndicalist consciousness into a successful recruiting drive. On the day the Longshoremen's Cooperative was announced, a reliable informant indicated that almost three-fourths of the port's dockworkers belonged to the MTW and that the local ILA hall had been converted into IWW headquarters for paying dues and issuing red cards.[35]

But momentum gradually slipped away from the longshoremen as the postwar slump in shipping activity deepened. Less than a month after walking out for "industrial democracy," they returned to work without the minimal protection of a hiring hall. Seattle's maritime employers then promptly instituted their own registration system designed to identify and eliminate "troublemakers" by requiring anyone seeking work on the docks to join the Waterfront Employers Union, pay an initiation fee, and provide a detailed employment history for the past five years. Still, the shipowners "experienced considerable difficulty weeding out the Reds." In 1921 they introduced a tighter, more centralized system for screening all longshore applicants. Within six months the labor force was reduced from 1,420 to 612 "eligible, skilled men" who, in the words of an employer spokesman, "had established a claim on the waterfront."[36]

Shipowners in nearby Portland, inspired by the "Seattle Plan," notified local union leaders in late April 1922 that all hiring would be conducted through an employer-run hall beginning in May. When the port's six hundred ILA members walked off the job in protest, they were joined by a group of about four hundred men, composed mostly of loggers and other casuals and led by the MTW. Following a poorly managed strike in which Wobblies and ILA members failed to honor each other's picket lines, union leaders were forced to accept the shipowners' original proposal, including the provision that all hiring would be carried out through an employer-run hall, known to the men as the "fink hall."[37]

Working conditions on the docks were dramatically transformed as control over hiring passed from the union to the employers. With the men toiling under an intense speed-up, numerous port production records fell: one nonunion crew, for example, stowed 38,000 sacks of flour in one fifteen-hour shift, averaging 63 tons per hour as compared with 40 to 52 tons per hour before the strike; another gang set a port record by handling 110,000 feet of lumber in less than eight hours.[38] Veteran longshoremen saw their coveted job control, achieved through two decades of struggle, wiped out in a matter of months. Jack Mowrey, a former cabin boy who joined the Wobblies shortly after he began longshoring outside Portland in 1916, recalls that conditions before and after the strike differed "like heaven and hell. The employers had the whip and if you didn't do the work, why, you didn't get no jobs. They'd work you sometimes until midnight and call you back at seven the next morning. . . . They had control and you either done it or you had no job." [39]

With the ILA increasingly on the defensive, MTW organizers renewed their agitation for a union-controlled hiring hall. By October the local MTW branch had been rebuilt into a powerful force on the docks, representing almost three hundred longshoremen. Alarmed by the resurgence of IWW activity, Portland's shipowners decided to begin registering all dockworkers in an effort to identify "Confermed [*sic*] Radicals, Soap Box Orators, and Wobblies." [40] On October 14, the day registration was to begin, members of the ILA and the MTW called a joint strike. As preparations were being made to broaden the walkout by including grain handlers and Teamsters, Portland's mayor hastily ordered a roundup of all suspected MTW members. Carefully combing the waterfront district, police arrested 275 Wobblies within a few hours; subsequent raids brought the total to 350—virtually the entire membership of the local MTW branch. [41] While union leaders languished in jail, charged with offenses ranging from simple vagrancy to criminal syndicalism, the shipowners brought in more and more strikebreakers, until nearly six hundred were working on the docks. When the remaining ILA members, leaderless and dispirited, drifted back to work through the fink hall later that autumn, Portland's long tradition of job control came to an end.

The battle lines then shifted from the Northwest to San Pedro where the Wobblies were beginning to organize against the shipowners' Marine Service Bureau, an open-shop system of hiring modeled after Seattle's Waterfront Employers Union. Early in 1923 the IWW launched a highly effective educational campaign, distributing to every household in the city literature that set forth in clear and simple language "how to do away with the tyranny of the scab hall" and extolled the advantages of industrial organization and the IWW program for emancipating labor. Membership in the MTW grew "by hundreds" as a result of this agitation. When the IWW called a national strike on April 25 to secure the release of all "class war prisoners," most of San Pedro's 3,500 maritime workers walked out, idling more than one hundred vessels. Locally, the demands included recognition of the MTW, improved working conditions for all marine workers, and abolition of the Marine Service Bureau.[42]

Rank-and-file longshoremen enthusiastically answered the strike call: ILA members, by a five-to-one margin, voted to walk out, while the independent Marine Transport Federation recorded a 184-to-48 vote of cooperation. As port congestion worsened, with ship arrivals outnumbering departures threefold,[43] MTW organizers stepped up their agitation. Following a routine street meeting, a Wobbly correspondent noted that "the port delegate and others were busy on the street making out little red cards and several of the delegates commandeered a small store in order to take care of the line-ups." Local press accounts conservatively placed the number of Wobbly longshoremen at around three hundred.[44]

City officials, approaching a state of near panic, responded with mass repression. All street meetings in the harbor area were banned and scores of strikers arrested. In support of their jailed comrades, workers formed an angry procession three blocks long and marched to the county jail singing the revolutionary British transport workers' anthem, "Hold the Fort."[45] More than six hundred longshoremen were arrested the next day on suspicion of criminal syndicalism. Though only about one-third of them actually carried IWW membership cards, a police spokesman stated that many of the others had displayed "radical proclivities." This well-coordinated police action had a chilling effect on the resolve of many strikers. A few days later, after voting to return to work but to continue the fight on the job, San Pedro's longshoremen reluctantly signed up for employment at the Marine Service Bureau.[46]

The Wobblies immediately began a campaign of guerrilla warfare on the docks, participating in numerous slowdowns and spontaneous job actions. As a measure of their continuing support, three hundred marine workers staged a brief walkout in July to protest the conviction of twenty-seven IWW leaders for criminal syndicalism.[47] In response, the shipowners began registering all longshoremen. Through "judicious weeding," the original complement of 3,500 men was sharply reduced to 1,200. If registration "was not altogether a plan to weed out radicals," observed one maritime historian, "it is true that in practice the troublemakers were dropped. Since none but registered longshoremen could obtain work, employers hoped the great number of radicals among the casual workers would soon drift away and the waterfront would be troubled no more by labor agitators."[48]

In San Francisco the struggle for control was pursued on the job rather than through the hiring hall. During the summer of 1919, as dockworkers in Seattle were fighting for rotational hiring, the Riggers and Stevedores Union of San Francisco, a loose affiliate of the ILA, was drawing up a list of even more far-reaching demands, two of which stipulated changes in working conditions that directly challenged the central role of the employer in organizing production. In loading and discharging cargo, the rhythm of work was determined by the size of the draft, or sling load, and by the number of men assigned to handle it, thus making control over these two conditions tantamount to control over the labor process itself.[49] The Riggers, striking at the heart of traditional managerial prerogatives, demanded a reduction in sling loads from the existing 1,800-pound limit to 1,200 pounds while increasing the size of gangs from twelve to sixteen men. A third demand, prefaced with rhetorical flourishes about the United States "running Red with revolution . . . until the worker gets the product of his labor," committed the union to seeking a 10 percent interest in the ownership of the industry, representation on all corporate boards, and a 25 percent share of all future dividends. The final demand was dropped in the early stages of negotiations, but the fact that a majority of longshoremen supported it on at least two occasions conveys a sense of the combative mood then prevailing on the docks.[50]

With neither side willing to compromise on the remaining "control" issues, the port's longshoremen were locked out on September 15 after reporting for work in gangs of sixteen men. A strike was formally authorized later in the week when scabs were put to work under heavy police protection. Leadership of the walkout was then delegated to a special Conference Committee elected from the floor of a mass meeting and composed mostly of rank-and-file militants and Wobblies.[51]

The shipowners wasted no time in beginning their attacks on the Conference Committee. Charging that the Riggers and Stevedores "is at present dominated by a radical group," they flatly refused to negotiate with the union "as now constituted." As the number of strikebreakers grew to almost two thousand, the employers escalated their attacks on the Conference Committee, branding it "a

lawless and radical group of irresponsible persons who have no re-
gard for contracts." The next day nearly four thousand rank-and-
file longshoremen met to discuss the impasse. After four hours of
rancorous debate, a motion to transfer responsibility for negotiations from the radically inclined Conference Committee to the
union's regular executive officers was narrowly carried by a voice
vote.[52]

But the employers were scarcely in a conciliatory frame of mind.
They refused to open talks with the newly constituted negotiating
committee on the pretext that one of its members was under indict-
ment for conspiring to murder a strikebreaker. Incensed, rank-
and-file longshoremen unanimously elected a prominent radical
member of the now defunct Conference Committee as temporary
secretary of the union. The shipowners remained firm, however,
and by the end of October were privately boasting that the once
powerful union had been "busted higher than a kite."[53]

Most union men remained out for another two months before
finally capitulating in mid-December when a contract was signed
with a recently formed company union. Issuing a pale blue membership book, in sharp contrast to the flaming red book of its pre-
decessor, the company union signed an unprecedented five-year
agreement that included a ten-cent reduction in hourly wages and
restoration of the same working conditions that had precipitated
the strike.

Still deeply concerned about the continuing radical presence on
the docks, San Francisco's employers closely monitored membership in the so-called Blue Book union in order "to keep out all the
reds that were in the old Riggers and Stevedores." Preferential employment was selectively extended to Blue Book members, each of
whom had been carefully screened for any history of union activism. In this respect, the company union was indistinguishable
from the employer-run hiring halls that were set up elsewhere on
the coast. Significantly, the Blue Book union had one other thing in
common with the employers—its founder, longshoreman Jack
Bryan, who later became president of the Pacific American Shipowners Association.[54]

The triumph of company unionism in San Francisco brought to
a close the golden age of syndicalism on the docks. As the last vestige of organization on the coast, the Blue Book stood as a vivid

reminder of how great a distance the longshoremen had traveled, from the exhilarating heights of workers' control after World War I to the sobering depths of shipowner hegemony a short time later.

But the fighting spirit of the Wobblies lived on, surviving the open-shop 1920s and blossoming again with the resurgence of maritime unionism on the Pacific. In San Francisco, several MTW veterans, most notably Harry Bridges himself, came forward in the summer of 1933 to lead the fight for union recognition on the docks. Elsewhere on the coast, former Wobblies, some of whom were now working with the Communists, played key roles in helping to get the struggling ILA off the ground. In San Pedro, for example, the first person to sign the formal petition requesting a local ILA charter was Chris Johannson, a former Wobbly. Paul Ware, a prominent MTW activist who served time in San Quentin for violating California's criminal syndicalism law, also signed the original petition and assumed responsibility for mailing it off to ILA headquarters in New York. In Seattle, aging Wobblies joined with ILA loyalists to launch the new union, while in Portland, "men of IWW persuasion and background" were "the most active and influential members of the local."[55]

Besides individual heroics, the Wobblies bequeathed an enduring legacy of militant industrial unionism that profoundly shaped the political contours of longshore unionism in the West. Virtually every demand in the original MTW program was taken up and fought for in the 1930s: union control over hiring was effectively secured in 1934, an industrial federation encompassing all marine crafts on the West Coast was organized in 1935, and uniform load limits and manning schedules were adopted coastwide in 1937. In fact, much of what the longshoremen sought to accomplish in later years was inspired by the IWW's pioneering efforts. As Rosco Craycraft, former ILWU international vice-president, observed, "the Wobblies laid a hell of a good foundation" on the West Coast.[56]

Occupational Recruitment and Port Ecology in New York

The MTW never became a significant social force on the New York docks. Even when objective conditions seemed clearly favorable, as in the dramatic portwide walkout led by rank-and-file in-

surgents in 1919, fewer than 5 percent of all striking longshoremen sided openly with the Wobblies. The relative weakness of
syndicalism on the docks, and the resulting inability of the Wobblies to wean disgruntled rank and filers away from conservative
leaders, was largely attributable to the distinctive sources of occupational recruitment in New York, which, together with the
port's inhospitable social ecology, diminished the attractiveness of
radicalism.

Certainly the most striking feature about occupational recruitment in New York was the virtual absence of men with seafaring
backgrounds. In practically all other parts of the country, including the West Coast, there was considerable movement between sea
and shore, as most seamen typically took up longshoring at some
point in their lives. In New York, however, offshore and dockside
workers appear to have led parallel but widely separated existences.

New York's seafarers inherited a rich tradition of labor radicalism. The port had the distinction of giving birth to the MTW in
1913 when five thousand marine oilers and firemen, mostly of
Spanish descent, voted to leave the hidebound AFL in order to affiliate with the IWW. New York soon became the center of IWW
insurgency among East Coast seamen. The threat to established
leadership grew to such proportions that the national headquarters of the International Seamen's Union, the main AFL union in
the industry, was moved from New York to the less threatening en-
virons of Boston in 1921. Repeated attempts to bar MTW sympathizers from New York failed to uproot the indigenous radical movement among the port's seamen, who would later play a
pivotal role in founding the Communist-led Marine Workers Industrial Union in 1930 and the left-wing National Maritime Union
in 1937.[57]

The port's militant seamen viewed conditions on the docks as
singularly uninviting. With longshore agreements consummated
verbally in the years before World War I, the local ILA had failed to
obtain any measure of job control. The first written contract, signed
by the New York district of the ILA in 1916, included a small wage
increase and an unenforceable preference-of-employment clause
for union members. Otherwise this landmark contract was silent
regarding all aspects of hiring, manning, and safety.[58] Experienced

seamen found the working conditions intolerable. "When a seaman retired in New York," Bill Bailey recalled, "that was it."

> Longshore work there was a son of a bitch. I did a little bit of it when I was a kid. . . . You were going all the time. The work was very hard. You know, you got a bale of cotton on a [hand] truck that weighs six or seven hundred pounds and if you didn't know how to handle it, you flew up in the air and lost your load. Somehow, no matter what you did, the son of a bitch boss was always standing there. So you're runnin' all the time, there was no walking or taking it easy. . . . The longshoremen really produced. Their first step was a walkin' step. No free time. As soon as they got onto the pier, bam, right to the gate without even taking off their coats.[59]

Such deplorable conditions mirrored the shape of the port's labor supply, which was marked by an unusually high proportion of surplus workers or "extra men." The 1920 census turned up some thirty-seven thousand longshoremen in the city of New York. Yet they handled fewer tons of cargo every year than on the West Coast, where the labor force numbered slightly less than eight thousand. Even allowing for the greater weight of many lumber shipments in the West, labor redundancy was a much more acute problem in New York.[60]

The glutted condition of the labor market in the East placed unions at a real disadvantage. With a large pool of workers to choose from, local employers had a relatively easy time recruiting strikebreakers whenever the need arose. At the same time, surplus labor dampened militancy on the job. The ease of securing replacements undermined the disruptive potential of direct action tactics, such as wildcat strikes. And finally, the large reserve of job seekers made restrictionist practices—the lifeblood of American unionism—unpopular with the rank and file and that much more difficult to enforce.

In the West, unionization had flourished under more favorable labor market conditions. From the very beginning, unions did everything in their power to restrict the size of the labor force. Locals of the ILA limited union membership to the regularly employed, thus keeping the number of extra men to a minimum, whereas the Wobblies, who represented many extras, practiced a more political form of restrictionism by excluding from the MTW all sorts of "labor fakirs, phonies, and pie cards." Even with the waning power of organized labor after World War I, restrictionist practices continued in full force as waterfront employers, attempting to root out remaining union sympathizers, limited and closely monitored the growth of the labor force.

These regional differences were magnified by the laws of supply and demand. On the supply side, New York was home to thousands of unskilled immigrants, many of whom were attracted to the docks, where the hourly wage rate for day labor was among the highest in the city. The West Coast also had its armies of unemployed drifters and vagabonds. But, compared to New York's huge immigrant population, they were far less numerous and, what was even more important, their search for unskilled work took them not only to the docks but also to the silver mines of Arizona, the lumber camps of the Pacific Northwest, and the farms of California's agriculturally rich Imperial Valley.[61] As a result, the supply of dockside labor was never anywhere near as great on the West Coast as it was in New York.

Even more significant were regional differences in the demand for labor. On both coasts, employment opportunities fluctuated from day to day depending on the type of ships being worked. In general, vessels confined to domestic routes were the most stable, making regularly scheduled and frequent stops at a number of ports, whereas those engaged in foreign trade, because of the infrequency of sailings and greater distances covered, were considerably less stable, often arriving late, singly or in groups, or sometimes not at all. With these unpredictable deepwater vessels accounting for as much as two-fifths of all maritime traffic in New York—almost twice as much as in the West—dockside employment levels fluctuated more radically. In the course of a single month, the demand for labor was so erratic that three times as many men were hired at the peak as at the lowest point in the demand curve. Faced with such extreme elasticity, local employers, rather than limiting the supply of labor as in the West, insisted on having at their disposal a large reserve of men who could be deployed as needed. The greater economic uncertainties in New York thus gave rise to a more expansive labor market that included a standing army of casual workers numbering close to twenty thousand by World War I.[62]

The industry's chronic problem of job insecurity, already worsened by the large surplus of men, was further exacerbated by the system of hiring in New York. Longshoremen were hired directly off the piers by "shaping-up," sometimes as often as three times a day, in a semicircle around a hiring boss. The shape-up, as later government investigations confirmed, fostered corrupt hiring practices in which workers were required to "kick back" a percentage of their earnings to the hiring boss as a condition of employment.[63]

And once workers were hired, they had no guarantee of steady work. Except for a small group of "regular men" who were attached to some of the larger companies, New York's longshoremen floated from one job to another, rarely spending more than a few days at any one. The extent of turnover is indicated from a sample of payroll records collected by a government research team. An unnamed "Company 3" provided the most complete set of records, covering ten consecutive weeks in 1919. Of 2,030 men employed by Company 3 during this period, a mere 249 showed up on the payroll as often as once in each of the ten weeks surveyed. In other words, close to 90 percent of the labor force could be legitimately classified as "floaters," men who routinely drifted from one company to another in search of work.[64]

This large mass of highly mobile, desperate job seekers drove New York's longshoremen into poverty. As competition for jobs increased, work was spread thinner and thinner until hardly anyone was able to make an adequate living. By 1915, the city's dockworkers were averaging between $520 and $624 in annual earnings, well below the $800 level set by the government as the minimum income necessary to maintain a typical family in "health and decency."[65]

Adverse labor market conditions and the resulting weakness of unions made the docks an unattractive place to work, transforming the New York waterfront into a vast receptacle for an eclectic assortment of displaced workers from varying social backgrounds. A special committee appointed by the mayor of New York in 1916 to investigate hiring practices on the city's docks reported that "men of all kinds of stature, health, previous occupations" were employed as longshoremen.[66] A later, more comprehensive study of occupational histories was based on actuarial data collected by a large New York life insurance company. The forty-five policyholders in this sample who were classified as longshoremen or stevedores in 1924 had originally been recruited from twenty different occupations representing every level of skill, including carpenters, machinists, engineers, laborers, iron workers, stablemen, teamsters, storekeepers, janitors, and bookkeepers.[67]

The prewar labor force in New York was assembled from not only a more diverse but also a less politicized population than on the West Coast. Whereas occupational recruitment in the West drew from a select group of workers whose earlier experiences made them more receptive to syndicalist thought and action, no such pattern of selective recruitment and radicalization was evident in New York. There, labor force recruitment was shaped less by common occupational origins than it was by successive waves of European immigration.

Around the middle of the nineteenth century, as the first wave of European immigrants poured across the waterfront threshold of New York, many sought work on the docks where wage rates were relatively high and employment, though irregular, was easy to come by. During this formative period the city's longshore industry came to depend almost exclusively on immigrant labor. By the turn of the century, three-fourths of New York's dockworkers were foreign-born, compared to roughly half of all longshoremen in the principal West Coast ports. As late as 1920, fewer than one of every ten native-born longshoremen in New York had parents who were also born in the United States, whereas one of every four longshoremen in the West was a second-generation American.[68]

The actual ethnic composition of both regions presented an even more glaring contrast. On the West Coast, longshoremen were overwhelmingly of northern European stock. Scandinavians, many of them former seamen, were the most numerous: in San Francisco and Seattle, they constituted the largest single group on the docks; in Portland, Scandinavians and men bearing Anglo-Saxon surnames together accounted for 80 percent of the port's longshoremen. Aside from a small colony of northern Italians who settled near the San Francisco waterfront, and an even smaller number of Italian fishermen and Yugoslav hardrock miners clustered around San Pedro, longshoremen on the West Coast traced their ancestry to the countries of northern and western Europe.[69]

The ethnic configuration in New York was not only more complex but also far more critical in shaping the character of longshore unionism. Longshoring began as one of the city's most ethnically homogeneous occupations; in 1880 a reliable source estimated that 95 percent of all longshoremen in the port were of Irish descent.[70] Although Irish control of the docks was gradually loosened over the course of several decades, longshore unionism in New York bore an unmistakable Hibernian imprint, reflecting the cultural heritage of its founding members.

Catholicism was perhaps the most significant piece of "cultural baggage" carried by Irish immigrants to America. Religion figured prominently in all phases of their lives in the New World, exerting a particularly strong influence on attitudes toward radicalism and organized labor. Church proselytizing against the "heresy of socialism" turned large numbers of devout Irish Catholics away from radical and left-wing unions. Opposition to socialism, labor theorist Selig Perlman observed, thus came to be seen as "a matter of religious principle" to many Catholic workers.[71]

Catholicism, of course, was not unique to the Irish working class. Yet compared to other Catholic immigrants, the Irish generally appear to have been more receptive to the conservative blandishments of their priests. Indeed, their intense hostility to radicalism made Irish workers "the missing factor" in the city's flourishing socialist movement during the first decades of the century. Between 1908 and 1912, when fully 80 percent of all Socialist Party members in New York City were foreign-born, Irish recruits made up less than 1 percent of the party's total membership. Leaders of the city's struggling Irish Socialist Federation readily acknowledged that religion played a critical role in undercutting the appeal of socialism, and they consciously tried to "downplay any anti-religious elements in socialism."[72]

The extreme conservatism of Irish workers may be partly attributed to their high degree of ideological accessibility to the church. This accessibility varied over time, depending on the presence and relative strength of popular ideologies that placed Catholicism within the context of a broader commitment to Irish national identity. The once powerful force of Irish nationalism, which during the nineteenth century had helped to draw the Irish in this country into various union and reform activities, had been dissipated by cultural assimilation and the slowing of immigration from Ireland. By the end of World War I its impact among second- and third-generation Irish-Americans was negligible. The church's ideological hegemony would not be challenged again until the late 1920s, when a large wave of IRA supporters emigrated to New York, bringing with them as part of their cultural baggage a strong commitment to radical Republicanism.[73]

This view suggests that New York's MTW organizers simply missed the boat, arriving on the waterfront too late to take advantage of Irish nationalism and departing before Republican ideology had a chance to take hold. The absence of a secular alternative to Catholicism after the war left many Irish dockworkers highly accessible to the church—an accessibility enhanced by an extensive network of church shelters and self-help institutes, where destitute marine workers received sanctuary in exchange for religious enlightenment on the evils of "foreign radicalism" and "IWWism."

Around the turn of the century the port's ethnic balance began tilting perceptibly toward more recent immigrants from southern and eastern Europe. Rivulets of Poles, Greeks, and Russians flowed into the much larger stream of Italians coming into New York. By 1900 one of every four newcomers was from Italy and, unlike earlier immigrants from the industrialized countries of northern Europe, a majority had agricultural backgrounds. Between 1901 and 1911 more than 80 percent of all Italians entering New York were from the semifeudal region of southern Italy. One study estimated that three-fourths of the males in this group were of peasant origin.[74]

Unaccustomed to urban life, these immigrants fell victim to the enterprising padrone. Typically a fellow villager, he tutored his non-English-speaking countrymen in "the ways of this strange land," providing many of life's necessities, including jobs. In his role as a labor contractor, mediating between native employers and foreign workers, the padrone reinforced Old World patterns of obligation and deference. To the extent that this paternalistic arrangement shielded the laborer from the excesses of employers, the system of padronism functioned as a culturally familiar, often benign substitute for unionization.[75]

At other times, however, padronism was subject to serious abuse. On the New York waterfront, many Italian stevedoring contractors brazenly exploited the dependent status of their compatriots, forcing them to accept the most onerous and hazardous job assignments under the worst conditions. Working at a feverish pace under the watchful eye of the "boss stevedore," Italian dockworkers were reportedly "more tractable" than their Americanized Irish counterparts. The economically secure Irish were "not always dependable," noted a contemporary source. But the Italians "could be relied on to turn up when wanted, and to hang around as long as there was any chance of work." [76]

In time, perhaps, the developed sense of occupational solidarity so often displayed by the port's Irish dockworkers might have led them to embrace the Italians, just as they later learned to accept other nationalities who took up longshoring. But in the case of Italians, the process of assimilation was complicated by the historical circumstances surrounding their appearance on the waterfront.

New York's Italians were introduced to longshoring as strikebreakers during a portwide walkout in 1887. What began in early January as a local job action by 150 Manhattan dockworkers over a pay dispute had mushroomed by the end of the month into a general strike consuming the entire New York–New Jersey waterfront and involving an estimated 50,000 harbor workers led by the Knights of Labor. Once the port was completely tied up, Italians and blacks were recruited as strikebreakers. Rioting flared along the waterfront as strikers tried desperately, often violently, to prevent the movement of cargo. Following rumors of an impending settlement, there was a frantic rush for the piers. Thousands of demoralized Irish longshoremen "jammed the gates of the docks, pleading for jobs—any jobs, at any price—shoving and thrusting each other aside." The "Big Strike," as it was remembered, inaugurated a period of ethnic-based rivalry that undermined any future prospect of portwide unity. [77]

Italians, now viewed as a form of strike insurance by the shipowners, were deliberately hired in large numbers until by 1912 they constituted one-third of all longshoremen in the port. Separated by language and culture from the more Americanized Irish longshoremen, "a gang of Italians was found to have a deterrent effect upon them. The Irish were afraid of Italian competition. This fear lessened the likelihood of a strike and kept the men from actively resisting abuses." Ethnic cleavages were reproduced on the job by placing Italians in segregated gangs, paying them less, and assigning them the most offensive cargoes. Residential segregation gradually led to a physical separation of the two groups, with Italians congregating in Brooklyn and the Irish concentrated in the

Chelsea district on the lower west side of Manhattan. Living in separate neighborhoods and isolated from each other at work, Irish and Italian longshoremen exhibited a strong ethnic consciousness, or "sectional feeling," as a contemporary observer described it.[78]

The existence of distinct ethnic enclaves throughout the port illustrates what Hobsbawm has termed "the built-in tendency of dockside unionism to grow up as a mosaic of locally based unions."[79] On the New York waterfront, local self-sufficiency was rooted in the lack of any natural geographic or occupational focal point for union organization. Regions of the port, even individual piers, survived as organized islands within a sea of disorganization. As a result, the strength of unionization varied widely among the port's fifty-four ILA locals. The Chelsea district was generally better organized than Brooklyn, but there was immense variation within both areas. One of the strongest and most militant locals in the entire port, for instance, was located in Brooklyn within walking distance of the United Fruit docks, which remained an open-shop stronghold well into the 1930s. This pattern of localism, together with the developed "sectional feeling" of both ethnic groups, made portwide solidarity—and hence effective unionism—virtually impossible.

Insurgency, Defeat, and Conservative Renaissance in New York

Dockside localism was overcome in England at the turn of the century, according to Hobsbawm, by a progressive leveling of skill differentials along with a vigorous socialist leadership that unified harbor workers organizationally as well as ideologically. In New York, significant skill differences for most categories of longshore work had long since been obliterated by waterfront mechanization. There, it was the failure of radical leadership that perpetuated port localism and the consequent stunted development of dockside unionism.

Radical insurgents in New York were handed a seemingly ideal situation in the fall of 1919. Earlier in the year representatives from the ILA's North Atlantic District Council had submitted wage demands calling for a thirty-five-cent hourly increase for straight time and ninety cents for overtime. When shipowners dismissed the union's demands as exorbitant, the matter was referred for arbitration to the National Adjustment Commission, which had been assigned the responsibility of regulating wages and conditions on the docks during the war. In October, after several weeks of deliberation, the commission awarded a wage increase of five cents an hour for straight time and ten cents for overtime. Chelsea's four thousand dockworkers expressed their dissatisfaction with this five-and-ten-cent "Woolworth raise" by failing to return from their afternoon meal break. Within two days the walkout was portwide, involving close to forty thousand dockworkers.[80]

Union officers, denouncing the work stoppage as unauthorized, asserted that it had been "engineered by the IWW." International ILA President T. V. O'Connor, who had reluctantly accepted the commission's award on behalf of the union, made several ineffectual attempts to get the recalcitrant strikers back to work. When he spoke before a gathering of longshoremen in Brooklyn, reminding them of the union's pledge to abide by all commission rulings, the angry crowd responded by calling for his resignation. "I can do nothing at present," O'Connor explained later. "The men are dominated by Bolsheviki and IWWs combined with radical elements in the union. When they come to their senses, the strike will be over." Supporting his contention that radicals were behind the walkout, O'Connor produced a handbill, signed by the MTW, urging the formation of "One Big Union" for all maritime workers.[81]

Any notion that the walkout had been instigated by radicals was dispelled at the first mass meeting. With more than three thousand longshoremen in attendance, John Reilly, president of the ILA's New York District Council, was unanimously elected chairman of the strike committee. Reilly, a conservative protégé of O'Connor, had been opposed by the men only a few days before. But as the leaderless walkout evolved from a desperate act of defiance into a full-scale strike, Reilly's position within the union as well as his contacts with influential employers suddenly became more important than his obvious lack of militant credentials. When a member of the audience, presumably a Wobbly, rose to denounce Reilly, cries of "throw him out" filled the hall, and the intrepid speaker was chased down two flights of stairs and out onto the street. The meeting was then adjourned, following a formal motion censuring the IWW.[82]

None of the available evidence supports O'Connor's contention that the IWW was deeply involved in the strike. Identifiable Wobblies constituted a tiny fraction of all those arrested during six weeks of violent confrontations between unionists, strikebreakers, and authorities. Among the scores of longshoremen taken into police custody, only four young Italians from Brooklyn were found to possess the IWW red card. Nor did the Wobblies have much of an organized presence in the leadership of the strike. Indeed, if IWW sympathizers had any role at all in planning the walkout it was not apparent from the nature of the strikers' demands, which contained no mention of anything remotely suggesting IWW influence. There were none of the obligatory references to industrial solidarity, nor was there any attempt to broaden the scope of the wage demand to include other maritime workers. Control over hiring, improved working conditions, and recognition of the MTW were never raised as issues.[83] But perhaps the most compelling argument comes from the Wobblies themselves, who reported that twelve hundred longshoremen were "lined-up" by the MTW in New York during the period of the walkout. If we assume that this number is roughly equivalent to the MTW's sphere of influence, Wobblies and their supporters represented less than 5 percent of all strikers.[84] By every conceivable measure, then, the walkout had little to do with the alleged machinations of radical agitators.

Wobbly-baiting, it turns out, was nothing more than a smokescreen to cover up the strike's underlying dynamic, which in fact reflected a developing faction fight between O'Connor and an equally conservative group of challengers based in Chelsea. Led by Richard Butler, formerly an official in the rival Longshoremen's Protective Association, and Paul Vacarelli, an international vice-president of the ILA until his expulsion earlier in the year, dissident forces backed the original wage demand primarily as a means of solidifying opposition against the union's international officers. They insisted that O'Connor lacked formal authority to accept the commission's award, to which the embattled president responded by suspending Butler's home local.[85]

The dissidents emerged victorious a few days later, however, when Mayor Hylan of New York passed over O'Connor and appointed Vacarelli to represent striking longshoremen on a Special Conciliation Commission that was formed to help end the walkout. Having thus discredited O'Connor's leadership, Butler and Vacarelli lost their enthusiasm for the strike. Early in November they ordered the remaining strikers to report for work "not in a surly or vindictive spirit, but with the determination to give the employers a full dollar's worth of work for every dollar they pay."[86]

In their efforts to contain the walkout, Butler and Vacarelli had benefited enormously from the persistence of port localism. Shortly after the strike broke out, several ILA locals had announced their intentions to resume work. One week later twelve locals were already back on the job. Localism was especially strong among Brooklyn's longshoremen, who had been polarized into warring camps almost from the beginning. By the middle of October the waterfront there was crisscrossed with intersecting zones of strike activity and scabbing. The situation degenerated to the point that one pier would be completely tied up while an adjacent pier, under jurisdiction of the same local, was busily handling cargo. Although Manhattan's dockworkers were more solidly behind the walkout, small groups of 50 to 180 men returned to work at scattered piers along the Chelsea waterfront as the strike progressed. Given the existence of numerous "safe harbors" throughout the port, the employers were able to move ships and cargo around with relative freedom, shrewdly playing one group off against another until the strike was broken.[87]

Defeat taught the longshoremen the importance of self-reliance. In their eyes, they had been misled by radical agitators, sold out by union leaders, and even abandoned by some of their fellow workers. The lesson was clear: survival meant self-reliance. Turning ever more inward, they looked to their immediate co-workers for support, steadfastly refusing for more than two decades to participate in another portwide job action of any kind.

Conclusion

Rank-and-file insurgencies, erupting almost simultaneously on both coasts after World War I, reduced the ILA to impotency in New York and all but eliminated it as a force on the Pacific. Yet despite these superficially similar outcomes, there were important differences in the historical significance and political consequences attached to the union's defeat in these two regions. On the West

Coast, where the rank-and-file upsurge was unleashed by syndicalist forces grouped around the IWW, dockworkers fought long and hard under radical leadership to fundamentally redefine their relationship to the job by acquiring greater control over many of the most important features of their work environment. In New York, however, where the mass movement was harnessed by opportunistic secondary leaders of the ILA, syndicalist agitators found the going much rougher; instead of leading the insurgency, they trailed behind it, and, as a consequence, the longshoremen ended up fighting not for workers' control but rather for the narrowest of wage demands.

Reflecting on their failure in New York, a veteran MTW activist cited "the lack of mental effort" on the part of the longshoremen.[88] But if mental sluggishness or, in the Leninist idiom, "false consciousness" appeared as the proximate cause of their failure, the relative strength of syndicalism on both coasts was materially grounded in the characteristics of the dockside labor force itself. The labor force in the West—composed mainly of former sailors and loggers, whose earlier experiences had left many of them open to radicalism—was already predisposed to the Wobblies' rough-and-tumble brand of syndicalism. In New York, however, dockworkers were far less responsive to similar IWW overtures. Weighed down by conservative cultural baggage, confronting an unfavorable labor market, and balkanized into warring factions by longstanding ethnic rivalries and urban geography, they denounced "IWWism" and rejected the Wobblies. The character of this initial contact with radical leadership supplied the basic raw material out of which longshoremen on both coasts began fashioning their distinctive and contrasting political cultures.

The important question of who got there first may thus largely depend on the particular circumstances under which workers first encounter a potential leadership. Simply being present from the beginning is rarely enough. Indeed, whatever advantage comes from being first can be realized only when the workers themselves are favorably predisposed toward fresh ideas and new leaders. Getting there first, then, has less to do with timing per se than with the receptivity of the rank and file, as determined by intersecting patterns of personal biography, history, and social structure.

Chapter Three

Shipowners Organize

One of the principal "staging areas of Communist penetration" during the 1930s, notes a leading specialist, was "violent employer opposition to unionism."[1] Where reactionary employers aggressively resisted the extension of economic citizenship, as, for example, in auto, hardrock mining, and the marine industry, workers embraced a more combative and politically radical leadership than in such industries as rubber, glass, and wood products, where opposition to union recognition was less strenuous.[2] Given that capital's initial response to labor is so crucial, why is it that some employers embark on a course of conflict while others follow a path of accommodation?

In the longshore industry, employers traveled down both roads during the formative stages of unionization. Whereas shipowners in New York maintained uninterrupted and harmonious relations with the ILA during the open-shop 1920s, their counterparts on the Pacific, including representatives from many of the same shipping lines, systematically suppressed any signs of independent unionism on the docks. Comparing employer responses in 1930, Joseph Ryan, ILA international president, commended shipowners on the North Atlantic for not taking "undue advantage" of the union and chastised steamship interests on the Pacific Coast for "not yet display[ing] sufficient confidence in our organization."[3]

These contrasting employer approaches solidified the divergent political cultures that were already taking shape in these two regions. In the West, where recently recruited seamen and loggers began interpreting and understanding their new surroundings as working longshoremen, their views were increasingly influenced by the particular way they experienced class relations on the docks. Protracted shipowner resistance served only to strengthen their existing syndicalist beliefs—providing, as two students of the industry observed, "powerful, practical support for the view that the interests of the employers and those of the men were deeply opposed."[4]

In this way, the intransigence of West Coast shipowners fueled the fires of radicalism on the docks. As San Francisco longshore leader Henry Schmidt put it: "The union was made radical by the employers. They really left us no choice." Whether or not a choice actually existed, the rank and file, having endured years of employer abuse, did not see one. Once the longshoremen got the upper hand following the 1934 strike, they went after the shipowners with a vengeance. After being "exploited for years," admitted one old-timer, "it felt real good to spit in the employer's eye."[5] This explosion of class consciousness in the West stood in sharp contrast to the continuing passivity of dockworkers in New York. There, in the absence of both syndicalist traditions and employer resistance, a working-class culture had taken hold that was as conservative as the West's was radical.

This chapter examines the sources of shipowner resistance and accommodation on the docks, arguing that employers' responses reflected their relative organizational capacities as shaped by regional differences in industry economics.

Determinants of Capital's Response to Labor

Early attempts to understand employer responses grew out of a voluntaristic conception of industrial relations in which the quality of face-to-face interaction between capital and labor, rather than the structural properties of the two, became the primary focus. Borrowing liberally from the human relations school, these analyses saw labor and management as mirror images of each other, with the actions of one conditioning and reciprocally influencing the other. This position was forcefully argued by Clinton Golden and Harold Ruttenberg in *Dynamics of Industrial Democracy*, their seminal study of prewar collective bargaining. "Management as a general rule," they observed, "gets the kind of union leadership it deserves. A tough management begets tough union leaders, while a patient, friendly, cooperative management begets a like type of union leadership." From this perspective, "employer ideologies" were viewed as critical determinants of industrial peace or conflict. Others attached greater importance to the behavior of union leaders in first determining employer ideologies, but both approaches—whether they began with capital or with labor—were premised on a "strict parallelism" between the responses of both parties.[6]

The interactive quality of this argument is at once its major strength and its major weakness. By drawing attention to the reflexive character of union and employer actions, the "mirror analogy" offers a dynamic model that is especially well suited for understanding changes in labor relations over time. But in treating unions and employers as simple reflections of each other, it becomes difficult if not impossible to distinguish cause from effect. Without a theory about the *sources* of union and employer behavior, we cannot know whether management created labor in its own image or whether in fact it was the other way around.[7]

The question of causation would be of little consequence were it not for the fact that the quality of face-to-face relations is initially structured by the surrounding industrial environment. Thus, labor-management cooperation and low levels of conflict are more characteristic of some industries than others. To make sense of these interindustry patterns, economists came up with a more structuralist explanation linking employer responses to the character of the product market. The argument is that, ceteris paribus, firms whose markets are protected from cost-cutting competition are in a better position to promote cooperative relations with labor. Not only do they receive higher rates of profit with which to "buy" labor peace, but they are also, as sheltered producers, able to pass on added labor costs to consumers through higher prices.[8] Much the same reasoning underlies the claims of "revisionist" historians who contend that the largest and most monopolistic firms—the so-called corporate liberals—have traditionally been the most supportive of collective bargaining and labor's right to organize.[9]

Both arguments assume that sheltered producers, once they recognize the importance of pacifying labor, will choose to do so by allowing some portion of their "monopoly rents" to trickle down to "their" workers. But they may also choose a more belligerent route to working-class pacification, using their vast economic resources not to co-opt but to destroy unions. Or, more commonly, they may alternate between the two strategies: monopoly rents that one year are used to raise wages may be used the next to recruit strikebreakers. The conclusion seems inescapable that, as Randy Hodson put it, concentrated market power "appears to operate as a double-edged sword, providing an expanded base of revenues, from which wage increases may be secured, as well as providing heightened corporate power, which may be used to undermine worker power."[10]

This element of indeterminacy is greatly reduced in situations where market power is low. For unprotected firms earning smaller rates of profit, the "corporate liberal" strategy of attempting to buy labor peace simply is not an option that individual employers are willing to entertain; and even if it was, the competitive reality of the market would require them to respond in the way that is perceived as most cost-efficient in the short run. As a result, competitive-sector employers normally face more uniform economic pressures, which compel them to resist unions.

But it would be misleading to explain employer actions simply as results of product markets, even highly competitive ones. Indeed, some of the most accommodating employers in the country have been found in traditionally competitive industries such as bituminous coal mining, building construction, and long-distance trucking. In such cases, the lack of fit between market characteristics and employer behavior is no accident. It does, however, reflect the failure of most economically oriented observers to consider the intervening role of organizational processes; as economist Almarin Phillips notes, few of his colleagues ever look beyond the interests of individual firms to the conditions affecting interfirm coordination and organization.[11]

The study of interfirm collaboration has been taken up by organizational theorists, mostly through research on corporate networks. Various dimensions of intercorporate life have been systematically examined, particularly the strength and direction of interlocks, the centrality of finance capital, and the processes of political mobilization.[12] Although this research has shed considerable light on the interorganizational structure of corporate capitalism, we still know relatively little about the conditions that allow employers to organize themselves within the industrial relations arena.

The following analysis illuminates the process of employer organization through a comparison of shipowner responses on the two coasts. Incorporating the insights of the interactive model as well as certain arguments advanced by labor economists, it acknowledges the influence of union-employer interaction on the one hand and product market competition on the other. But, as we will see, neither of these variables adequately accounts for the pattern of employer responses on the waterfront. Our analysis therefore turns to an investigation of organizational dynamics, in which differences in employer responses are traced to the shipowners' relative capacities for self-organization.

Employer Responses on the Waterfront

During the interwar years, the maritime industry closely approximated the economist's model of perfect competition. With a large number of suppliers and little to differentiate one from the other, shipping was a risky, highly competitive undertaking. Profit margins, never very wide to begin with, all but disappeared with the slump in shipping activity following the stock market crash. In 1931, 83 percent of all American-owned intercoastal carriers lost money, as did 36 percent of coastwise companies (servicing either the Pacific or Atlantic seaboard) and 37 percent of operators engaged in overseas trade.[13] For individual shippers already operating close to the margin, failure to "hold the line" meant financial ruin, while for the industry as a whole, stiff competition from alternative modes of domestic transportation as well as from foreign shipping lines exerted a strong downward pressure on wages and other variable costs of production. The competitive nature of the product market severely limited most employers' ability to afford unions, thus creating an industrywide intolerance to labor organization.[14]

Within the constraints imposed by industry economics, water-

front employers were far more intransigent on the Pacific than in
New York. In part, this reflected the different character of the initial
contact between labor and capital on the coasts, with employers in
the West reacting more aggressively to the strength of syndicalism
on the docks—"matching fire with fire," as the shipowners saw it.
But whether the first spark was actually struck by the union or by
the employers is difficult to say. What is clear, though, is that employer fires raged on waterfronts all across the country regardless
of the character of the union. On the Gulf Coast, shipowners "energetically opposed" the ILA, despite the union's unquestionably
"conservative philosophy and moderate actions." Before World
War I, Southern shipowners fought the conservative ILA with determination, deploying the full range of anti-union weapons then
available to "eradicate any vestige of organized labor" from the
waterfront.[15] It was much the same story on the Great Lakes, where
the ILA, led by District President Daniel Keefe, was characterized
as "anti-radical to the point of being radical." Keefe's collaborationist policies, marked by his absolute refusal to authorize any
form of strike action, earned for him "only the strongest words of
commendation" from local employers.[16] And yet, as on the Gulf,
union moderation failed to elicit a like response from employers.
Instead, Great Lakes employers "displayed a solidarity, determination, and ruthlessness unequaled on the coasts." If, as the interactive model suggests, labor gets what it deserves, then clearly the
noncombative unions on the Gulf Coast and the Great Lakes were
shortchanged.[17]

　　Thus it is not likely that labor radicalism alone caused employer
resistance on the West Coast; rather, it merely brought such resistance to the surface. So, too, did the competitive nature of the
product market, which compelled shipowners on both coasts to
oppose unions. The reason they were so much more aggressive in
the West than in New York had less to do with the organization of
labor than with the organization of capital—specifically, the shipowners' relative abilities to constitute themselves as a class of actors
in opposition to the longshoremen.

　　In shipping—as in most competitive product markets—the
capacity for employer self-organization grew as the industry itself became more concentrated. In England, for example, ship-

owner associations did not really take hold until after the turn of the century, when the process of concentration had advanced far enough to create a few large firms whose consolidated economic strength and more expansive vision enabled them to provide leadership as well as organizational direction for the industry as a whole. Summarizing these developments, Hobsbawm writes: "On the waterside, employers had to achieve a degree of concentration which allowed them to see the problem as one of the industry as a whole, and not merely as one of individual entrepreneurs or sections within it; or else sections of large employers, with wider views, had to be effectively counterposed to the multiplicity of small ones with a narrower outlook."[18] In the United States, too, the industry had to reach a high degree of concentration before employer organization became possible. On the Great Lakes, the massive Isthmian Line, a corporate subsidiary of U.S. Steel, was the driving force behind the Lake Carriers Association. The powerful Lykes-Ripley shipping combine took charge of organizing its smaller Gulf Coast competitors, while on the Pacific Coast, this crucial leadership role was collectively assumed by the "Big Three" firms of Matson, American-Hawaiian, and Dollar.[19] In each case, capital concentration enhanced the shipowners' capacity for self-organization, which—given the competitiveness of the product market—manifested itself in vigorous employer opposition to unions.

In New York, the port's largest domestic lines confronted a similarly competitive product market. However, unlike shipowners elsewhere, they ended up cooperating with the union. Although the conservative character of the East Coast ILA may have moderated employer hostility to some extent, what set the port's employers apart from other shipowners was the wider dispersion of capital, which left local shipping interests leaderless and without direction.

Table 1 compares the extent of capital concentration in New York and on the West Coast for 1930. Compiled from records of the American Bureau of Shipping, it ranks, on the basis of vessel ownership, the ten largest domestic lines headquartered in both regions. The aggregate vessel tonnage of the ten largest companies in each region was approximately the same: 1.2 million tons on the

TABLE I. *Number and Gross Tonnage of Vessels Owned by the Ten Largest American Lines Headquartered on the Pacific Coast and in New York City, 1930*

Pacific Coast Lines	Number of Vessels	Gross Tons	Percentage of Total Tonnage
Matson Navigation Co.	50	301,206	24.8
American-Hawaiian SS Co.	41	262,891	21.6
Dollar Co.	24	203,439	16.7
Pacific Atlantic SS Co.	17	99,639	8.2
American Mail Line	5	70,730	5.8
Pacific SS Co.	21	68,260	5.6
States SS Co.	12	67,600	5.6
Alaska SS Co.	14	54,311	4.5
Tacoma Oriental SS Co.	7	44,072	3.6
Alaska Packers Assn.	14	43,561	3.6
Totals		1,215,799	100.0

New York City Lines	Number of Vessels	Gross Tons	Percentage of Total Tonnage
United States Lines	11	187,871	16.2
Luckenback SS Co.	19	147,443	12.7
Export SS Co.	24	126,308	10.9
Munson SS Line	26	125,848	10.8
United Fruit	24	110,924	9.6
Grace SS Co.	18	108,702	9.4
Moore & McCormack	20	98,512	8.5
Eastern SS Line	29	92,647	8.0
American Line SS Corp.	3	81,693	7.0
Bull SS Co.	24	80,585	6.9
Totals		1,160,533	100.0

Sources: American Bureau of Shipping, *1930 Record of American and Foreign Shipping* (New York: American Bureau of Shipping, 1930) (figures limited to nonindustrial carriers of at least 1,000 gross tons). Company totals include all subsidiary holdings as identified in *Moody's Manual of Investments. American and Foreign Industrial Securities* (New York: Moody's Investors Service, 1931), pp. 304, 2762.

Note: The preferred measure of industrial concentration would be standardized industry concentration ratios based on the market share controlled by the top four firms. Unfortunately, such ratios are not calculated for transportation industries. Therefore vessel ownership—the next best indicator of market power—is used as the measure of concentration here. Shipping, like any transport industry, also raises special problems for regional comparison because the means of production (ships) are not permanently fixed in one location. Two criteria for locating companies—where they conduct most of their business and where they are headquartered—were used in assigning companies to either the Pacific Coast or New York.

Pacific as compared to 1.1 million in New York. But as Table 1 reveals, the overall distribution of vessel tonnage was very different. In the West, vessel ownership was concentrated among the Big Three—Matson, American-Hawaiian, and Dollar. Together they accounted for more than three-fifths (63 percent) of the tonnage held by the ten largest West Coast lines. The concentration was so marked that Dollar, the third-ranked firm, had more than twice the holdings of the next largest company. In contrast, vessel ownership in New York was more evenly distributed, with no single line enjoying more than a 20 percent advantage over its nearest-ranked competitor. The top three New York lines held about two-fifths (40 percent) of all tonnage on the East Coast, considerably less than their counterparts on the West Coast.

These differences in the levels of capital concentration significantly shaped employer responses in each region. The more concentrated structure of shipping in the West allowed the Big Three lines to play a decisive leadership role on the Pacific Coast. Already backed into a corner by the industry's low tolerance for unionism, then forced to confront a well-organized and militant labor force, the Big Three came out fighting, using their superior economic muscle to galvanize the many smaller firms around an uncompromisingly anti-union program. In New York, however, the more even distribution of shipping capital produced a leadership vacuum. Without an organizational center of gravity, the many medium-size employers were scarcely able to initiate, much less enforce, any plan of portwide action for dealing with labor.

The organizational ability of New York's domestic lines, already diminished by the wider dispersion of capital, was undermined still further by the deep fragmentation of the local maritime economy. Unlike the West Coast where the largest American commercial lines clearly dominated the industry, shipping in New York was more evenly parceled out among domestic commercial operators, subsidized U.S. government lines, and powerful foreign shippers. Though trade agreements and international maritime law prevented certain classes of shippers from directly competing with one another, the presence of three distinct groups of employers made the search for portwide unity that much more elusive. Lacking both a core leadership group at the top and an enduring basis for solidarity at the bottom, the shipowners' intolerance toward unionism was expressed not in collective resistance—as on the West Coast—but rather through informal modes of accommodation between individual shipping lines and the port's conservative union leadership.

The Big Three Organize the Pacific

Employers on the West Coast vigorously opposed organized labor from the very beginning. In 1914, well before the MTW was a force on the docks, San Francisco shipowners formed the open-shop Waterfront Employers Association, the first such organization of its kind anywhere in the country to deal exclusively with longshore labor. Within a few years, employers in each of the major ports had established separate negotiating bodies for sailors and longshoremen. This "departmentalization" plan altered the basic contours of the emerging marine working class, splintering an already fragmented labor force along traditional craft lines and reasserting the primacy of occupation over industry as the basis of collective action. In the words of a leading maritime historian, this formal reorganization "made it appear that there was no common interest between shore workers and the men who sailed the ships— a strategy which prevented all the waterfront workers from uniting along industrial lines for many years."[20]

The Big Three were prime movers in these early reorganization efforts. Through their control of the San Francisco employers' association, which provided leadership to local associations in the Northwest and San Pedro, they exercised a significant influence on coastwide policy. According to Thomas Plant, past president of the San Francisco association, American-Hawaiian was the "moving spirit" behind the city's waterfront employers, with Matson, Dollar, and two smaller lines playing an important supportive role throughout the 1920s.[21]

Pacific shipowners grew restive with the onset of the Depression. Plant, a corporate vice-president with American-Hawaiian, assumed the presidency of the San Francisco waterfront employers group. Under his aggressive leadership, West Coast shipowners adopted an increasingly belligerent posture toward longshore unionism. In March 1934, with twelve thousand longshoremen on the Pacific Coast preparing to walk out in support of closed-shop recognition of the ILA and union-controlled hiring, Plant defiantly announced that "thousands of men now unemployed will be glad to get the jobs." When the strike finally broke out two months later, Roger Lapham, president of American-Hawaiian, took an equally firm line. Branding strike leaders "out and out Communists," he characterized the demand for union recognition as an attempt to "break down the walls of government."[22]

The employers at first welcomed the 1934 walkout as an opportunity to finally rid the waterfront of longshore unionism. A government mediator directly involved in pre-strike negotiations later wrote to his superiors at the National Labor Board that "the shipowners were confident of victory and gave me to understand that even if they lost two or three million, it would be worth it to destroy the union."[23] But the cost of doing battle with the ILA proved far greater than the employers had anticipated. The paralysis of maritime commerce during the first month of the strike idled an estimated $45 million of coastwise cargo. Besides incurring huge losses in revenue, shipowners paid considerable sums out of their own pockets to maintain small-scale, largely symbolic strikebreaking operations in several ports. In San Pedro, where these efforts were most successful, provisions for housing, feeding, and protecting scabs cost local employers nearly $7,000 a day.[24]

Yet the shipowners remained adamant. Early in the walkout, the mayor of San Francisco convened a meeting with the city's most "prominent shipping men" to discuss the impasse. The shipowners, represented by an officer from each of the Big Three firms and one other company, flatly refused to concede any ground to the union. With these hard-liners dictating employer strategy, the walkout dragged on for three months before the shipowners reluctantly agreed to recognize the ILA.[25]

Settlement of the 1934 strike failed to soften employers' opposition to the new union. Instead, the shipowners attempted, as the La Follette Committee later described in its report to the U.S. Senate, "to drive a wedge between the radical and conservative elements" in the ILA. Harry Bridges, the fiery young leader of the San Francisco local, was the principal target of this campaign. Early in 1935, Lapham traveled to Washington to personally urge the Secretary of Labor to initiate deportation proceedings against Bridges, an Australian immigrant and alleged communist.[26] When government cooperation was not readily forthcoming, San Francisco employers turned to conservative union officers for help in dislodging Bridges. Over a period of several months, the shipowners—again led by the Big Three—covertly supplied money, organizing resources, advice, and encouragement to conservative ILA leaders at both the district and the international levels. Summing up these efforts in a confidential memo in the spring of 1935, Plant wrote:

> We have worked all angles—the Department of Labor, J. P. Ryan, Lewis, Peterson, and other conservative ILA leaders on this coast. Our only apparent hope of progress lies in trying to persuade the conservative leaders that if they wanted to preserve anything for the ILA, they would have to set their own house in order. . . . We have had reason to believe that [conservatives] Lewis and Peterson and some of the others are really making progress. It is, of course, a slow process. It is obvious that if we do anything to hurt Lewis and Peterson and the other conservatives at this time, we nullify all the work they are doing in their efforts to clean out the radicals.[27]

But conservative ILA leaders were in no position to rally the rank and file behind any such anti-radical crusade. Recognizing this, the employers embraced a more confrontational approach. "I am for decisive action at this time," Lapham declared in presenting his "suspension program" before a strategy meeting of the waterfront employers in the fall of 1935. His proposal called for unilaterally suspending relations with the ILA until its radical leadership publicly agreed to clamp down on unauthorized job actions. In this way, Lapham argued, they would pit Bridges and other union leaders, who were contractually bound to enforce the existing agreement, against an increasingly restive rank and file. Lapham's proposal encountered strong opposition from many smaller employers who saw it as dangerously provocative. Reservations were also expressed by several New York–based intercoastal lines. But the Big Three once again prevailed. In December, representatives from American-Hawaiian, Matson, and a leading British line were sent east to shore up support for the suspension program. Shipowners on both coasts "are said to be in constant contact," reported the *New York Times*, "and well informed sources indicate the employers are ready for a showdown."[28]

The shipowners patiently waited for an appropriate situation to execute their suspension program. Employer documents from this period, as summarized by the La Follette Committee, reveal "a somewhat startling spectacle of a group of employers, who, having determined to engage the unions with which they had agreements in a struggle that would interrupt commerce and business on a wide scale, were unable to find a pretext for initiating the conflict that could be put reasonably before the public and the unions."[29] A suitable opportunity finally presented itself in April 1936, when the *Santa Rosa,* an intercoastal steamer with a crew of strikebreakers, docked at San Pedro. Declaring the *Santa Rosa* "unfair," local marine workers refused to service the nonunion vessel. The employers decided to discharge all passengers and mail in San Pedro and then reroute the *Santa Rosa* north in an attempt to unload its remaining "hot cargo." When the disputed vessel reached San Francisco, it was greeted by an angry crowd of pickets dispatched by the Maritime Federation of the Pacific. Even though the port's longshoremen voted not to join the picket line on the grounds that the entire incident "was a bum beef," the shipowners used the boycott of the *Santa Rosa* as an excuse to suspend relations with their union.

It immediately became apparent that removing Bridges from office, rather than the public issue of contract compliance, was the employers' main objective, as they announced that the entire port would remain shut "until Harry Bridges is no longer head of the union." But this smoothly executed lockout backfired. Instead of discrediting Bridges, the employers' attack transformed him into a martyr, rallying to his defense not only rank-and-file longshoremen but also some of San Francisco's most conservative and respected labor leaders. After the port had been tied up for one week, "Bloody Mike" Casey, an old-line Teamster leader who had openly clashed with Bridges during the 1934 waterfront strike, presented a motion to the Central Labor Council condemning the shipowners. "We can't let the employers tell us who will represent us," he argued, "no matter what we may think of the particular leader who happens to be in question." With the rest of the labor movement contemplating sympathetic action in support of the longshoremen, the shipowners acquiesced, opening the port the following morning.[30]

Calm had hardly returned to the waterfront when battle lines began forming once again. In June, an eight-member "Coast Committee for the Shipowners" was assembled to coordinate employer efforts aimed at modifying the longshore agreement scheduled to expire in a few months. Chaired by Plant of American-Hawaiian and including both Dollar and Matson representatives, the Coast Committee approached contract negotiations with extreme inflexibility, issuing a series of relatively inconsequential but firm ultimatums to the union. In this acrimonious atmosphere, the ILA's "fairly moderate demands"—as the *Pacific Shipper,* a leading industry journal, characterized the union's position—were rejected outright by the Coast Committee. During the final days of negotiations, a coalition of twenty-six European and East Coast American lines broke with the Coast Committee and offered the ILA a separate agreement. Describing the offer as "virtually a capitulation," the commercial press reported that "it struck the waterfront like an earthquake."[31]

Buoyed by the prospect of an imminent settlement, the *Pacific Shipper* editorialized that the employers' conciliatory mood evidenced "the lessons which the shipowners have learned in more than two years of incessant contact with the modern labor problem. It explains why they are confident that the disputes will be settled by arbitration and conciliation in the long run; why they are neither as reactionary nor as craven as they have been painted ... why such of them as did not know the virtues of moderation before have discovered them now." But if some shippers had learned the virtues of moderation, the Big Three were not among them. Working feverishly behind the scenes, they patched up the schism within their ranks and pressed forward with strike preparations. As the union later charged, a "minority group ... known on the coast as the 'Big Three,' blocked all reasonable efforts for peaceful settlement." The rift among the employers was acknowledged even by industry sources. Midway through the ensuing three-month walkout, the *Pacific Shipper* conceded that the aggressive methods of the Big Three "have been questioned by other operators—even to the extent of breaking away from their leadership."[32]

The 1936–1937 strike ended without significant gains by either side. But the employers came away with a deeper understanding of the need for regional organization. The "go it alone" attitude of many shipowners, exemplified by the pre-strike defection

of twenty-six companies from Coast Committee policy, had produced only divisiveness and defeat. To combat the growing solidarity of the marine working class, individual lines, even local port
associations, were no longer any match. What the shipowners
needed, insisted Lapham, parodying the Wobblies, was nothing
less than "One Big Union of Employers." Lapham's continued
pleading for solidarity was finally heeded in the summer of 1937,
and the Waterfront Employers' Association of the Pacific Coast
(WEA) was born.[33]

Forming their own association was an essential first step on the
road to employer organization, but for the shipowners to reach
their intended destination the WEA still had to win over the very
constituents it was created to represent. First, however, the WEA
had to forge an industrywide consensus out of the immediate and
sometimes conflicting interests of its potential members. Organizational survival demanded proof that the new association, unlike
the short-lived Coast Committee, was capable of representing the
entire industry, not just a segment of it.

This issue of representativeness holds the key to any successful
combination of capital. If an employer association is to be effective, it must be clearly demarcated from its constituent members;
the association must acquire, in the words of Clark Kerr and Lloyd
Fisher, "an institutional character and identity somewhat distinct
from that of any of its member firms."[34] Transposed into the language of structuralist Marxism, the employer association—much
like the state in capitalist society—requires some independence or
"relative autonomy" from individual capitalists in order to func-
tion effectively as a representative of the industry (or class) as a
whole.

Such autonomy was especially critical for the WEA. The falling-
out between the Big Three and the twenty-six defecting lines made
it imperative that the WEA demonstrate at the outset its independence from either faction. Accordingly, its founding board of di-
rectors sought a neutral administrator from outside the industry to
head the organization. Almon Roth, comptroller of Stanford University for eighteen years, was ultimately chosen, not "for his ship
operating experience, but for his ability to solve public relations
problems and *to reconcile diverse points of view,*" observed the
Pacific Marine Review, a usually reliable industry journal. With an

industry "outsider" at its head, the WEA enjoyed greater organizational autonomy than any of its predecessors, including the many local port associations and the Coast Committee.[35]

But the concentrated structure of the industry sharply limited the WEA's independence from the largest employers. This was perhaps most evident in the procedures for allocating votes to each member company. Table 2, compiled from internal employer documents, shows the strength of the major voting blocks within the WEA at the time of its incorporation, as determined by the total volume of tonnage shipped through Pacific Coast ports during 1936. West Coast operators, including both deepwater and coastwise lines, held a clear majority of all votes. Within this majority block, the Big Three accounted for more votes than either the thirty-nine coastwise schooner companies or the six other deepwater lines. The Big Three, with fifty-one votes between them, directly controlled almost one-fourth of the total votes allocated to all member companies of the WEA. A more detailed breakdown of voting strength shows that only eight other companies received as many as three votes each and, of this small group, only two lines had more than six votes.

Underpinning the Big Three's political power within the WEA was, of course, their economic supremacy within the industry itself. Size alone was an important factor in their ability to dictate to other employers. Smaller companies, lacking the vast economic resources available to the Big Three, were in no position to challenge their leadership and risk provoking a costly rate war that they were sure to lose. The prospect of being slowly "starved out" of business kept many small firms in line.[36]

Although size was an important part of the Big Three's success, economic centrality was even more critical. By the early 1930s an expansive corporate network had developed in the West, with the Big Three constituting its core. Dollar's holdings included five vessels operated under the name of the Admiral Line, along with a half-million-dollar investment in the American Mail Line, the fifth largest company on the West Coast. American-Hawaiian's fleet included seven vessels belonging to the Williams Steamship Company, a wholly owned subsidiary; half ownership of the twenty-one-vessel Oceanic and Oriental Navigation Company; and ten thousand shares of stock, valued at half a million dollars, in the

TABLE 2. *Distribution of Votes in the Waterfront Employers' Association of the Pacific Coast, June 1937*

Operating Category	Number of Companies	Number of Votes	Percentage of Total Votes
West Coast deepwater lines	9	84	38
Big Three	3	51	23
Others	6	33	15
Coastwise steam schooners	39	41	18
East Coast deepwater lines	10	34	15
Foreign-owned lines	50	64	29
Totals	108	223	100

Source: Memorandum from A. Boyd to Mr. A. E. Roth, dated June 19, 1937, Waterfront Employers' Association Papers, Pacific Maritime Association, San Francisco.

Pacific-Atlantic Steamship Company, the fourth largest company on the Pacific Coast. Matson's holdings included the other half of the Oceanic and Oriental Navigation Company and an additional sixteen ships belonging to the Los Angeles Steamship Company and the Oceanic Steamship Company, both wholly owned subsidiaries. In short, the Big Three were really more than three, with sizable financial investments in at least a half dozen other lines.[37]

The Big Three were thus in a class by themselves. Large enough to discipline their smaller rivals and financially tied to a host of other firms, they had little difficulty imposing their views on the rest of the West Coast. Occupying the commanding heights of the industry, the Big Three were in a position to provide leadership and organizational direction for the multiplicity of smaller operators who passively, and sometimes reluctantly, followed them down a path of maximum resistance to unionism.

Employer Disorganization in New York

The maritime industry in New York was marked by a wider dispersion of capital than in the West. Whereas shipping on the Pacific was dominated by three large firms, the economic landscape in New York was cluttered with more than a dozen medium-size commercial American lines. Although they were as intolerant of

unionism as their West Coast counterparts were, New York's domestic shippers were handicapped by a lack of portwide leadership, which left them poorly and incompletely organized. Unable
to resist collectively, individual lines cultivated informal, often collaborative, relations with local ILA leaders whose deeply ingrained
conservatism prevented them from fully exploiting the employers'
organizational weaknesses.

The moderating influence of employer disorganization on the
New York waterfront was evident as early as 1907 when, during a
wildcat dock strike, several coastwise companies broke a "solidarity pact" with deepwater lines in order to accommodate union
wage demands. After settling the strike, the shipowners were still
unable to agree on a portwide labor policy, leaving the basic issue
of union recognition to be resolved by each company. Few lines
formally recognized the ILA, but its presence was tolerated on the
more solidly unionized docks. This policy of expediency underscored the importance of self-reliance to New York's already atom-
ized shipowners. Following a decade of such practices, seven separate waterfront associations had emerged to represent the port's
increasingly diverse employer interests. This factionalism, concluded a 1918 Labor Department study, is "not particularly favorable for any close association of boat owners. . . . The result has
been a more or less aloofness . . . and a jealously guarded independence on the part of private operators."[38]

Employer disunity, however, was conducive to the growth of
longshore unionism in New York. By sounding out weak spots
among the shipowners and then targeting the most vulnerable
lines, the ILA grew from six thousand members in 1914 to more
than forty thousand four years later. In the face of the advancing
union, waterfront employers offered little or no resistance, even
when the relation of forces was clearly favorable. During the 1919
portwide strike, for example, the shipowners never once threatened to sever relations with the ILA. On the contrary, the degree of
support given union leaders in the course of the walkout was, as a
contemporary observer noted, "almost without parallel in labor
history, and is evidence of the confidence which the shipping interests at the port have in the intention of the organization to observe
its agreements."[39] After the walkout collapsed, the shipowners still
failed to retaliate against the defenseless union. Such restraint may

have indeed been partly a measure of the employers' continuing confidence in the ILA's conservative leadership, but it also reflected their own capacity for self-organization—limited as it was by the absence of an industrywide leadership group on the waterfront.

This is not to say that leadership dynamics alone determine how employers will respond to unions. Particularly in competitive product markets, it is also necessary to consider how market forces differentially shape the economic interests of rival employers. Where individual firms compete on a more or less equal footing, industrywide resistance remains relatively easy to organize. This, it seems, was the key to employer organization in New York City's fragmented and leaderless garment industry. Down by the docks, however, where shipowners were internally divided by differing economic ability to tolerate unionism, unity in the face of organized labor was far more difficult to achieve and even harder to maintain.

A leading source of employer disunity on the New York waterfront was the sizable presence of government operators. Commissioned under renewable cost-plus contracts let by the United States Shipping Board, government lines were effectively insulated from market competition. Consequently, they found it easier to absorb the costs of unionism than did their commercial competitors. At the same time, Shipping Board operators, as representatives of the federal government, were necessarily more sensitive to public opinion than were private interests: they could hardly expect to treat their own workers as harshly as commercial operators treated theirs without being accused of harboring anti-labor biases.[40]

These conciliatory government operators were a force to be reckoned with in New York.[41] In 1929, government vessels carried almost 10 percent of all cargo handled through the North Atlantic custom district, compared to less than 1 percent on the Pacific Coast. As late as 1931, almost three years after the Shipping Board had transferred its entire Pacific Coast fleet to private ownership, regular government service to New York was still being provided by eight separate lines with a total of sixty-seven vessels. Adding to the government's already considerable influence was the fact that the port's largest domestic carrier—the 187,000-ton United States Line—was under exclusive contract to the Shipping Board.[42]

Alongside government operators stood some of Europe's most powerful commercial shipping lines. Before World War I, European influence had been so pervasive in New York that the port's overseas shippers organized a Foreign Commerce Club to promote their common interests. The withdrawal of most European vessels from the transatlantic carrying trade during the war afforded a brief respite from foreign competition. But the postwar resumption of commercial shipping restored European supremacy on the North Atlantic. By 1920, more than half of the nation's overseas waterborne commerce was being carried in foreign ships. To protest America's steadily deteriorating position in foreign trade, Herbert Hebermann, president of the Export Steamship Company, then the largest private New York line flying the American flag, resigned from the city's leading commercial association. In tendering his resignation from the New York Maritime Exchange, Hebermann declared that "it was time foreign interests ceased to have a share in the direction of the American merchant marine."[43]

Foreign influence on the East Coast can also be seen in statistics on overseas commerce. Table 3 compares the volume of domestic and foreign cargo shipments reported for the Port of New York and the Pacific Coast for 1930. The figures on coastwise and intercoastal trade provide a negative measure of foreign penetration, for both categories of domestic shipping were reserved by federal maritime law for American flag ships. On this basis alone, more than three-fourths (80 percent) of all cargo passing through Pacific Coast ports was legally protected from foreign competition, compared to less than two-thirds (62 percent) of all shipments in New York. The volume of overseas trade represents a more direct measure of foreign influence. Table 3 shows the profound regional disparity in foreign trade, which, in relative shares, was almost two times larger in New York (38 percent) than on the Pacific Coast (20 percent).[44]

What these aggregate tonnage figures only begin to suggest is the greater economic power wielded by foreign lines in New York. The heavily trafficked North Atlantic shipping corridor connecting Europe and the United States, already supporting many of the world's largest steamship lines, experienced a wave of corporate consolidations as a result of the Depression. In 1930, Germany's two largest lines pooled their enormous resources, bringing three-fourths of that nation's tonnage directly under their control. Brit-

TABLE 3. *Distribution of Waterborne Commerce by Type of Service for Ports on the Pacific Coast and in New York City, 1930*

	Pacific Coast	New York City
Total cargo shipments (in thousands of cargo tons)	98,843	69,535
Percentage of total shipments carried by foreign lines	20	38
Percentage of total shipments carried by domestic lines	80	62
Coastwise	70	56
Intercoastal[a]	10	6

Sources: Data for foreign and coastwise shipments are from United States Department of Commerce, Bureau of Foreign and Domestic Commerce, *Statistical Abstract of the United States, 1932* (Washington, D.C.: Government Printing Office, 1932), p. 400. Data on intercoastal shipments are from United States Shipping Board, Bureau of Research, Maritime Records Division, *United States Water Borne Traffic by Port of Origin and Destination and Principal Commodities* (Washington, D.C.: Government Printing Office, 1930).

[a] Intercoastal shipments are reported only in "long" cargo tons of 2,240 pounds in the source listed above. Thus the estimates for intercoastal shipments presented here are based on the number of long tons plus an added 10.7 percent to account for the difference between long tons and regular cargo tons of 2,000 pounds.

ish shippers retaliated with rationalized transatlantic sailings and mergers. Less than a year later, Britain's four largest companies held in excess of two million gross tons. France's largest line then met this challenge by augmenting its fleet with modern combination passenger-cargo vessels.[45]

Whereas New York's commercial shippers were, according to one industry observer, "hard-pressed to hold a footing" against such established maritime powers as Great Britain, Germany, Italy, France, Norway, and Sweden, American lines engaged in the transpacific trade confronted a more decentralized, less competitive Japanese fleet, along with a small number of tramp steamers and European vessels engaged in round-the-world service.[46] Restricted to the West Coast's comparatively small overseas market, foreign lines lacked both the means and the motives to challenge their American hosts. Instead, they tried to "get along," as Paul St. Sure, former head of the Pacific Maritime Association, explained in a 1957 interview:

The foreign lines on this coast represent a minority of tonnage. They've always taken the position, at least until recently, that "we are visitors in your country. We are a minority group, even on the waterfront. We should not dictate to you how you should handle your labor problems. We would like to get along, but if we can't, we're not going to tell you how to do it."[47]

In sharp contrast, the highly concentrated European lines servicing the East Coast operated far more independently of domestic shipowners. And, as in the case of government operators, their independence took the form of a more accommodating stance toward dockside unionism. Foreign lines were better able to absorb higher stevedoring costs. With most voyages originating overseas, European vessels typically covered greater distances, spending more of their time on the open seas than in port. Unlike domestic carriers confined to the intercoastal trade, whose routes took them from port to port, discharging and taking on cargo along the way, foreign lines docked only at ports of origin and destination. Consequently, cargo handling costs constituted a smaller, and therefore more affordable, expense for Europe's deepwater lines. Then, too, foreign operators had a stronger interest in cooperating with dockside labor. With their own offshore crews, they had little to gain by engaging an American longshore union in an extended and possibly costly confrontation. Their main concern was keeping the lid on offshore labor costs, which they attempted to do by fighting unionization aboard ship, not on the docks.[48]

The presence of so many competing interests undermined employer solidarity on the waterfront. When conciliatory foreign and government operators clashed with the port's more intransigent commercial operators, the resulting employer factionalism often worked to the advantage of the union. Such was the case during contract negotiations in 1931. The shipowners opened negotiations that year by demanding a significant cut in wages. After the union balked, industry leaders hastily assembled a Committee of Ten to bargain on behalf of all waterfront employers in the port. But the appearance of unity masked deep-seated divisions, particularly between foreign and subsidized government lines, on the one hand, and domestic commercial lines, on the other. The former, generally more tolerant of unionism, openly voiced their desire to avoid a costly work stoppage. ILA leaders then promised that, in the event of a walkout, they would continue supplying union labor to any company willing to meet their counterproposal. In the absence of a few powerful American lines capable of enforcing discipline—as the Big Three in the West would be able to do when faced with a similar situation in 1936—the threat of a selective strike shattered the employers' fragile unity. Within hours, Ryan reported that several transatlantic lines had "expressed a willingness to meet the demands of the men." As more foreign companies defected, all seven Shipping Board lines in New York promptly signed with the union. The Committee of Ten, now representing the more intransigent private American operators, reluctantly accepted the union's wage offer, although two of the largest domestic shippers, Grace Lines and United Fruit, refused to sign a union contract.[49]

This experience drove home the importance of establishing some form of portwide organization, if only as a defensive measure to prevent the union from playing off one shipowner against another. A few months later the New York Shipping Association (NYSA) was formed for the explicit purpose of representing all of the port's deepwater lines, both foreign and domestic. Its inclusive membership finally enabled the shipowners to contest the union's effective use of "whipsaw" tactics. One of the association's principal objectives was to secure an agreement stipulating that the contract could not be changed through "individual action on the part of a company or union official." This provision was "mainly inserted to deter the union from concentrating on the weakness of an individual employer to establish a precedent-setting action to bind all employers and the New York Shipping Association."[50]

The NYSA provided a formal instrument for collectively responding to the union. But its voting procedures, reflecting the fragmented state of the industry, rendered it all but powerless. Unlike the employers' association in the West, which codified the influence of the Big Three through proportional representation, each member of the NYSA received one vote, regardless of size. To further restrain powerful minorities, all major policy decisions required approval by three-fourths of all members. With numerous small voting blocs exercising effective veto power, no single inter-

est group possessed sufficient strength to formulate basic policies
on any controversial matters. Hamstrung by excessive democracy,
the NYSA succumbed to bureaucratic inertia, capable only of passively reacting to union overtures.[51]

Many of the port's larger lines, frustrated in their attempts to
influence the direction of the employer organization, established
informal bargaining relations with the ILA. Thus during the 1930s
the powerful Clyde-Mallory Line and nine other coastwise companies formed an unofficial negotiating committee to deal directly
with the union. A confidential investigation conducted by the
United States Maritime Commission elaborated:

> The representatives of the ten principal coastwise operating lines
> find it convenient to meet as a body and negotiate basic terms and
> conditions with the ILA. The same group acts in the same informal
> manner in settling disputes of a major character that arise under the
> agreement. . . . All other disputes are settled individually between
> the companies and the union—in most instances it is a matter of a
> telephone call—no records of settlements or disputes are kept.

Similar informal relations later developed between the employer
association itself and the ILA. In 1939 the chairman of the NYSA
told a government interviewer that the written contract between
both parties was supplemented by "gentlemen's agreements or
understandings." Describing their collective bargaining relationship as "one of perfect harmony," the interviewer added that from
the standpoint of the employers, "everything is lovely—they
wouldn't change anything even if they had a chance. No problems—no trouble—just peace and contentment all around."[52]

Although these harmonious relations were fundamentally
grounded in employer disorganization, the port's urban geography
also came into play. Antiquated and congested piers created inor-
dinate delays in discharging cargo, inadequate railroad connections to piers complicated the transfer of rail shipments, narrow
surface streets caused trucks to back up for several blocks on main
waterfront arteries, and limited space for maneuvering vessels inside the harbor forced additional delays as costly "time charges"
piled up. These cramped spatial arrangements provided, in Daniel
Bell's phrase, an "economic fulcrum" for industrial racketeering

through the unique system of "public loading" that arose during the 1920s as a response to port congestion. Explaining the origins of loading, Bell writes:

> The most expensive cost item in trucking became waiting time. Rather than pay a driver's helper for snoozing on the truck, the practice arose of sending a driver alone to the pier and having him hire a loader from among the "shenangos" or barflies at the nearby saloon. Gradually, through a process of squatters' rights, various individuals began to assert a monopoly on loading at each pier. At first they offered a service; later they began to charge, literally, all that the traffic would bear. . . . So the toll-gate was established. Whether you needed a loader or not, you had to pay for the service, and on each ton of goods an extra tax was levied.[53]

Time-conscious shippers were thus placed at the mercy of local union leaders who controlled the loading rackets and who, for an extra fee, could guarantee that a client's shipment would be expedited. Payoffs of this sort, totaling hundreds of thousands of dollars, became an economic fact of life in New York, tolerated by most shipowners as a necessary cost of conducting business in the world's busiest port. Of course, their generosity was repaid in kind by conservative union leaders who signed "sweetheart" deals, failed to enforce legitimate contracts, and in countless other ways neglected their members' interests. In words that perhaps best convey the collaborative nature of labor relations on the waterfront, a prominent New York stevedoring contractor told a Citizens' Waterfront Committee in 1945 about the collective bargaining process. "We call Ryan in once a year or so," he explained, "and say, 'Joe, how much of a raise do you need to keep the boys in line?'"[54]

Conclusion

Maritime employers on the two coasts responded very differently to the emergence of working-class opposition on the docks following World War I. Whereas shipowners in the West waged a protracted struggle against longshore unionism, their counterparts in New York established close, and at times openly collaborative, relations with the same union. These differing approaches reinforced the contrasting political cultures that were taking shape on both coasts.

Shipowner intransigence in the West nourished the rich Wobbly legacy on the docks. Combining the experience of employer resistance with the preexisting syndicalist beliefs of the labor force produced a militant, politically radical working-class culture out of which the union's left-wing leadership emerged in the course of the 1934 strike. As former Wobbly and strike activist Jack Mowrey put it, "The employers organized the longshoremen. No question about it. They were the best organizers we had. It got so bad you couldn't take it any more. They organized the whole West Coast." [55]

The employer's role in "organizing" the men is also suggested by the evolution of longshore unionism in Tacoma, Washington, where local waterfront employers were the least combative on the coast. Refusing to join the coastwide open-shop crusade after World War I, they instead maintained close and friendly relations with the local ILA, "using entirely Union men and practically working under closed shop conditions." In 1921, while the rest of the West Coast was convulsed in industrial warfare, the port's leading shipowner boasted of the "splendid co-operation between the men and the managers," adding that they had done "everything possible . . . to foster good fellowship in Tacoma." [56] This cooperative atmosphere continued well into the 1930s, sparing Tacoma's longshoremen the radicalizing experience of employer resistance during the crucial years of union building. Consequently, in 1937, when fifteen thousand West Coast dockworkers followed Bridges into the CIO to launch the ILWU, six hundred longshoremen in Tacoma and two smaller satellite ports—still firmly anchored to the conservative AFL—voted to remain behind with the ILA.

Employer moderation in the East had much the same effect. Having seen the shipowners on their best behavior—as men of reason and restraint—New York's longshoremen maintained their healthy skepticism toward ideologies of class conflict. Coupled with the lack of a syndicalist tradition, employer moderation pointed to the reconcilability of class interests. This combination, unlike the West's, spawned a distinctly nonmilitant and conservative political culture, which Ryan skillfully wielded against leftist insurgents for more than two decades.

The very different ways in which shipowners on the coasts responded to unionization were partly influenced by their interactions with labor. In the West, worker radicalism and employer resistance reinforced each other. With the growth of syndicalist, and later Communist, agitation on the docks, the shipowners themselves grew more determined to resist unionization. Just as radicalism galvanized employer opposition in the West, union conservatism in New York moderated somewhat the anti-union inclinations of the port's shipowners.

This is not to suggest, however, that waterfront employers responded like mirrors in simply reflecting the character of dockside unionism. On the contrary, the image cast by labor was never that compelling. Thus ILA leaders on the Great Lakes and the Gulf Coast, as conservative as any in New York, drew considerable heat from local shipowners—more heat, in fact, than those on the West Coast, the hotbed of labor radicalism.

In responding to organized labor, the shipowners were guided not only by the character of the union but by stubborn economic realities as well. The competitive nature of the product market squeezed profits to the point where unionization posed a serious economic threat, particularly for unprotected domestic operators, who proved to be the most intransigent on both coasts. In the West, their intransigence produced militant coastwide resistance, whereas in New York it dissolved into union-employer cooperation. Part of this difference was a result of the conservatism of New York's union leaders and their greater willingness to cooperate. But no matter how cooperative local ILA leaders may have been, driving the union from the docks remained the overriding objective of American commercial shippers everywhere. whether on the Pacific, the Gulf Coast, the Great Lakes, or the North Atlantic. If New York's employers ended up being the most conciliatory, it was not because the local union was that much more conservative than in other parts of the country, nor was it because the economic interests of the port's shipowners differed that much from those of commercial operators elsewhere.

Rather, the most telling difference between New York and the West Coast was the relative ability of shipowners to constitute themselves as a cohesive social force in opposition to waterfront labor. These varying "class capacities" were determined initially by differences in industry structure. Concentrated ownership in the West created favorable conditions for unifying individual ship-owners, whose limited horizons were subsumed under a broader and more militant vision forcefully articulated by the largest firms. Conversely, the wider dispersion of capital in New York meant that no single leadership group was powerful enough to transcend the many smaller employers and initiate portwide organization.

The relative organizational potential of shipowners was then transformed by regional economic processes into markedly differ-ent policies toward organized labor. On the Pacific Coast, employ-ers' intransigence, though spurred on by labor radicalism, was mostly a product of their greater capacity for self-organization set within the context of an industrywide intolerance toward unions. In New York, however, the industry's low tolerance for unionism was never realized in employer resistance. There, against a back-drop of labor conservatism, the port's lack of capital concentration created a leadership vacuum at the top, while at the bottom deep economic cleavages among commercial, government, and foreign operators reproduced conditions for employer disorganization. Un-able to resist collectively, New York's maritime employers, includ-ing even the staunchly anti-union commercial lines, sought instead to neutralize the union by establishing close working relations with local ILA leaders whose control over the loading rackets pro-vided a particularly durable foundation for union-employer col-laboration for many years to come.

Although product market competition created strong incentives to resist unions, shipowners on the two coasts were not equally capable of doing so. Effective resistance had to be organized, and that required a sufficient concentration of capital to create regional leadership roles. Capital concentration fulfilled the shipowners' need for centralized leadership in much the same way that the vari-ous "vanguard" parties provided the longshoremen with much-needed leadership of their own. But in neither case was the presence of leadership sufficient to ensure durable organization. Lasting and effective organization also required rank-and-file solidarity based on shared economic interests. For domestic shipowners, such soli-darity was achieved on the West Coast but not in New York, where the greater presence of foreign and government lines fractured their ranks. Leaderless and divided, the port's employers responded in much the same way that disorganized workers have responded throughout history—by cutting the best possible deal they could as individuals.

The organization of capital, then, may not be so different from the organization of labor. On both sides, internal stratification, cross-cutting pressures, different organizational capacities, and other obstacles make the transition to a "class for itself" most uncertain. Facing many of the same challenges, each class will respond differently, in ways that reflect its particular strengths and weaknesses. But the likelihood that either one will succeed in actually constituting itself as a collectivity of actors with a single unified will may be only marginally greater for capital than it is for labor. Whatever organizational advantages employers enjoy are partially offset by the potentially higher costs—including bankruptcy—that may result from coalescing with weak allies, or taking on too powerful an adversary, or committing any number of other tactical blunders in the course of waging the class struggle. To even admit such contingencies into an analysis of class relations is to remind ourselves that capital's own organizational capacities, like labor's, are far from absolute.

Chapter Four

The Strategic Pivot

Communist influence in the American working class depended not only on the receptivity of certain workers—as a result of either earlier radical traditions or employer resistance—but also on the particular organizing strategies that local Communist Party cadre chose to follow in their daily work. Not that there was any one path to success, as might be inferred from the party's tireless search for the "correct line." The fact is that the same "line" that worked so well in one setting often proved disastrous in another. Indeed, if there was any formula for success it was that the Communists were most effective when they operated with no formula at all and instead fashioned organizing strategies to best fit local conditions. Earl Browder, who guided the party through its period of greatest growth and influence, only to be expelled in 1947 for "revisionism" and "opportunism," concluded much the same years later. "One thing you can always be sure of," he told an interviewer in 1955, "where the Communists succeed it's not because they're dogmatic; dogmatic followers are their own ruin. Where they succeed they almost always have to depart from their own rule." [1]

The willingness of local waterfront Communists to depart from their own rule in formulating strategy was a key factor in the widening regional split in longshore unionism. In 1930 the national Communist Party dispatched small nuclei of organizers to both the San Francisco and the New York waterfronts. Party functionaries in the West, displaying considerable flexibility in their choice of organizing tactics along with a keen sense of timing, sank deep roots in the ideologically fertile soil on the docks, whereas their comrades in the East, pursuing a more rigid and sectarian approach, never overcame their isolation from New York's longshoremen.

The Communists' deeper penetration in the West had far-reaching political consequences. Having cultivated a large following during the early years of the Depression, left-wing organizers were able to translate their support on the docks into a powerful mass movement capable of challenging the newly-installed conservative leadership of longshore unionism on the West Coast. With ILA leaders on the defensive by 1934, Communist-supported activists seized the moment, coming forward that spring to lead the rank and file into the pivotal coastwide maritime strike out of which Bridges and the left rose to power.

This chapter traces the evolution of Communist strategy before the strike, focusing on the complex interplay between the national policy handed down by top party leaders and how this official line was interpreted by front-line cadre and then modified to fit local conditions, thus producing very different opportunities for leftist insurgents on each coast.

Rooting the Party on the West Coast Docks

Communists on the West Coast inherited generally favorable conditions for organizing the longshoremen. Although both the IWW and the ILA had been driven from the waterfront following World War I, traditions of syndicalism and militant craft unionism survived in the major ports. The resulting union orientation toward job control and direct action, coupled with vigorous employer resistance, provided a solid foundation on which to rebuild.

Deteriorating working conditions on the docks underscored the need for organization. Union-controlled hiring, which had been established after the war in Seattle, Portland, and San Pedro, had given way in each case to employer-operated hiring halls or "fink halls," as the workers referred to them. During the 1920s the principles of scientific management were also introduced on the docks in the form of "labor-saving machinery and rationalization techniques . . . designed to get the most out of the workers on the waterfront." Following the stock market crash of 1929, dockside employment opportunities diminished as the economic crisis deepened. The demand for casual labor vanished almost entirely in the early Depression years, as total coastwide cargo shipments plummeted by more than one-third between 1929 and 1932.[2] Longshoremen who managed to find work often drove themselves to exhaustion while working thirty-six-hour and forty-eight-hour shifts. The men were treated "like animals," recalls San Pedro longshoreman Al Langley. "And that's the way any of them bosses looked at the men, like animals—to be used in any way it was possible to attain their end. They didn't care if they killed you or not. You were just so much scum."[3]

Conditions were worse in San Francisco, where the degrading shape-up system of hiring had been in force since the defeat of the Riggers and Stevedores Union in 1919. By 1930 West Coast shipowners could openly boast that labor output per worker was higher in San Francisco than in any port in the world. "Short gangs" of four to six men were working on the docks and in the holds of vessels where formerly eight to ten men had been employed. "Accidents occur constantly," noted a contemporary source, "due to the speed-up, overloading, and rotten gear." The large surplus of men who shaped up for work every morning along San Francisco's fog-shrouded embarcadero was swollen by the nationally depressed economy into a sizable army of four to five thousand desperate job seekers.[4] "The waterfront was just full of people looking for work," recalls San Francisco longshoreman Germain Bulcke, "and if you got into any kind of an argument with the boss or if he didn't like you, he'd point and say: 'Look, if you don't shape up there are fifty men out there waiting to take your job,' which was true." A rank-and-file newspaper, reporting on the resulting speed-up in San Francisco, observed in 1933: "While only a few years back 18 to 20 tons was the average for a gang, and 25 tons was considered exceptional, today 60 to 75 tons an hour is common—a three-fold increase." That same year wages were slashed to seventy-five cents an hour, the lowest rate in twenty-five years.[5]

Although objective conditions may have been conducive to radicalization, the Communists' political line was not. The party was in the midst of its ultra-left "Third Period," following a line initiated by Moscow in 1928 to capitalize on the expected revolutionary upsurge of working-class activity in the West. In effect, this policy lumped all progressive forces to the right of the Communists into the enemy camp. Socialists and their allies were attacked as "social fascists" for leading workers down the dead-end path of reformism. Worse still, this line claimed, were the tiny sects of left-wing socialists and independent Marxists masquerading as revolutionaries. These "left social fascists" were even more dangerous than plain "social fascists," who, in turn, were more dangerous than outright fascists.[6] In this heady atmosphere, political sectarianism was no longer a deviation, but the road to truth.

The doctrine of social fascism had important consequences for trade union organizing in the United States. Influential Soviet leaders expressed their displeasure with the American party for "dancing a quadrille around the AFL," as a high-ranking Profintern official put it. To counter the reformist influence of the AFL and the Socialist Party, which were now characterized as "vital parts of the expanding fascist organization of the capitalists," Communists began in 1929 to organize revolutionary "red" unions, affiliated with the Communist-led Trade Union Unity League, in several industries.[7]

It was during this sectarian "revolutionary" phase that the Communist Party established a national presence in the longshore industry with the formation of the Marine Workers Industrial Union (MWIU). Organized in the spring of 1930 at the height of Third Period ultra-leftism, the MWIU was a product of the excesses that characterized Communist trade union efforts throughout the early 1930s. Its preamble committed the union to "fight not only for better immediate conditions but also for ultimate freedom from wage slavery." Recognizing further that "the liberation of the marine workers from exploitation is only one part of the revolutionary struggle of the whole working class against the capitalist system," the red union boldly condemned "the treacherous 'class collaboration' policy of the A F of L, which seeks to delude workers that it is possible to live 'in peace' with the capitalists."[8]

Such revolutionary posturing won few converts on the docks. Even in San Francisco, where the party was most active, dockworkers had little interest in politics at the expense of pork chops. Lashing out against the speed-up, low wages, and blacklisting, Communist agitators had "the sympathy of the men right away," Bridges explained in his 1939 deportation hearing. But when they urged longshoremen to join the party as a means of improving these conditions, "that was too far-fetched for the men at that time and they didn't pay much attention to that point." Novelist Orrick Johns, one of several eloquent soapbox orators carrying the Third Period message of class struggle to the waterfront during the early 1930s, later acknowledged the party's limited appeal on the docks. Longshoremen who were otherwise "rebellious against their working conditions," he wrote, "were often sullen and indifferent" at Communist street meetings held along the embarcadero.[9]

While the party ran up against serious obstacles in its work on the San Francisco waterfront, the red marine union was facing extinction. In fact, the MWIU was unable to recruit even one working longshoreman during this period. Sam Darcy, leader of the Communist Party's District 13 (California, Nevada, and Arizona), attributed the failure to "serious sectarian errors" committed by the MWIU. "Because of this," he observed in 1934, "we approached the situation from the outside, and were not able to break down the agitation against our union and against the Party on the waterfront."[10]

To overcome their outsider status, Darcy and three others formed an "initiating group" late in 1932 as part of a concerted effort to establish closer contact with the rank and file. In December, Darcy's group joined with the small MWIU branch in San Francisco to produce the *Waterfront Worker,* a lively agitational bulletin directed mainly at longshoremen. The first issue was so well received that all 350 copies, selling for a penny each, were gone within half an hour. "There was an undercurrent of restlessness on the waterfront when we started putting out the paper," remembers Mitch Slobodek, one of its founding editors, "but no direction. The paper gave one."[11]

But the *Waterfront Worker*'s direction was not yet clear enough for the majority of longshoremen to follow. Even national party leaders in New York, often blinded by their own revolutionary vision, could see that the paper was too advanced; reviewing the first issue, the CP's national shop-paper editor criticized its format of exposing routine job grievances without "telling the workers how to organize" against them. Similar criticisms were leveled against the *Waterfront Worker* a few months later in a formal statement from the National Bureau of the MWIU in New York. Recent issues were faulted for not addressing "*immediate grievances* and what to do about them NOW. There should be no hesitation on how to conduct small struggles."[12]

If the *Waterfront Worker* appeared hesitant to address immediate grievances, it was most likely because the paper's small group of editors and writers, most of whom were full-time Communist functionaries or MWIU organizers with little or no firsthand experience as longshoremen, had only the vaguest notions about the sources of discontent on the docks. Three members of Darcy's originating group, for example, had never worked in the industry, and the fourth had only brief stevedoring experience.[13] Lacking direct involvement in the working lives of ordinary longshoremen, the Communists' understanding of dockside culture as it was expressed in the workers' aspirations and goals was still largely that of a distant outsider.

Darcy's group finally managed to touch base with rank-and-file militants on the docks following a series of closely related developments during the summer of 1933. Under the Roosevelt administration, the National Industrial Recovery Act was passed in June. Section 7a provided legal sanction for employees "to organize and bargain collectively through representatives of their own choosing." Under cover of the NIRA, ILA loyalists and former Wobblies resurfaced to lead the organizational drive on the docks. With ILA supporters beginning to attract large followings in the major ports, the MWIU once again found itself on the outside, isolated from the mass movement developing around the "fascist" ILA.

The dilemma confronting red unionism on the West Coast was played out in other industries within the AFL's jurisdiction. Section 7a, which party leaders railed against as "slave legislation," ended up freeing thousands of workers to join the ranks of organized labor. The Communists benefited handsomely. Their union in the needle trades grew from 12,000 to 20,000 members, while red unions in the shoe and steel industries reported even more dramatic gains. In all, TUUL affiliates absorbed 100,000 new members within a year of the NIRA's enactment. But the real beneficiary was the more established AFL, which added 500,000 workers to its rolls by the end of the year, bringing its total membership to more than 2.5 million, compared to roughly 125,000 enrolled in the TUUL. The time for strategic reappraisal was at hand.[14]

Communist leaders on the waterfront in San Francisco were

sharply at odds over the wisdom of dual unionism. Radicalized seamen, led by the MWIU's charismatic spokesman Harry Jackson, clearly favored the Third Period revolutionary formula. In supporting the MWIU, West Coast seamen were responding not only to ideology but also to the moribund state of the existing AFL organization, the Sailors Union of the Pacific (SUP). By the early 1930s, the once proud SUP had been reduced to "nothing more than a building," with only a few hundred members in San Francisco and no contracts except on some of the Australian lines. Because a seamen's union had to be built from scratch anyway, Jackson and other militants argued that it might as well be one that had a real future. Their choice was the MWIU.[15]

The view from the shore was different. Unlike the SUP, the ILA was on the rebound, generating considerable excitement and interest among the rank and file. As the AFL union began picking up supporters on the docks, the *Waterfront Worker* boldly asserted its independence from Third Period orthodoxy. The May issue featured a cartoon with a longshoreman scratching his head in obvious confusion as he stood before divergent roads labeled ILA, BB (Blue Book), MWIU, IWW, and Independent. Without offering any directions, the caption simply read: "Which Way?"[16]

Such indecisiveness grew out of the political space that had been temporarily created by the intraparty conflict between Jackson's dual unionist seamen and an emerging core of longshore activists, led by Darcy, who saw their task as building a mass movement inside the ILA. Unable to resolve their differences, both sides pursued their own agendas—until the strategic "line" of the San Francisco Communist Party became little more than a blur. The resulting confusion even found its way into the pages of the Communist press. Reporting on a July meeting of the port's longshoremen, the *Western Worker,* an official party organ, noted approvingly the advice of several speakers who urged recent ILA recruits to "organize fighting groups" within the new union. Then, in a last-ditch stand for dual unionism, the article concluded by calling on all marine workers to join the MWIU as well.[17]

As the debate over dual unionism dragged on within the party, Darcy turned his attention to the rank and file and began recruiting some of his contacts among the longshoremen into a study group. Darcy took this original group of fifteen or so (known subsequently as Albion Hall, for the name of the German hall where they met every Sunday morning) through a course on union history, structure, and tactics. "What I was trying to do," he recalls, "was provide these guys with some experience in trade unions which they didn't have. . . . I tried to give them a brief background to trade union history in the United States, how trade unions are organized, the difference between industrial and craft unions, and how we should organize a strike." One of Darcy's pupils at the time was Harry Bridges.[18]

Albion Hall, as a base of organized radicalism on the docks, was just the vehicle the party needed to make contact with the rank and file. To have continued "competitive MWIU recruiting at that point," Darcy wrote in 1934, "would have been suicide. . . . The Party, therefore, took a determined stand against it." Actually, it was Darcy and the longshoremen who took a determined stand against the MWIU, while the national party took a determined stand against Darcy. Chairman Browder still vigorously insisted that the red marine union was as appropriate for the longshoremen as it was for the seamen. When Darcy persisted, Browder dispatched a high-ranking comrade from the furriers union to the West Coast to straighten him out. Within hours of his arrival, Darcy sent him packing. The next Browder emissary did not get off so lightly: he was thrown out of a second-story window. Browder got the message and backed off.[19]

With the MWIU no longer in the picture, the party was finally in a position to shed its outsider status. From inside the ILA, the ten or so Communist activists exerted growing influence on the docks through the indigenously rooted Albion Hall group, which had grown now to almost fifty members. As the group expanded, experienced longshoremen came forward to provide leadership. Bridges, for example, soon emerged as an unofficial leader of Albion Hall. Former member Ben Jones recalls "there was never any question" about Bridges's leadership role:

> He had a lot of good ideas, he was always there when meetings were called, and most important, he'd had more experience than any of the rest of us had had. . . . That goes for those of us who were in the party, too. We used to study a lot, and we had a pretty good theo-

retical grasp of what it was all about, but when it came to practical knowledge and what to do from one day to the next, we just naturally turned to Harry. He always had an answer.[20]

The first task confronting Albion Hall was to reinvigorate the *Waterfront Worker*. Editorial responsibility was transferred to working longshoremen, producing a noticeable change in the paper's style and content. Written in colorful waterfront vernacular, articles concentrated more on issues of immediate concern to the men. With this new format the paper became "so well known," remembers marine worker Jim Kendall, "that the guys would look for it because it spoke in terms the guys couldn't help but respect. It was their own language."[21] Circulation jumped from several hundred copies each month to more than fifteen hundred every other week.

Albion Hall's presence was also felt on the docks and in the holds wherever its members worked. "Before we got to be generally known along the waterfront," Bridges said in 1939, "we were letting our presence be felt on the docks where we regularly worked. We were the ones who received complaints from the men and relayed them to the foremen. We took specific action against the speed-up by slowing up at the winches and in the hold. . . . Other men on the docks watched and saw that we were getting away with it and began to imitate us."[22] Albion Hall built a substantial following by leading many such job actions throughout the summer of 1933.

The left became an integral part of the union-building process later that fall when Albion Hall helped to establish the ILA at the Matson Navigation Company, the port's largest employer and a stronghold of the Blue Book company union. In September the Blue Book delegate put in a rare appearance at the Matson dock to inspect union books and collect dues. When several men refused to display their books, as a protest against the company union, they were promptly ordered off the ship. The delegate then went from man to man, asking to see each one's book and firing anyone who refused. Streaming off the ship, workers headed for a vacant lot across the embarcadero where hundreds of blue books were set ablaze in a roaring fire. Matson had seen enough. From aboard the ship, a company foreman called out to the men, pleading with them to return to work, with or without their books.[23]

Two weeks later Matson fired four workers for wearing ILA buttons. Local ILA President Lee Holman, seeking to avoid a confrontation with the powerful Matson company, advised the four to remove their offending buttons and return to work. With the union's leadership unwilling to act, the *Waterfront Worker* appealed directly to the men, calling for a strike against Matson. The next morning Albion Hall members showed up at the Matson terminal and pulled the entire crew, almost four hundred men, off the job. On the fifth day of the walkout Matson capitulated, and all four men were soon reinstated. "From that time on," Bridges said later, "the union was established, it was recognized, it was in business."[24] And for that San Francisco longshoremen had Albion Hall to thank.

Albion Hall's influence radiated out from its base in San Francisco through a coastwide rank-and-file convention held in that city in early 1934. Late in February, delegates from twenty-four ports met to map a plan of attack. Conservatives, fearing a possible challenge from San Francisco, concentrated on retaining their formal organizational control of the ILA's Pacific Coast district. This focus left Albion Hall free to push through a number of radical political resolutions along with its militant contract demands for union-controlled hiring, a thirty-hour week, a coastwide contract, and improved wages and conditions.[25]

The shipowners' response amounted to an open declaration of war. Charging that the convention had been dominated by "Communist elements," and citing as proof their claim that sixteen of the twenty members of San Francisco's delegation were known Communists, they refused to bargain over any of the union's substantive demands.[26] In response, the longshoremen voted overwhelmingly to strike all Pacific Coast ports on March 23, 1934. On the evening of March 22, however, district ILA leader William Lewis acceded to President Roosevelt's last-minute request to postpone the walkout until a government fact-finding board could be appointed to hear both sides of the dispute.

Roosevelt's intervention inflamed the rank and file. In San Francisco, longshoremen gathered in front of the union hall that evening, shouted against cancellation of the strike, listened to vehement harangues directed at "weak-kneed" union leaders, and then called for a mass demonstration the following morning. "Radical agitation on the waterfront began to assume alarming proportions," Paul Eliel, an employer representative, later wrote. "The workers were being told that their employers were selling them out. They were being goaded to take radical and drastic action and a general state of unrest was being created."[27]

Albion Hall finally consolidated its position in April when San Francisco longshoremen voted to suspend local ILA President Holman for being "too conservative." In his place they elected a fifty-member rank-and-file strike committee. Chaired by Bridges, the strike committee took over the most critical functions of relief, defense, picketing, and negotiations, thereby effectively stripping Holman and other conservatives of any say in the direction of the strike.[28] This time there would be no last-minute cancellations, no sell-outs. On May 9, when twelve thousand West Coast longshoremen walked out, Bridges and his supporters were in a position to challenge and, in the course of the ensuing strike, supplant San Francisco's conservative leadership.

The CP's successful strategy for shedding its outsider status in San Francisco was not applied elsewhere on the West Coast. In Seattle and Portland, where small bands of ILA supporters had been organizing since 1931, Communist activists maintained a politically correct distance from the "social fascist" AFL. Unlike their comrades in San Francisco who played a key role in establishing the ILA, Communists in the Northwest poured most of their energies into building the MWIU, often at the expense of the ILA. In Seattle, for example, MWIU activists launched a major organizing drive as late as November of 1933, when most of the port's dockworkers had already declared for the ILA. Guided by such sectarian tactics, the local branch of the MWIU could not claim even twenty-five longshoremen as members after almost three years of organizing.[29] By the time the MWIU was scrapped early in 1934, the ILA was already firmly established in Seattle, and the party, having been isolated for months in its tiny red marine union, could claim little of the credit and none of the rewards.

The story was similar in San Pedro, where pre-strike conditions more closely approximated the situation in San Francisco. Before the reemergence of the ILA in the summer of 1933, the contest for local leadership had been wide open in both ports. But the Communists made less headway in the south, partly because of their failure as strategists. Rather than leading the rank and file into the ILA as the party did in San Francisco, they obediently followed the official Third Period line on dual unionism. Thus while the ILA was being organized from the ground up, San Pedro's Communists remained on the sidelines cheering on the MWIU, yielding much the same results as in the Northwest.[30]

The party's relatively limited influence in these outlying ports after 1934 was not solely attributable to the belated entry of Communists into the ILA. Clearly, such factors as the quality of local ILA leadership and the strength of radical traditions also played a part. Yet in many important respects conditions in the major ports during the early 1930s were strikingly similar—except for the strategies leftist organizers pursued. And on that score, if the San Francisco experience is at all telling, the strategy of remaining outside the ILA during its formative stages certainly cost the party some degree of influence later on.

Perhaps the most compelling evidence for the importance of strategy comes from a comparison of the ILA and the SUP on the San Francisco waterfront. The port's seamen, having been exposed to the city's left-wing political culture, were hardly strangers to radicalism, but they never really warmed up to the Communists as the longshoremen did. Looking back on the divergent political trajectories of the ILA and the SUP in San Francisco, Darcy now attributes the "more limited gains" among the seamen to the sectarian policy of dual unionism that guided the party's offshore organizing efforts until 1935.[31]

The strategic lessons of San Francisco were not lost on the national leadership of the party. Darcy's approach of working inside the AFL, which had been condemned as a "right deviation of the most serious kind" before and even during the 1934 strike, was later singled out as the party's crowning achievement. In trying to understand why, among the three major strikes led by radicals that spring (the Auto-Lite strike in Toledo, the Teamster strike in Minneapolis, and the maritime strike in the West), only San Francisco answered the party's call for a general strike, Browder argued that "the difference is to be found, not in any different level of radicalization of the workers" but rather in the particular organizing strategies that were followed. In Toledo, he explained, the party was outside the striking union, based mainly among the city's unemployed. Similarly, in Minneapolis, where leadership of the strike was in the hands of the Socialist Workers Party, the demand for a general strike was promoted "from outside" by members of the CP. In San Francisco, Browder pointed out, the relationship of forces was different. There, "organized left-wing groups . . . played a most decisive role" from inside the strikers' own ranks. "The lesson," he wrote in the fall of 1934, "is the supreme, vital importance of work inside the A. F. of L."—a lesson Browder himself had a difficult time learning.[32]

Applying the "Correct Line" in New York

Communist organizers on the New York docks were hardly blessed with ideal conditions. The conservative cultural traditions, ethnic antagonisms, and adverse labor market conditions that had so effectively blunted the Wobblies' earlier efforts were still very much in evidence when the party arrived on the scene in 1930.

But the situation was far from hopeless. None of the basic grievances that had sparked the 1919 portwide wildcat had been resolved. Work was still highly erratic, with alternating periods of unemployment and intense activity ruling the men's lives. Earnings remained unevenly distributed, despite the relative prosperity of the 1920s. But above all else, the position of the hiring foreman was as secure as ever by the end of the decade. His "powers in selecting or rejecting the men," noted a 1930 government study, "are still unabridged."[33]

The insecurity, poverty, and abuse that had driven the workers to revolt in 1919 were all greatly intensified by the Depression. As on the West Coast, thousands of job seekers flooded the waterfront hoping to pick up a few hours of work. By 1930 the dockside labor force had mushroomed to nearly fifty thousand. What little work there was went mostly to a small number of experienced, steady men. The rest tried to make do on one or two days of work a week. Competition for jobs turned morning shape-ups into near-riots. At the larger terminals "there was such a mob," recalls New York longshoreman Johnnie Dwyer, "that the hiring boss would take the [brass hiring] checks and throw them up in the air. . . . He just couldn't go out there, so he'd throw 'em up in the air and the people would scramble for them . . . and then you were hired." [34]

Despite the crying need for organization on the docks, the party's waterfront section in New York concentrated its forces on offshore workers. Of the dozen or so full-time MWIU functionaries assigned to the port in 1930, only one, Sam Madell, was instructed to work with the longshoremen. At the time, Madell says, the policy of offshore concentration "made sense. The seamen were much more advanced than the longshoremen. . . . A lot of seamen began to join the Communist Party. There was a great response to the program of the MWIU." [35] But what appealed to the seamen did not appeal to the longshoremen. Madell was able to recruit a few rank and filers directly into the party, but the MWIU, as in the West, had no takers on the docks.

The fact that, on both coasts, dual unionism was an unmitigated disaster did not mean that local organizers responded in precisely the same way. On the West Coast, party leaders in San Francisco recognized the failure of dual unionism and modified their strategy accordingly by entering the ILA in the summer of 1933. In New York, facing a similar situation, party leaders diagnosed the same condition as a failure of political will on the part of local cadre who were simply proceeding too cautiously. Summing up the problem in the East, the national MWIU secretary observed early in 1934 that "what New York needs now more than anything else is maybe an Open Letter on Bolshevik tempo." [36]

The decision to go along with dual unionism was to some extent forced on New York's Communists by conditions on the docks. Given the conservatism of the labor force, the best that any organizer could realistically hope for was to win over a few enlightened workers—an approach that meshed perfectly with the revolutionary pretensions of dual unionism. Ironically, then, it was the very weakness of radicalism on the docks that, rather than moderating the party's extremism, drove it further to the left. Politics aside, there were also more practical objections to "boring from within." The growing influence of criminal and racketeering elements within the union, the lack of democracy, and especially the noninvolvement of the rank and file led some insurgents to question whether the ILA was worth capturing. In Madell's words, "You were not really dealing with a union. The ILA was not a union at all. They didn't even collect dues regularly. It was strictly a racket organization."[37] As such, Communist organizers were understandably reluctant to bore from within what was obviously a rotten apple.

Revolutionary dual unionism remained the Communist Party's official line on trade union work through the fall of 1935, precipitating many disagreements between national leaders and front-line cadre. Browder, as we saw, clashed with Darcy over that issue on more than one occasion. But Darcy prevailed, partly because his position as district organizer gave him significant leverage in internal party fights, and partly because his district enjoyed a certain degree of organizational autonomy owing to its distance from national headquarters in Manhattan.[38]

Strategic innovation was more problematic in New York, especially for someone like Madell. As a rank-and-file Communist working under the shadow of "the Kremlin," as party headquarters was sometimes called, Madell had neither the power of position nor the organizational autonomy to question his superiors—men such as Roy Hudson, national MWIU secretary, and Al Lannon, chairman of the party's waterfront section in New York. For Madell, the only real options were to accept party discipline and dutifully carry out his assignments or be temporarily "removed" from his position as longshore organizer. In more than thirty years on the docks, Madell was removed at least a half dozen times for refusing to toe the line.

Madell's first run-in with party leaders concerned "Bolshevik tempo." After investing almost two years on the docks with little to show for it, he became convinced that the party's Third Period stance was much too advanced for the average rank and filer, whom he now saw as "backward" and lacking even a rudimentary trade union consciousness. So although he continued to pay lip service to dual unionism, Madell began quietly reorienting his work toward progressives within the ILA. Near the end of 1933 he befriended two old-timers, both charter members of Local 791 in Chelsea and highly respected by the men. With his two friends as escorts, Madell, a known Communist, was able to attend local meetings. At that point his strategy was to "stay in the background" and "cultivate these guys." But the leadership of the party had other ideas. They told Madell that if he was unprepared to provide revolutionary leadership, they would find someone who was. Madell was removed a short time later. His replacement, a "gung-ho party guy," walked into his first union meeting and, when the agenda was open for new business, began lambasting "sell-out" union leaders. Madell recalls:

> The first thing that happened is the delegate says, "Who the hell are you? Are you a member of this local?" Because nobody knew him. He said he was a member, he walked up, showed them his book. The delegate looked at the book, closed it, tore it up, and threw it in his face and said, "You get the hell out of here fast or you'll go through that window." That was the end of that guy. I couldn't even ask my two contacts to defend the guy because I thought it was wrong.[39]

Nevertheless, party leaders in New York believed what they wanted to believe. On the heels of the debacle in Local 791, an organizing report came in from the port's waterfront section telling of "progress" and "crystallization" on the docks. "Quite a few of the longshoremen," it read, are beginning "to come towards us." A screening of the Russian revolutionary epic *Potemkin* had attracted a crowd of almost a thousand Brooklyn longshoremen whose "greatest applause" erupted when Stalin's picture graced the screen. Conditions were ripe, the report concluded, for building a strong party nucleus on the docks.[40]

The first signs of doubt began appearing early in 1934. Openly acknowledging the "extreme weakness of the Party" on the East Coast docks, the Central Committee convened a special conference in January to salvage the situation in the North Atlantic ports. Summarizing the proceedings, Roy Hudson wrote that the assembled delegates "emphasized the need for developing a strong opposition movement" within the ILA. "At the same time," he added, "the conference combated tendencies that have prevailed which minimized the possibilities of organizing the unorganized longshoremen directly into" the MWIU. So there would be no misunderstanding, Hudson reiterated that "the establishment of a strong longshore section of the Marine Workers Industrial Union and the strengthening of the forces assigned to this work [are] of the utmost importance."[41]

Hudson continued vigorously advocating dual unionism for the next several months. As late as June 1934 he was still criticizing the party's approach in San Francisco, which had resulted in "1,200 longshoremen join[ing] the ILA. It does not help to say we are *beginning* to do opposition work there," he wrote, revealing his own ignorance of the party's long history of involvement in building the ILA. Dual unionism, it seemed, was sacrosanct among the party elite. Citing the example of the MWIU's successful efforts to organize offshore marine workers in the East, Hudson concluded that it is "possible . . . at this time for us to build revolutionary unions here in the United States." Although he wrote that spring that the "experience we have had among the seamen especially proves it,"[42] the party's experience with longshoremen in the West, who were at that moment leading one of the most significant labor struggles of the decade from inside the reformist ILA, pointed to a very different conclusion.

The 1934 maritime strike was celebrated in the Communist press as a "Great Historic Battle." And indeed it was. On the West Coast, particularly in San Francisco where Albion Hall had established a base of support from inside the strikers' ranks, conservative ILA leaders were thoroughly discredited and later driven from office by radical insurgents. In New York, however, the strike failed to galvanize an oppositional movement inside the ILA. A few locals, including 791 where Madell was concentrating, formally endorsed the West Coast demands. But nothing more came of it. When Ben Jones, an original member of Albion Hall, went back East to build support for the walkout, his motion for a sympathy strike died on the floor of a Brooklyn union hall for lack of a second.[43] The Great Historic Battle came and went, causing hardly a ripple on the New York waterfront.

Communist leaders in New York finally abandoned dual unionism as 1934 was drawing to a close, but by then the brief historical opening for mass insurgency had passed. Looking back on the party's missed opportunity in the East, Hudson concluded that longshore work had "received inadequate attention from the Center, and especially from myself." Despite Hudson's admirably self-critical tone, he either missed or chose to ignore the obvious lesson of their failure in New York—not that the Communists had neglected the importance of longshore work but rather that "the Center" had tried to guide the party's work on the docks by mechanically applying Third Period organizing strategies. Hudson himself, in a thinly veiled attack on the doctrine of social fascism, implicitly acknowledged the CP's strategic shortcomings in New York. "It is only in recent months," he wrote in December 1934, " . . . that many of us have learned that there are such things as 'progressives' amongst the lower officials of the I.L.A.; that there are also a few Socialists on the dock with whom we can work, and that it is possible for us to develop activity inside the unions."[44] Unfortunately, like Browder and other party leaders, Hudson rejected dual unionism too late to benefit Communist longshore organizers in New York.

Conclusion

The few years leading up to the 1934 maritime strike were perhaps as critical to the future of longshore unionism as the strike itself. On the West Coast, Communist-supported insurgents built a mass-based oppositional movement on the docks, out of which Bridges and the left eventually rose to power. In New York, despite the presence of Communist organizers, popular resistance to Ryan's conservative leadership never developed, thus giving him a free hand throughout the early 1930s to tighten his grip on the port's longshoremen.

The relative success of rank-and-file movements on the two coasts was partly attributable to the strategies Communist organizers adopted before the strike. In the summer of 1933, Communists and their supporters on the San Francisco docks abruptly broke with the national party's Third Period strategy of building revolutionary unions and instead joined the growing stream of workers flowing into the "social fascist" AFL. From inside the ILA, they patiently worked to overcome their outsider status by helping to build the new union, organizing job actions, and maintaining pressure on both the shipowners and the conservative union leaders. Having earned their union cards the hard way, leftist organizers won the respect and trust of the rank and file, who followed them into the 1934 strike and later into the ILWU.

The content and timing of strategy was equally significant in New York, where a policy of dual unionism remained in force through 1934. Isolated in the MWIU, Communist organizers were understandably viewed with suspicion as opportunistic outsiders, or worse, during the 1934 strike. Because of the Communists' self-imposed isolation on the docks, they were unable to grasp the historical moment, however brief, that was created for mass insurgency during the early 1930s.

The fact that strategic differences of this sort even existed is a reminder that organizing strategies were never simply given—either by Moscow or by the class struggle.[45] In the West, the Communists' strategic reorientation was set in motion by a ranking member of the party, Sam Darcy, who was prepared to take on Browder and, if necessary, sacrifice the revolutionary purity of dual unionism for the opportunity to establish close working relations with the rank and file. Yet the decision to enter the ILA was not Darcy's alone to make. Conditions on the docks—particularly the strength of syndicalist traditions, the years of employer resistance, and the viability of the reinvigorated ILA—also played a part in redirecting strategy on the West Coast. The absence of such conditions in New York, together with the dogmatism of Communist leaders, bound the party ever so tightly to the strategy of dual unionism, a situation from which it never fully recovered.

Dual unionism was not necessarily a recipe for failure during the early 1930s. Outside the longshore industry radical insurgents were sometimes undermined by prematurely abandoning dual unionism. In the steel industry, for example, the party's decision in 1935 to back an organizing committee of the CIO drew precious resources and support away from rank-and-file steelworkers just as they were about to launch an industrial union of their own. The long-term consequences of this decision came back to haunt the party: the organizing committee evolved into the United Steel Workers of America, whose president, Philip Murray, led the campaign to expel Communists and their supporters from the CIO after World War II.[46]

Strategy, then, does make a difference. Indeed, the ability to formulate workable strategies—like many of the more tangible organizational resources identified in the social movement literature—can have an important bearing on the success or failure of any mobilization effort.[47] In some cases, simply knowing how to organize may be one of the most important resources of all.

Chapter Five

Generations in Motion

The social forces that ignited the industrial insurgency of the 1930s grew out of the collective experiences of an entire generation of American workers. For the millions of men and women who came to political maturity during the Great Depression, the only alternative to a life of broken dreams was to struggle actively against the poverty, unemployment, and personal tragedy that filled their daily lives. Their fight for a better world gave us the progressive social legislation of the New Deal, a solid Democratic majority in Congress, and the CIO. Sharing in these decisive political experiences, the generation of the 1930s developed a common worldview and interpretive framework anchored in their unique place in history.

Although longshoremen on both coasts occupied the same place in history, they experienced the world of the Depression in different ways. In the West, the 1934 strike gave rise to a distinct generation of workers whose loyalty to one another, including their radical contemporaries like Bridges, rested on their participation in the violent conflict that reestablished unionism on the Pacific Coast. This generation of "'34 men," forged in the heat of battle, was then tempered and politicized by a protracted struggle, under leftist leadership, to fundamentally transform class relations on the waterfront. In New York, the generation that came of age during the 1930s confronted a different historical reality. Lacking traditions of working-class solidarity, highly skeptical of leftist agitators, and cowed by repression, this group made its peace with Ryan's conservative machine, learning that survival on the docks meant accepting his often corrupt ways, collaborationist policies, and ties to industrial racketeers. By the end of the decade, long-shoremen in the East had come to embrace a union leadership as conservative in its vision and practices as the West's was radical. This chapter explores the politically relevant generational experiences of the rank and file as the basis for the contrasting "political generations" that emerged on the two coasts during the watershed of the Depression.[1]

The '34 Men: A Generation Forged in the Crucible of Violence

The 1934 maritime strike on the West Coast has been treated extensively by historians, and not without good reason. When the longshoremen walked off the job on May 9, they did much more than shut down commerce. Nationally, the walkout coincided with important strikes involving Teamsters in Minneapolis and electrical workers at Auto-Lite in Toledo. Together, these three struggles represented a radical break with the past: each was influenced by some faction of the left—Communists on the West Coast, Trotskyists in Minneapolis, and followers of A. J. Muste's local Unemployed League in Toledo; each relied on rank-and-file mobilization to challenge conservative AFL leaders; each resulted in violent confrontations with public authority; and each was successful. In their leftist leadership, mass participation, and confrontational tactics, the walkouts that spring set a pattern that was to become the dominant expression of working-class struggle for the remainder of the decade, paving the way for the organization of basic industry and the rise of the CIO.

The effects of the maritime strike were also felt locally. Workers in other West Coast industries, inspired by the longshoremen's heroic example, began organizing and demanding union recognition. Loggers in the Northwest, warehouse workers in California, and fishermen in Alaska all won important union victories after the maritime strike. And down on the waterfront where it had all started, industrial organization and working-class solidarity were becoming more than empty rhetoric, as evidenced by the dramatic four-day general strike that broke out in San Francisco at the height of the walkout and by the subsequent formation of an industrywide trade union federation encompassing all marine workers on the West Coast.[2]

But the strike's significance ran deeper still, especially for the generation of marine workers who remember it as one of the bloodiest confrontations in the history of the American working class. Indeed, the walkout that year epitomized class warfare. A physician who attended to several strike victims later commented that many of the casualties "were far worse looking than some of the war casualties in World War II. . . . There were many broken arms from forcefully breaking an opponent's arm who was engaged in the attack. There were head wounds caused by the blow of a heavy hand implement such as pick handles. These were common implements of warfare that one saw on the piers, on the ships, and elsewhere." During the three-month walkout nine marine workers lost their lives, hundreds were arrested, and thousands were clubbed or teargassed by Pinkertons, police, and national guardsmen. In San Francisco, scene of some of the most violent clashes, close to five hundred longshoremen were arrested on charges ranging from malicious mischief to felony kidnapping.[3]

Collective violence drew the embattled longshoremen together in much the same way that a popular war unifies an entire nation. In the words of urban anthropologist William Pilcher, whose father was active in the strike, participation in the walkout gave the men "a great feeling of being engaged in important historical processes and working together towards a common goal."[4] This "great feeling" of making history provided the veterans of the "Big Strike" with their own identity as a generation, while tying them closely to Bridges and other prominent strike activists who led the '34 men into the violent social struggle out of which the ILWU was later born.

Violence began in San Francisco on May 9, the day the longshoremen walked out, when one hundred police, many on horseback or motorcycles, rode into a group of two hundred strikers, knocking several down and taking others into custody. Confrontations with police also broke out in the Northwest during the first week of the strike. In a climax to three days of scattered violence along Portland's waterfront, several hundred longshoremen and sympathizers charged through police lines, boarded the steamship *Evans*—which was being prepared to house and feed strikebreak-

ers—and repulsed twenty-four private guards before setting the
vessel adrift. In Seattle an estimated two thousand strikers swept
across the waterfront in a wave of violence that lasted from dawn
to dusk. Small contingents of police stood by helplessly as the
crowd surged from pier to pier, tearing down dock gates, smashing
freight, and routing strikebreakers from the holds of ships.[5]

Strike violence claimed its first victim hours later in San Pedro.
Twenty-year-old "Dickie" Parker was shot through the heart while
leading three hundred men in a daring nighttime raid on a heavily
fortified "scab stockade" where four hundred strikebreakers were
sheltered. Several others in the raiding party sustained serious in-
jury at the hands of club-wielding police and private watchmen.
Six men were hospitalized with broken bones, fractured skulls,
and bullet wounds, including Tom Knudsen, who later died from a
perforated intestine.[6]

Parker's death galvanized the working-class population of San
Pedro. With many regarding the "dead youth and injured as martyrs to the cause," local press accounts described an atmosphere of
"seething unrest" along the waterfront. On the day of Parker's funeral, more than ten thousand mourners lined both sides of the
city's main street to pay their respects. Leading the solemn procession was a separate detail of a thousand longshoremen, headed
by an ILA color guard bearing the American flag and the union's
blue and white standard. The full cortège of five thousand marchers
presented a "grim spectacle" as it moved slowly and silently toward the cemetery. It was San Pedro's largest such gathering in
more than a decade.[7]

The killing of a striking longshoreman and the spilling of union
blood brought to the surface long-submerged feelings of solidarity
from other marine workers. As news of Parker's death traveled up
the coast, seamen, itching for a showdown with the shipowners,
spontaneously quit work in San Francisco, Portland, and Seattle.
Bowing to mounting rank-and-file pressure, officials of the various
offshore unions formally authorized strike action. Seafarers now
joined longshoremen in demanding union recognition, a closed
shop, increased wages, and reduced hours; and—in a rare display
of waterfront unity—all ten striking marine unions pledged to remain out until all received a satisfactory settlement.[8]

San Francisco was the site of the next violent outburst, precipi-

tated by an unprovoked police attack on a group of pickets. Setting
out as usual from the Ferry Building on the afternoon of May 28, a
spirited crowd of one thousand strikers began their daily parade
along the embarcadero. When they reached Pier 18, a squadron of
police ordered them to either detour from their customary route
or immediately disperse. Instead, Communist longshoreman John
Schomaker, who was leading the procession, pressed forward.
When mounted police charged, unarmed pickets answered with
bare fists. Schomaker, meeting the charge head-on, pulled two
policemen from their mounts before being beaten to the ground
and arrested. Advancing under a heavy barrage of bricks and
bottles, marine workers engaged more than two hundred police in
what local newspapers described as a "bloody pitched battle" that
produced numerous casualties on both sides.[9]

The use of such excessive force against lawful pickets escalated
the conflict. Now there would be no turning back. When Ryan announced his signing of a "compromise agreement" on June 16,
longshoremen up and down the West Coast voted overwhelmingly
against it, except in San Pedro where, with vigorous sponsorship
from local leaders, it passed by a mere fifty-four votes. In San Francisco an angry crowd of three thousand strikers rejected Ryan's
latest handiwork by acclamation, then elected their own rank-and-
file committee to conduct all future negotiations with the shipowners.[10] Continued meddling by Ryan and other salaried officials
drove growing numbers of strikers into the insurgent camp and
closer to the Communists. Following the collapse of the June 16
agreement, the San Francisco local voted to make the *Western
Worker*—the newspaper of the California Communist Party—its
official organ for carrying strike news. The party itself even began
to look attractive. Internal party documents indicate that, in California alone, nearly 125 marine workers joined the CP during the
month of June.[11]

Wary public officials began taking a more direct role in the
strike. The mayor of Seattle, declaring his intention to open the
port, assumed personal command of the police. More than five
hundred officers were deputized, nearly doubling the size of the
city's regular police force. An additional one hundred men were
secured through the largess of the Citizens' Emergency Committee,
an anti-union organization funded by the local Chamber of Com-

merce. On the morning of June 21, pickets and police clashed in front of Pier 40, the terminal point for most railroad lines servicing the waterfront. Isolated skirmishes continued throughout the afternoon as more than four hundred strikers contested an equal number of police for control of the ramp leading up to the pier. By nightfall, both sides were digging in for a siege expected to last several days.[12]

Seattle's Central Labor Council condemned the strikebreaking activities of the police as evidence of the "undemocratic and antiquated policies" of the waterfront employers. Union teamsters immediately imposed an embargo on all cargo unloaded with police protection. As Pier 40 became congested with discharged cargo, city officials mobilized several hundred reserve officers to open an adjacent dock. On June 30, a mile-long caravan of police descended on Pier 41. Warning his men that "today's the day," the chief of police explained that "we are not looking for trouble but we are prepared for it. Some of you are armed with tear gas, some with guns. See that your guns are in good shape. But use them only as a last extremity, for the protection of life and property."[13]

Pier 41 was opened without incident. But violence erupted that evening at a Standard Oil storage facility located about ten miles north of Seattle at Point Wells. Longshoreman and strike leader Shelby Daffron was fatally wounded—shot in the back—during a brush between pickets and company guards. Although a Standard Oil spokesman was unable to explain what he termed "the sudden and unexpected" onslaught of pickets, the longshoremen insisted that they had been ambushed. According to Fred Richardson, a participant in the raid, an unconfirmed report had come into the union hall that evening that strikebreakers were on the job pumping oil at Point Wells. Piling into a large truck, a group of pickets headed out to the refinery, where they overpowered a lone security guard, cut the telephone lines, and then proceeded down a ramp leading to the main pumping station. But "when we walked down this incline," remembers Richardson, "the cops all of a sudden started shooting. The guy next to me was Shelby Daffron. They killed him, shot him in the back."[14]

Daffron was eulogized in the local Communist press as a courageous and militant activist. The *Voice of Action,* a weekly newspaper put out by the Seattle Communist Party, treated his "murder by company thugs" as a tragic lesson in class analysis. Daffron's real killers were "the entire force of capitalism: the shippers, the Chamber of Commerce, the 'Citizens' Emergency Committee—and the exploiters' hirelings: scabs, gunmen, police and deputy sheriffs." His killers were "the same gang" that murdered Dickie Parker and, "swathed in judges' robes," condemned the Scottsboro boys to death. "Daffron's death," the statement concluded, "is an attack upon every worker and every farmer." On the day of his funeral, an overflow crowd of fifteen hundred mourners attended memorial services. The funeral cortège, with flags and banners waving in the breeze, stretched over four blocks and tied up traffic for half an hour.[15]

Violence escalated sharply on July 3 when West Coast city officials and shipowners launched a coordinated drive to open the major ports. In San Francisco, maritime workers and police were poised for a resumption of hostilities following a one-day truce in observance of Independence Day. Fighting resumed the morning of July 5 as punctually "as if the combatants had punched in a time clock." Promptly at 8 A.M. police hurled teargas bombs into a picket line of four thousand strikers who had assembled in front of Pier 38 to block several freight trains loaded with scab cargo. Fleeing the enveloping cloud of gas, a large group of pickets retreated to the higher ground of nearby Rincon Hill. From their advantageous position overlooking the embarcadero, they showered the police with bricks, bottles, and other projectiles. After two unsuccessful assaults on the steep slope, the police laid down a thick fog of tear gas, igniting the parched hillside. Gasping and choking, the pickets conceded the "Battle of Rincon Hill" and retreated en masse to the recognized neutral zone in front of the ILA hall a few blocks uptown on Steuart Street. The police then sealed off both ends of the street and, with guns drawn, closed in on the trapped strikers. Without either warning or provocation, they fired directly into the milling crowd, killing two and injuring many more.[16]

By midday the entire waterfront was consumed in violence. Journalist Royce Brier, recording his impressions in the *San Francisco Chronicle*, compared "the savagery of the conflict" to "a Gettysburg in miniature. . . . Don't think of this as a riot. It was a hundred riots, big and little, first here, now there. Don't think of it as one battle, but as a dozen battles." San Francisco's final toll from "Bloody Thursday" was two dead, thirty-one wounded by gunfire, and seventy-eight seriously injured by bricks, clubs, or tear gas. Bridges, speaking as chairman of the rank-and-file Joint Marine Strike Committee, characterized the confrontation as "an attack by the shipowners, through the police, on the strikers. From the very beginning," he explained, "the forces of the city and the state have been arrayed on the side of the shipowners. They have instituted a reign of terror under which peaceful pickets have been arrested and beaten without cause. Police department thugs have committed murder and gone unpunished." [17]

Nearly two thousand steel-helmeted national guardsmen, armed with bayonets, automatic rifles, gas equipment, and machine guns, took up positions that evening along the entire length of the waterfront. With soldiers stationed every five feet behind barbed-wire enclosures, "the Embarcadero looks like a section of wartime France," an unnamed West Coast labor organizer reported to her national office. [18] Deploying the national guard to break union picket lines and protect the movement of scab cargo rallied the marine workers "against the public itself. A less obvious effect," noted two veteran labor correspondents, "was to suggest to the strikers that the government was not impartial. Communists were not slow to point this out to the men." In this politically charged atmosphere, liberal reformism and the promise of a New Deal for American workers rang increasingly hollow to seamen and longshoremen who were being gunned down by state troopers for exercising their "right" to organize. "Ryan is about as popular here as Roosevelt," observed the West Coast labor organizer, "and whenever Roosevelt's name is mentioned he gets the bird. The strikers here are redder than any communist I ever saw." [19]

An aroused San Francisco labor movement paused on July 9 to bury its dead. Longshoreman Howard Sperry and fry cook Nick Bordoise, a member of the Communist Party who was on duty in the ILA's relief kitchen when the shooting began, had been transformed by death "into heroic symbols of Labor." A somber procession of mourners, conservatively estimated at fifteen thousand, "flowed up Market Street" like "cooling lava." Marching eight and sometimes ten abreast, the funeral cortège stretched from the Ferry Building on the waterfront to Seventh Street, almost two miles uptown. "Line on line they came," read a typical newspaper account, "their bared heads in view as far as the eye could see . . . in a silent orderly march, a mass demonstration of protest which transcended anything of the like San Francisco has seen." This spectacular display of working-class solidarity culminated two weeks later in a citywide general strike directed against the continuing presence of state troops on the waterfront.[20]

The Puget Sound ports were also opened on July 5. Tacoma longshoremen peacefully returned to work after city police withdrew from the waterfront. Violence was likewise avoided in neighboring Seattle, where strikers had not yet regrouped from their earlier rout at Pier 41 and the recent killing of Daffron, whose funeral was scheduled for the next day. Three squads of heavily armed police, standing shoulder-to-shoulder in front of the pier, encountered little resistance from a small but noisy crowd of strikers. When three freight trains moved onto Pier 41 that morning to unload, it marked the first successful passage of landborne cargo through the port of Seattle in nearly two months.[21]

In Portland, bloody clashes between police and strikers attended the opening of the waterfront. Violence erupted, as elsewhere on the West Coast, when local law enforcement agencies abandoned any pretense of neutrality and openly entered the strike on the side of the shipowners. On the morning of July 5 a loaded tanker train pulled out of the Union Oil plant on its way to Terminal 4, a city-owned dock. Striking marine workers, having received assurances from the engineer and brakeman that they would reverse the train rather than break a union picket line, massed midway along the route. But "the first time they started backing up," recalls longshoreman Jack Mowrey, "the damn policemen jumped out of the cars and turned loose. Actual fire: shootin' shotguns, rifles, and pistols. We had two guys wounded, one of 'em pretty serious, hit in the mouth. Another one was hospitalized for a while." The *Portland Oregonian* reported that "freely employed" nightsticks "cracked available skulls," as police were drawn into fierce hand-to-hand combat, climaxed that evening by a teargas attack on five hundred workers.[22]

Marine workers assembled the next afternoon at a strategic point along the tracks where the railroad bed was hemmed in on either side by steep natural embankments. The sun-soaked rails leading up to the gulch glistened with a thick layer of grease, oil, and soap that had been applied by the strikers. An estimated two hundred men, most armed with clubs and rocks, crowded together at "Greasy Gulch" to form a human barricade in front of the advancing locomotive. The slow-moving engine ground to a halt as it approached the greased railing. A police captain, backed by twenty-five officers, got off the train and ordered the men to clear the track. "If we let you move this train to the dock," answer a striker, "our cause is lost. You can kill us if you want to move it any further. We are ready to give our lives, if necessary, to prevent it." A bloodbath seemed inevitable as the train inched forward. But after losing traction on the slick railings, the train was forced to turn back. The police then retaliated with a massive teargas attack. Alternating volleys of rocks and long-range gas bombs were exchanged for several hours until both sides retreated.[23]

Strike violence became more serious a few days later when armed police, stationed on a flatcar preceding a train en route to Terminal 4, opened fire on several hundred pickets, seriously wounding four. That afternoon, enraged union leaders marched into the city council chambers during a meeting and, waving the bloodied shirt of one of the strikers, demanded the immediate resignation of the chief of police. A motion to remove him from active duty was passed without dissent by all three city commissioners. The mayor's subsequent vetoing of the resolution unleashed a storm of protest, including a threatened general strike by the Central Labor Council.[24]

The mood on the waterfront turned ugly. Many men regarded the police attack as the last straw. "Nobody liked it," remembers longshoreman Joe Werner, who was at the union hall right after the shooting to record the men's reactions. "They would have done crazy things. They would have risked their lives to get revenge. . . . Fanatics would have taken hand grenades, machine guns, rifles and stormed the police station. But you can't do that. It's revolution. . . . We had to hold them back."[25]

With the situation in Portland remaining tense, the Seattle waterfront exploded once again. On July 18, several hundred pickets broke through police lines and reclaimed control of the railroad tracks leading to piers 40 and 41. More than five hundred men remained camped outside the pier gates that night. Additional marine workers, many from smaller Puget Sound ports, poured into the strike zone throughout the pre-dawn hours, swelling the ranks to more than two thousand. At sunrise, police with teargas equipment took up positions on a bridge overlooking the piers, with reinforcements stationed 800 yards upwind. When the strikers refused to disperse, teargas bombs rained down from the bridge into the picket line, scattering the men in all directions. An eyewitness described the fighting as "a wartime battle. I could hear the shooting plainly. There were clouds of gas. I saw several men falling." Three police and three longshoremen were hospitalized, and scores of less seriously injured pickets were treated by companions. Fred Richardson recalls that "the men got a real education that day." [26]

Indeed, the three-month walkout amounted to one big lesson in labor solidarity for the '34 men. Fighting side by side taught them the importance of trust. Risking their lives on an almost daily basis forced them to confront the limits of human courage. Seeing their friends fall in battle drove home the meaning of personal sacrifice. And, like any veterans of warfare, the dockworkers came out of their ordeal changed. Having been transformed by collective violence from an odd assortment of individual combatants into a finely integrated army, the '34 men developed the kind of intense loyalty to one another that is usually found only on the battlefield. [27]

The close interpersonal bonds that were forged in the heat of battle endured long after the fighting was over. "Remember Bloody Thursday" became the rallying cry for an entire generation. "We will never forget" the events of that day, Bridges swore at his first deportation hearing. And the longshoremen never did. Several locals erected small memorials on the ground where union blood had been spilled. In San Francisco, an American Legion post was renamed after Howard Sperry, one of two workers gunned down by police on July 5.

More telling than any of these symbolic gestures, however, was the first anniversary of Bloody Thursday. Up and down the West Coast, longshoremen and other marine workers walked off the job in a silent protest commemorating the martyrs of the Big Strike. In Portland, pickets roamed the waterfront from 7 A.M. until midnight, virtually shutting down loading operations for the day. Nearby in Seattle, "5,000 tanned, windswept, grim, and silent men" marched to the strains of the "Marseillaise," while in San Francisco 25,000 turned out for a "monster parade" up Market Street that "awed" tens of thousands of onlookers. This one-day

work stoppage inaugurated a tradition that West Coast longshoremen have stubbornly continued: every July 5 they stop work to
honor the '34 men who sacrificed their lives in the cause of militant
industrial unionism.[28]

The '34 men who lived to tell about their experiences enjoyed a
privileged status within the union. In an organization of equals,
their views carried the most weight, and when they spoke others
listened. Their "attitude toward us—who they called 'Johnny-
come-latelies'—was, in a sense, nasty," recalls Asher Harer, who
entered the union during World War II. "If you got in an argument
or even a discussion about something that was political or something that had to do with the trade union movement, one question
they would always ask you: 'Where were you during the 1934
strike?' . . . I must have had that directed at me a hundred times.
And others went through it too."[29]

For the generation of dockworkers who lived through the Depression, the Big Strike was unquestionably the single most important event of their working lives. In many cases, it changed the way
the '34 men looked at themselves and their world. Joe Werner, for
example, relates how, in the course of the walkout, he became more
open to new ideas. "If you fight a battle and you are convinced you
are in the right position and you're doing the right thing," he explains, looking back on his involvement in the strike, "you would
be surprised how quickly your mind will grasp ideas that will lead
you forward." Others were more explicit about the strike's impact
on their thinking. "I've always been afraid of strikes," admitted a
"stevie" in a letter published in the *Waterfront Worker* during the
walkout. "But now I like it, for it proves what power the workers
have if they will only use it when it becomes necessary. Even the
shipowners must have learned by now where the power lies; if they
haven't, I'm sure they will by the time the strike is over."[30] In fact,
the shipowners' education was just beginning.

Tempering The Generation: Transforming
Class Relations on the Docks

The maritime strike ended when the dispute was submitted to an
arbitration board. None of the major issues that had provoked the
violent eighty-three-day walkout had been resolved when the long-

shoremen reported for work on July 31. Yet "somehow or another," remembers Henry Schmidt, an original member of Albion Hall, "the men discovered that . . . they had terrific power; they also had some courage and they changed the working conditions immediately." Employer representative Paul Eliel later acknowledged that the shipowners "were faced with a revolution in the thinking of their men." Firms that "attempted to operate as they had in the past found a new and militant spirit" on the docks.[31]

Riding this wave of militancy, radical insurgents displaced incumbent ILA officers in several locals. In San Francisco, where the left was most active, Bridges was elected local president by a comfortable three-to-one margin over a conservative challenger, while twenty-three of thirty-seven candidates endorsed by the *Western Worker* were also swept into local office after the strike.[32] This growing radicalization combined with employer intransigence to produce a highly combustible situation on the docks: during the seventy-four-day period from July 31 to October 12, when the arbitration board rendered its decision, West Coast longshoremen initiated twenty-nine separate job actions aimed at driving former scabs from the waterfront and revising pre-strike work rules to reflect the changing relations of power on the docks.[33]

These immediate job control gains were consolidated, extended, and gradually transformed into a basic realignment of class forces through two key provisions in the October 12 award. The first, section 11 of the award, stipulated that all employees "shall be free to select their own jobs." Under terms of this "choose your job" clause, as it came to be known, men could decline work assignments or even quit a job any time during the life of the contract.[34]

Section 11, however, was unenforceable without union control over hiring, for the "choose your job" clause was meaningless so long as the employers had the right not to hire men who exercised their right to refuse work. In this battle of "right against right," control over hiring would determine the winner. Recognizing this, the arbitration board wrestled long and hard with the issue of hiring before finally deciding in favor of "neutral" hiring halls, so named because they were to be jointly funded and operated by employer and union representatives for the purpose of regulating the supply of labor and dispatching men in each port. But the principle of joint operation was negated by another key provision of the award, section 5, which specified that all job dispatchers were to be selected by the ILA. Thus, although the shipowners were permitted to place an observer in the hall, all crucial decisions regarding job assignments were made by ILA representatives, resulting in what an employer spokesman later characterized as "100 percent union control" over hiring.[35]

Together, sections 11 and 5 insulated the longshoremen from conventional forms of industrial discipline. Under terms of the final award, any employee who was discharged for engaging in a job action simply returned to the hall and reregistered for work. The only disincentive was a temporary loss in pay. Moreover, his replacement, invariably a sympathetic '34 man, could still continue the original dispute by refusing employment under section 11. With no provision for deregistering men who refused work, employers were pressured into negotiating unfavorable on-the-job settlements. This unique institutional arrangement, combining control over hiring with the right to refuse work, placed the union in the unusually powerful position of being able to exploit the economic security provided for in the contract without suffering any attendant loss of rank-and-file initiative on the job.[36]

The direct action guarantees contained in the contract were underwritten by the competitive nature of the shipping industry. For all but the largest and most well-heeled companies, economic survival depended on efficiency in loading operations, which—as the Wobblies had discovered earlier—left individual employers highly vulnerable to any kind of work stoppage. Faced with the possibility of losing business to a hungry competitor, few shipping lines were prepared to "take a strike" over some relatively minor work rule violation. The workers, however, ran almost no risk in calling a "quickie" strike: if they did not win outright, they at least stood to earn overtime pay as the employer tried to make up for lost time. "The quickie," as an experienced longshore arbitrator concluded, "was a weapon almost cost-free in the eyes of the men but wickedly effective in the eyes of the employers."[37]

Years of accumulated grievances and suppressed hostilities found an outlet after the 1934 strike in hundreds of these hit-and-run quickies. More than five hundred job actions—most aimed at reducing sling load limits, regulating the pace of work, or challenging abusive foremen—were recorded coastwide in the two-year period following the October award. By 1936 most of the remaining "scab bosses" had been driven from the waterfront, and sling load limits, the real measure of employer hegemony, had been drastically reduced.[38]

With the balance of power tilting away from the shipowners, productivity fell off sharply. The *Marine Workers' Voice*, national organ of the MWIU, conceded that efficiency was down "in some places 50 percent" on the Pacific, "but," continued the Communist newspaper, reflecting the rebellious mood along the waterfront, "to hell with boss efficiency and speed-up." In Portland, where longshoremen conducted thirty-seven recorded job actions over sling loads, labor productivity declined on the order of 30 percent between 1934 and 1936. San Francisco longshoremen led the West Coast with forty work stoppages directed at reducing sling loads during this same two-year period.[39] After slashing load limits from almost three tons to a mere 1,800 pounds—the lowest limit anywhere on the coast—the port's longshoremen, in the words of one old-timer, "done as we damn well please" on the waterfront. "No more do the docks of San Francisco hear the booming echo of some boss's voice," observed the *Waterfront Worker*, "the winches do not groan with their heavy loads as before." Even in San Pedro, where employer resistance during the strike had been most intense, the longshoremen "were taking over the waterfront. The employers didn't have no say at all," according to Al Langley. "We just said: 'Look, that's the way it is and that's the way it's gonna be.' And we had enough power to enforce it."[40]

This power found institutional expression in a tightly organized network of job stewards that coordinated the workers' activities in each port. With the "authority to direct work upon the docks passing from the hands of the foremen into the hands of dock and gang stewards," shipowners complained that the longshoremen were taking over the waterfront by deciding "the manner in which, and the speed at which, work is to be performed." For the longshoremen, the transformation in class relations was no less monumental, as men who only a few years before had been regarded as lowly "wharf rats" had suddenly become, in the words of one especially proud stevedore, "Lords of the Docks."[41]

From their lofty heights, the longshoremen were now able to more clearly see as well as act on their common interests as members of a class. When ILA militants embarked on an ambitious campaign to organize freight handlers employed in the many uptown warehouses far removed from the waterfront, the dockworkers lent their full support to the drive, refusing to handle "hot" cargo that had been declared unfair by organizers of the "march inland."[42] Longshore militants also pushed for labor unity on the waterfront. In 1935 the Maritime Federation of the Pacific was formed to more closely coordinate collective bargaining and job action on an industrywide basis. Despite an arbitrator's ruling that sympathy strikes in support of other unions constituted a violation of the ILA's most recent contract, the men steadfastly refused to cross legitimate picket lines. When "agreements conflict with labor solidarity," Bridges told a mass meeting of longshoremen, "agreements must go."[43]

Left-wing ILA activists were instrumental in focusing this diffuse syndicalist mood on more political targets, particularly the rise of fascism overseas. When the swastika-flying German cruiser *Karlsruhe* steamed into San Francisco Bay in March 1935, the longshoremen, in a dramatic application of the "choose your job" clause, refused to service the Nazi vessel. German sailors finally had to put ashore to fasten their own lines. In Seattle, longshoremen stopped work to protest the overseas arrest of American seaman Lawrence Simpson by Gestapo agents for allegedly possessing communist literature in his shipboard locker. Then in October San Francisco longshoremen refused to load an Italian ship unless they received assurances that its cargo of airplane spruce was not "destined for Mussolini's bombing planes." In justifying this action, Bridges declared: "We emphatically agree with President Roosevelt that the United States should do all in its power to prevent war material being shipped to Italy to aid the Italian government in this uncalled war of aggression" against Ethiopia.[44]

This reasoning was more significant than it appeared. Bridges, who had previously sided with left-wing critics of Roosevelt, was now couching his defense of the union's boycott in terms of supporting the president's opposition to war shipments—an indication that something big was in the wind.[45] In fact Bridges did move toward the political center during the latter half of the 1930s, reflecting the left's growing sense of urgency in building broader unity to contain the spread of European fascism. The consolidation of Nazi political power under the Third Reich, followed by the rapid militarization of the German economy, had decisively altered the international balance of power—forcing Comintern officials, in particular, to reconsider their policy of benign neglect toward nazism, exemplified in the German Communist Party's slogan "After Hitler—Our Turn."[46] During the winter of 1935 an emergency meeting of the Communist International was held in Moscow to assess the rapidly changing global situation. Clearly making defense of the "socialist motherland" the cornerstone of its new policy, the communist movement shed its Third Period ultraleftism for the more moderate Popular Front strategy of building a broad, multiclass alliance of all democratic political tendencies opposing fascism.

With the international campaign against fascism heating up, the class struggle at home began to be pushed to the back burner. On the West Coast docks, Popular Frontism led to a relaxation of the ILA's confrontational posture. "Prospects for peace on the waterfront," wrote *New York Times* labor reporter George West in February 1936, "are brighter than they have been at any time within the past year, as San Francisco tries to accustom itself to the spectacle of Harry Bridges exerting all his influence on the side of moderation and peace as against militants on his own side." As part of the union's "strategic retreat," Bridges ordered striking longshoremen in Hawaii back to work, opposed the six-hour-day demand of the sailors' union, and twice provided replacement gangs for longshoremen who quit work in San Francisco.[47]

The Communist Party's role in actively discouraging job action was roundly condemned by anti-Stalinist leftists on the waterfront. In the fall of 1935 when the *Waterfront Worker* introduced a distinction between acceptable forms of direct action "confined to the job itself" as opposed to disruptive "premature" strikes involving other marine crafts, left oppositionists within the Maritime Federation attacked the "Stalinite freaks" on the waterfront for their growing conservatism. "I am opposed to the Communist Party," wrote the departing Trotskyist editor of the *Voice of the Federation*, "not because of its 'radicalism,' but because I consider it a reactionary force and an enemy of militant industrial unionism. In spite of the radical phraseology of the Communist Party, its line has shifted so much to the right that if Samuel Gompers were alive today he would have to fight them from the left."[48]

Although it provoked a few such attacks from other leftists, the

CP's more selective advocacy of direct action hardly tarnished its image among the rank and file. San Francisco longshoreman Archie Brown recalls that when he and other Communists first spoke out against "anarchistic, irresponsible job actions," most men responded favorably. "You have to remember," explains Brown, "this thing is always a double-edged sword, so that we fought to better their conditions and now what they want is a more stable life than they had before" the strike. By exercising greater restraint on the job, the party was "meeting the wishes and feelings of the workers"—simply "stepping back to go ahead," as the *Waterfront Worker* described its new stance. This more accommodating posture provided ideological ammunition for a handful of anti-Stalinist leftists, but it apparently did little to undermine the party's active base of support on the docks.[49]

The Communists' vision of labor peace was shattered in the fall of 1936, however, when forty thousand West Coast marine workers walked off the job. Unlike the 1934 strike, this one was largely peaceful. But the central issue was the same, with unions and employers divided over who should control hiring. In pre-strike negotiations with the ILA, the shipowners, returning to the language of the 1934 award, demanded genuinely "neutral" dispatchers in each hiring hall. The longshoremen, voting in a coastwide referendum, rejected the employers' position and authorized strike action. At midnight on October 29, the entire marine labor force quit work. Confident in their ability to outlast the strikers, the employers calmly tied up their ships and closed down operations. But the marine workers hung together, and on February 4, 1937—ninety-nine days after the strike began—they returned to work with most of their demands met. The longshoremen retained their control over hiring in exchange for contract language outlawing most forms of job action.[50]

The party's presence was very much in evidence throughout the three-month walkout. Shunning the low-profile approach of the Popular Front period, the *Marine Worker,* mass publication of the San Francisco waterfront section, openly solicited striking marine workers to join the CP as "the only way—the REVOLUTIONARY way out—the COMMUNIST way out" of the present impasse. And the rank and file responded. Nearly 2,000 new members joined the party in California during the six-month period that included the strike. Of the 616 recruits in San Francisco, 316 belonged to various marine unions; in the Los Angeles area 48 out of 825 recruits were maritime workers. Although comparable recruitment figures are not available for the Northwest, total membership in Seattle's waterfront section stood at 153 after the strike. William Schneiderman, who at Browder's insistence had replaced Darcy as West Coast organizer in 1935, reported that "the Party came out of the strike stronger than ever."[51]

The left's increased strength was demonstrated a few months later. In June, as the Waterfront Employers' Association of the Pacific Coast (described in Chapter 3) was being formed, longshore delegates attending a coastwide ILA convention agreed to conduct a membership referendum on joining the CIO. Given the generally obstructionist role Ryan and his followers had played on the West Coast, the outcome of the voting was never really in doubt: when the ballots were counted, the CIO was the clear winner. Small pockets of anti-CIO sentiment developed in some locals, notably San Pedro, where fifteen ILA loyalists—known to CIO supporters as the "dirty dozen"—took their case to court before finally losing. The only other opposition to CIO affiliation surfaced in the Puget Sound ports of Tacoma, Port Angeles, Anacortes, and Olympia. When Olympia later voted to join the CIO, the AFL was left to represent roughly six hundred members in the remaining three "exception ports." By August, the Pacific Coast district of the ILA had become District 1 of the International Longshoremen's and Warehousemen's Union, with Bridges selected to head the new organization. West Coast longshoremen had moved en masse into the mainstream of the industrial union movement.

The longshoremen did not let their institution-building efforts interfere with the struggle against fascism. In the spring of 1937, they struck a symbolic blow for Spanish democracy, joining with other marine workers on the West Coast in a thirty-minute work stoppage called by the Maritime Federation of the Pacific to protest America's policy of nonsupport for the democratically elected Republican government in Spain. Pointing out that the work stoppage was explicitly forbidden under the recent contract, Almon Roth, newly installed president of the employers' association, expressed his profound sense of frustration: "If the majority of the membership of the maritime unions have become so social-minded that they are prepared to sacrifice their earnings and the stability of their own employment for the common cause of 'the Communist

Party' it is apparent that the sanctity of contracts and such items will mean but little."[52]

Contractual obligations were again subordinated to political goals a few months later when two European freighters docked at San Francisco to load scrap iron for Japan. Union leaders, acting on their publicly declared opposition to Japan's invasion of China, notified activists in the city's sizable Chinese community of the cargo's destination and its possible use in the production of military hardware. As loading operations were getting under way, two thousand boys and girls from Chinatown paraded onto the waterfront, where they formed an informational picket line in front of the two vessels. Several gangs of longshoremen immediately ceased work, stranding the entire shipment of scrap iron on the dock. "Our union wants to live up to its contract," explained local president Henry Schmidt, "but we cannot expect self-respecting men to push Chinese children out of the way and load scrap iron that will be used to slaughter their countrymen." The picket line was withdrawn after five days of public discussion and media attention focused on the issue of Japanese militarism.[53]

Scrap iron incidents occurred elsewhere on the West Coast. A 7,500-ton shipment of scrap destined for Japan lay untouched for more than two weeks on the Portland waterfront. In Seattle, dockworkers openly defied a court's restraining order to load scrap iron. After a similar protest in San Pedro, an arbitrator imposed a one-week suspension on sixty-one men for participating in an illegal work stoppage. But local union officers, instead of suspending the "penalty men" as ordered, dispersed them among regularly employed gangs in widely scattered areas of the port.[54]

The dockworkers' decade-long struggle against fascism ended on a confused and sour note. In August 1939 the Soviet-German nonaggression pact was signed, obliterating the Popular Front's central distinction between the forces of democracy and fascism. Comintern officials redefined the developing European conflict as imperialistic in nature rather than anti-fascist. Abruptly, the American Communist Party, which had been hammering away at the Roosevelt administration for its neutrality, became a bulwark of noninterventionism. "The present war is not a war against fascism," Al Lannon told a mass meeting of the waterfront section late in 1939. "It is not a war of the democracies against Hitlerism nor is this a war to right past injustices, as Hitler would have us believe. It is a war between rival imperialisms for the domination of the world."[55]

The sudden change of line following the Hitler-Stalin accord was one of the most dramatic reversals in the long zigzagging history of the communist movement. It was also the most alienating, at least for many independent radicals and sympathetic liberals who had supported the work of the party in the past. More than a few felt betrayed. The left-liberal *New Republic*, labeling the pact "Stalin's Munich," noted dryly that "fellow travelers are dropping like ripe plums in a hurricane."[56]

In the trade union movement, however, the extent of damage caused by the pact seems to have varied widely depending on the influence and personal reputations of local Communists. On the waterfront, the new line thoroughly discredited San Pedro's struggling left-wing forces, whereas in San Francisco, where the party enjoyed much firmer support on the docks, it caused hardly a ripple. When the issue of the pact arose on the floor of the San Francisco local, Schneiderman, the party's district organizer, compared Stalin's tactics to the union's approach during the recent strike. Stalin's intention, he explained, was not to make peace with fascism, but rather to shatter the anti-Soviet alliance of Western democracies who had earlier refused to sign a collective security treaty. By signing the pact with Hitler, Stalin was merely attempting to divide a united opposition in the same way the longshoremen had tried to undermine the unity of the shipowners by offering to sign with certain companies. Steve Nelson, a national leader of the party who attended the meeting, recalls that "most of the longshoremen thought that was a pretty good answer."[57]

The campaign against Hitler was over but not forgotten. Like the earlier pitched battles with police in 1934 and the ensuing struggle to wrest control of the waterfront away from the shipowners, opposition to fascism overseas was an important part of what it meant to be a longshoreman on the West Coast during the 1930s. The result was a generation of dockworkers skilled in the art of combat and determined to even the score with shipowners, other employers, reactionary politicians, and anyone else who stood in their way. Leading the charge was the one man who seemed to embody the experiences and hopes of an entire generation—Harry Bridges, whom the '34 men followed until he retired almost half a century later.

The "Lost Generation" in New York

Longshoremen in New York inhabited a world all their own during the 1930s. Untouched by the rank-and-file insurgencies, violent battles, and leadership challenges that shook the rest of the industry, they remained, as Walter Galenson put it, "incredibly quiescent" within the conservative ILA. While longshoremen in the West were actively building a new union under radical leadership, and seamen on the East Coast were doing the same through the National Maritime Union, New York's dockworkers hardly stirred. During their long sleep from 1919 to 1945, there was not a single major work stoppage anywhere in the port. If the longshoremen of that era left any mark at all on the waterfront, it was as the "lost generation."[58]

Older members of this generation had long since been tamed by the failure of the 1919 strike. Their humiliating defeat, though distant in time, remained fresh in their collective memory. What was painfully remembered as the "impossibility" of portwide solidarity in 1919 turned many old-timers into hard-nosed realists. Without any sense of the possible, they came across as "provincial and cynical," according to Meyer Baylin, who tried to organize the port's waterfront freight handlers during the 1930s. "They cut through ideas very quickly," he recalls. "They didn't go for long developed arguments. If their sense told them something was right, they followed through."[59]

Brooklyn's Italian longshoremen encountered additional obstacles. Those who had entered the country illegally as "ship jumpers" were disciplined by the constant threat of deportation. Ignorance also kept them in line. Among naturalized Italians, few had any understanding of their rights as American citizens. "They simply didn't understand the phenomenon of American democracy," recalls Vincent "Jim" Longhi, whose father worked on the docks. "The old-timers found it much more difficult to understand the idea that you can do many things in a democracy, even in a gangster-infested area like the Brooklyn docks."[60]

Democracy or not, waterfront society was ruled by a coterie of gangsters and corrupt union officials—a marriage of convenience consummated during the 1930s when Ryan began hiring power-fully built ex-convicts as "union organizers" to police the water-front. Their numbers increased steadily over the years until almost one-third of all ILA officers in New York had criminal records, ac-cording to a 1953 investigation conducted by the New York Crime Commission. Publicly, Ryan defended his hiring preferences with all the enthusiasm of a crusading rehabilitator. "Where are these poor devils to go?" he asked plaintively. "Because a man's done wrong once, don't show he's a criminal. Why, a man can't get pa-roled unless somebody'll give him a job."[61] In private, however, the shipowners offered a different rationale. One company official candidly testified that, if given the choice between "hiring a tough ex-convict and a man without a criminal record," he would "take the ex-con . . . because if he is in a boss job he'll keep the men in line and get the maximum work out of them. They'll be afraid of him." When another employer was asked why he had hired Albert Ackalitis, a former convict and waterfront tough, he answered: "We would like to have twenty Ackalitises. We get more work out of the man than anybody else. We're not interested in his personal life."[62]

Men with known ties to organized crime blasted their way into the leadership of several ILA locals in New York. So-called pistol locals—in which union meetings were called to order by banging not a gavel but the handle of a revolver—sprang up throughout the port. By the end of the decade the expansive New York–New Jersey waterfront had been carved up into separate fiefdoms, each ruled by warring mobs who looted union treasuries like modern-day pirates. "I started paying dues to these boys" in 1939, a rank-and-filer told the Crime Commission. "We got a membership book for $26, cut rate. The official rate was $50. The mob never put stamps in our book. I guess 2,000 men paid off in this way."[63]

In addition to skimming union dues, gangsters extorted an esti-mated $25 million annually in payroll padding, wage kickbacks, loan sharking, and other rackets. More came in from untold mil-lions of dollars in pilfered cargo—everything from small jars of imported caviar to, incredibly, a ten-ton shipment of steel that turned up "missing." The total take is anyone's guess. What is known is that the high incidence of theft drove freight insurance rates up 25 percent in New York, making it the most expensive port in the world.[64]

But the biggest prize was the loading racket. By gaining control over the various public loading systems, local union officers were able to impose additional "hurry-up" fees on all cargo shipments. It was an enviable business, almost risk-free and paying nearly a thousand dollars a week on each pier. As word got out, the loading racket became a magnet for the underworld, drawing increasing numbers of criminals into key positions within the union and fueling some of the port's bloodiest wars for control of the waterfront.[65]

If New York had more than its share of corrupt individuals, it was largely because they found the port so attractive: urban congestion provided racketeers with a secure niche through the system of public loading; chronic job insecurity allowed loan sharks and others to prey on the large surplus of casual men; stiff product market competition left many employers highly vulnerable to various forms of economic blackmail; and the existence of some two dozen union locals created numerous points of entry for well-armed waterfront toughs. Finally, the vast size of the port, spanning more than seven hundred miles of shoreline with 350 principal piers, made it extremely difficult to police.[66]

Yet it would be facile, and ultimately incorrect, to lay all the blame on the port itself. After all, many of the same conditions that fostered racketeering in New York also existed on the West Coast—bribery, extortion, theft, loan sharking, and kickbacks were common in San Francisco and other Pacific ports throughout the 1920s and early 1930s. What had changed, of course, was the union. With the consolidation of radical leadership after the 1934 strike, "the racketeers took flight from the San Francisco docks, terrorized," as one reporter put it, "by Harry Bridges' 'Red Guards.'" Ryan's "White Guards," in contrast, were not about to launch any such reign of terror in New York. There, facing at most mild opposition from ILA officials, the racketeers became the terrorists, intimidating the rank and file and all but destroying the union.[67]

By the mid-1930s, the ILA had degenerated into little more than "a dues collection agency," as the old-timers used to say. "All the ILA did on the East Coast was collect union dues, and they weren't even very concerned about that," recalls Sam Madell:

> They would come down to the pier at the end of the quarter. The delegate would come down there with the [union] buttons and distribute buttons for the dues. And that was the end of it. If you

avoided that particular shape-up, you could shape for the next three months without being a union member. . . . What the hell kind of union is that? [68]

Rank and filers were starting to ask themselves the same question. In 1935 Madell and a few supporters began putting out an agitational newsletter titled the *Shape-Up,* which was modeled after the *Waterfront Worker.* Early issues tediously injected global political questions into discussions of blacklisting, union corruption, and job conditions. But as its focus shifted toward more pressing concerns, the *Shape-Up* became more popular with the men. Sales and subscriptions soon exceeded one thousand copies every week, with hundreds more distributed for free along the New York waterfront. Rank-and-file "action committees" began forming throughout the port. By the end of 1936 two important locals had elected "anti-Ryan progressives." [69]

With Ryan on the defensive, Bridges was invited to New York by striking East Coast seamen. Hours before he was scheduled to speak at Madison Square Garden, Bridges was called into ILA headquarters and dismissed as West Coast ILA organizer by President Ryan, who reportedly called the fiery longshore leader a "punk" and told him he had no business coming East. That evening, addressing a capacity crowd of seventeen thousand unionists, Bridges repeatedly stressed the importance of intercoastal unity, pledging his full support to New York longshoremen "if you decide to join the fight with your brothers" on the Pacific. [70]

Bridges returned to the East Coast in the fall of 1937, this time as president of the ILWU, to gauge the extent of support for industrial unionism on the docks. Prior to his arrival in New York, representatives from eleven locals in Brooklyn and Manhattan had formally endorsed the organizational principles of the CIO. National CIO strategists, encouraged by the sudden groundswell of support, immediately committed $60,000 and forty-three full-time field organizers to the New York campaign. Ben Jones, an ILWU member and field organizer, reported that more job actions took place on the New York docks during the first five months of the CIO's drive than in the previous ten years. "In lots of places," he wrote, "the men feel like the West Coast longshoremen felt after the 1934 strike. They understand their power and ability to get better conditions." [71]

The situation on the docks had never looked more promising. Six months of organizing had netted ten thousand pledge cards for the CIO. Even if, as ILA leaders charged, most of those signing were "shenangos," or casual workers, the tide was at long last beginning to turn. In 1938 delegates from throughout the port came together to draft a "Rank-and-File Program." Agreement was reached on seven basic demands, including limiting the size of sling loads and establishing minimum manning levels. But "this swell program," warned one of the delegates, "will just stay on paper unless we all of us get out and get the boys on the docks and in the locals to back it up. The shipowners and their pal Joe won't hand it to us on a platter."[72]

This fighting mood was most evident in Brooklyn, where Pete Panto, a recent refugee from fascist Italy, came forward to lead the anti-Ryan movement. Many Italians regarded the feisty twenty-eight-year-old "pizon" as "their own Harry Bridges." Panto's open and increasingly bold attacks on organized crime and union corruption galvanized his followers into a real movement.[73] Local CIO organizers sensed "something really big in the wind." Reporting on a rank-and-file meeting in 1939, Madell wrote that it was a "tremendous success . . . the whole neighborhood resounded with the enthusiasm and the cheering of the longshoremen. The hall was jammed with nearly 800 men and the crowd overflowed into the aisles and the hallway. . . . [The CIO program] was cheered to the roof-top, every time union hiring hall and rotary hiring was mentioned the longshoremen went wild."[74] Joe Curran, NMU president, wrote Bridges that "the longshoremen in Brooklyn can be turned over to the CIO in a short time," insisting that "sentiment for the CIO in that area is extremely high." Field organizer Sam Kovnat was equally optimistic, describing Brooklyn's rank and file as "wild and rarin' to go." But, he cautioned, "it will be a slow process. Because in spite of the enthusiasm of the men, we have yet to see how they react when [gangster] Carmada's gunmen start to work."[75]

The gunmen went to work in the summer of 1939. Ten days after addressing fifteen hundred Brooklyn longshoremen in the largest anti-Ryan rally ever held in New York, Panto mysteriously vanished. His sudden disappearance had a chilling effect on the rank and file. "The workers were so scared," reported Kovnat, "that they locked their doors and windows to keep us away." Italian-speaking longshoremen asked, "dov'è Panto?"—where is Panto?—a message they scrawled all over the Brooklyn waterfront. They got the answer they expected when Panto's badly decomposed body was later found in a New Jersey lime pit.[76]

The threat of physical violence hung like a cloud over anyone who dared to speak out. Dissidents were routinely "dumped," or worse. In one case, two rank-and-file activists were found murdered, gangland style, in different parts of the city only hours after meeting with Communist leader Sam Madell. No one was safe, not even women party members, who were routinely roughed up by Ryan's "organizers" whenever they tried to distribute literature on the docks. Nor were left-wingers the only targets. Organizers with the anti-communist Association of Catholic Trade Unionists, reactionary Teamster bosses, and even rival ILA leaders were all victimized by waterfront thugs.[77]

This campaign of terror, culminating in Panto's execution, took much of the steam out of the rank-and-file movement. The sentiment for change that had seemed so widespread and so solid only a few months earlier disappeared as suddenly as had its leader. As old fears returned, New York's dockworkers were once again reduced to an easily intimidated mass over whom Ryan and the mob exercised almost complete control by the end of the decade.

Conclusion

The 1930s were a turning point on the waterfront, witnessing the emergence of a powerful radical insurgency on one coast and conservative retrenchment on the other. On the Pacific, longshoremen departed from the course of extreme caution charted by their international leaders back East and struck out on a more militant, politically independent path, forming their own union and electing Bridges, a prominent leftist, to its leadership. In New York, the growing chorus of voices calling for reform was effectively silenced by repression, leaving the port's dockworkers completely under the thumb of their conservative, racketeering leadership. The generations thus formed on the two coasts were as different as their collective experiences and, by the end of the decade, as politically distant from each other as their leaders were.

One thing they did have in common was the experience of being victimized by waterfront violence. On both coasts, blood was spilled and lives were lost in the struggle for a better union. But the similarity ends there, for the character of violence, and its impact on the longshoremen, differed markedly.

In New York, violence most closely resembled a form of terrorism. Its intended victims were few, limited to a handful of highly visible ringleaders, while its perpetrators, fewer still in number, often went unrecognized and unpunished. Following an episodic pattern that befits the criminal underworld, violence in New York destroyed the emergent rank-and-file movement on the docks by driving its leaders into hiding or to an early grave.

Compared to the selective terrorism found in New York, the violence surrounding the 1934 strike on the West Coast was much more widespread, touching practically all of the strike's participants and transforming the walkout into a life-and-death battle between marine workers and shipowners. For the most part exercised openly in the course of a mass social struggle, violence in the West unified its many victims, creating a cohort of battle-hardened militants whose deepening radicalization after the strike was grounded in a set of politically relevant historical experiences unique to their generation.[78]

The kinds of factors emphasized here are rarely considered by sociologists. An intellectual predilection for stable routines and structures has created within the discipline a major blindspot concerning the role of unique historical events.[79] Perhaps this is understandable, given the propensity for generalization that pervades contemporary social science. Yet, in the long run, such a view is theoretically shortsighted, for it ignores the fact that many abnormal occurrences—whether wars, popular mobilizations, or even natural disasters—produce institutional residues which condition the structures and routines that are the objects of so much sociological theorizing. By closing our eyes to the importance of exceptional events, we run the risk of missing much of what may explain the distinctiveness as well as the uniformities in social structure.

Chapter Six

From Hot to Cold War

World War II rescued the left wing of the industrial union movement from impending political isolation, only to destroy it a few years later. Indeed, the Japanese attack on Pearl Harbor, which helped bring about a fragile truce in the escalating war of words that had threatened since 1939 to divide the CIO into hostile political camps, ended up disarming the left for the more life-threatening battle that began shortly after the fighting was over.[1] As the hot war turned cold, Communist-supported forces suffered a string of defeats, beginning in 1946. In the politically pivotal United Auto Workers union (UAW), a progressive leadership bloc lost important ground to the growing anti-communist opposition led by Walter Reuther. Close on the heels of Reuther's ascendancy, East Coast transport workers, led by "Red" Mike Quill, broke with the Communist Party. Then, most devastating of all, the Communists lost control of the National Maritime Union when some of the party's most able and admired representatives, including several founders of the NMU, were defeated in union elections by three-to-one margins. Following similar anti-communist eruptions among furniture, wood, chemical, and shoe workers, rightward-moving CIO leaders confidently took matters into their own hands. In 1950 the remaining Communist-led unions—eleven affiliates with a combined membership of almost one million—were put on trial by the national CIO, convicted of "following the Communist Party line," and summarily expelled.[2]

In explaining the postwar rout of the left, most analysts focus on labor's experiences during the war. Their arguments run in two

general directions. One, a more structuralist explanation, traces
the left's defeat to the changing and increasingly conservative composition of the labor force. In this view, the key wartime development was the displacement of veteran CIO militants by new workers lacking union experience or ideological attachments to the
left.[3] The other leading explanation sees the demise of the left in
more historical terms. From this perspective, the fatal blow was
delivered by the left itself, as a result of the "class collaborationist"
policies pursued by many Communist-supported union leaders
during the war.[4] This chapter examines both arguments in the context of longshore unionism, focusing in particular on how left-
wing forces on each coast were affected by changes in union policy
and labor force composition during the war.

The Battle for Production in the West

The Communists' "plunge to disaster," writes Bert Cochran, began with party leader Earl Browder "taking on unsolicited the task
of war manager on the home front." Guided by the party's slogan
"Everything for Victory" and driven by his own single-minded ob-
session with maximizing productivity, Browder's enthusiasm for
the war effort knew few bounds. "We have to find out ways to
make the capitalist system work better," he pleaded before a gathering of New York unionists in 1943. "And since the capitalists
themselves, who are in charge of that, are not doing a job that sat-
isfies us, we have to help the capitalists to learn how to run their
own system under war conditions."[5]

Browder's stunning metamorphosis from one of the country's
leading class antagonists to its self-appointed "captain of industry" had been triggered by Hitler's invasion of the Soviet Union,
which, in the mysterious dialectic of communism, transformed the
basic character of the developing European conflict from an "imperialist squabble" into its opposite: a popular "war of national
liberation" against fascism. In calling for national unity to defeat
the Axis powers, Browder counseled union leaders to set aside
their peacetime differences with employers. Labor's enemy, he
stressed, was no longer capital per se but rather the small "defeat-
ist wing" of the bourgeoisie who failed to support the American-
Soviet wartime coalition. "If J. P. Morgan supports this coalition

and goes down the line for it," Browder declared in a burst of patriotism, "I, as a Communist, am prepared to clasp his hand on that and join with him to realize it. Class divisions have no significance now except as they reflect on one side or the other of this issue."[6]

Browder's support for the war effort was nothing if not sincere, stirring the party faithful in a way that the ignominious Hitler-Stalin pact never could. Within nine months of Pearl Harbor, fifteen thousand members of the party and its major youth affiliate, the Young Communist League, had enlisted in the armed forces, including fully 30 percent of the leadership. So as not to antagonize "progressive capitalists," Communists took the lead in liquidating their own presence in industry by abolishing Communist Party clubs, the basic unit of shop-floor organization. The next casualty of wartime cooperation was the party itself, which was officially dissolved in 1944 and replaced by the Communist Political Association. With the dissolution of the party, it was clear that the Communists would stop at nothing to realize their principal wartime objective of defeating fascism.[7]

This grand strategy hinged on winning "the battle for production" on the home front. Accordingly, many party loyalists in the labor movement called for relaxing hard-won work rules and voluntarily giving up any conditions that seemed to hamper the war effort. At the same time they vigorously advocated a number of proposals—including those traditionally opposed by unions, such as piece rates and no-strike pledges—that might speed up workers and raise output.[8]

This accommodating posture proved to be a serious liability in several unions. In the UAW, party support for incentive pay turned militant rank and filers into enemies. Communist autoworker Nat Ganley, a leader in the Detroit UAW, later admitted that the opposition's "most effective slogan was 'Down with Earl Browder's piecework.'" Still more damaging was the Communists' militant enforcement of labor's no-strike pledge. Wartime walkouts in auto were condemned by party leaders in the most vituperative terms as "disgraceful . . . nothing less than a stab in the back of our armed services." Striking UAW members were accused of sabotaging the war effort and, argued the *Daily Worker,* "should be treated as scabs." Even as the war in Europe was approaching a favorable

outcome late in 1944, Communist leaders clung tenaciously to
their policy of "labor sacrifice" by leading the opposition to a UAW
referendum aimed at rescinding the no-strike pledge.[9]

Communists were just as obstinate in other unions. In the East
Coast NMU they instructed new members on the essentials of
avoiding strikes and threatened to turn over the names of recalcitrant seamen to local draft boards. In the UE they supported both
incentive pay and the establishment of government-sponsored "War
Production Speed-Up Committees," which were later renamed
"Labor-Management Committees" in the interest of gaining rank-
and-file support.[10] Besides working to dampen militancy within
their own unions, Communist-supported leaders were kept busy
trying to stamp out insurgency in other industries as well. When
the nation's coal miners struck in 1943 over an unresolved pay dispute with the War Labor Board, Julius Emspak, UE secretary-
treasurer, urged President Roosevelt "to make it impossible for
John L. Lewis and his henchmen to continue to organize disruption of coal production." Lewis's failure to prevent the walkout
made him, in Bridges's opinion, "the single most effective agent of
the fascist powers within the ranks of labor."[11] In denouncing
Lewis this way, Emspak, Bridges, and other prominent leftists
merely echoed the sentiments expressed by more mainstream union
leaders. But if the left was no less timid than the rest of organized
labor, neither was it any bolder; and that in the end proved to be
its undoing.

The wartime absorption of the Communist Party into labor's
mainstream disoriented many rank-and-file unionists who had
previously looked to it for militant leadership. Disillusionment
turned increasingly to anger as CP functionaries, preoccupied with
their various productivity campaigns, neglected conditions on the
shop floor. With many CIO veterans deriding the party's new approach as a form of "red company unionism," younger workers
who might have been won over to the left on union issues were
instead driven into the growing anti-communist camp. Where
these disaffected forces coalesced around a militant and charismatic leader—such as Reuther in the UAW, Curran in the NMU,
or Quill in the Transport Workers—the party suffered some of its
worst setbacks after the war.[12]

In the ILWU the pro-Soviet left heartily embraced the "labor sacrifice" line, at least in words. "The program for production and supply and victory must supersede all things and all desires," Bridges told a group of civic leaders in 1942. "Labor's enemy is not management," he explained. "Its enemy—our enemy—is Hitler and Japan. Only that employer or that representative of management—or union representative, for that matter—who is not first of all concerned with the full war effort and victory is the contemporary enemy of all of us." Getting down to brass tacks, Bridges told the San Francisco CIO council exactly what it had to do to win the war: "The majority of the time of officers, of grievance committeemen, of the unions as a whole must go to winning the war. How? Production. I'd rather say speed-up, and I mean speed-up. To put it bluntly, I mean your unions today must become instruments of speed-up of the working people of America."[13]

Bridges's rhetoric aside, the reality of the war for most longshoremen was not all sacrifice or speed-up. In fact, as we will see, the ILWU's left-wing leadership managed to strike a fairly reasonable balance between the demands of increased production and the protection of the rank and file's immediate economic interests. Carefully avoiding the kind of superpatriotism that contributed to the CP's demise in auto and elsewhere, these leaders met their wartime obligations without sacrificing the union's coveted job control. As a result, Bridges and the left came out of the war in a more secure position, with their trade union credentials intact and their stewardship of the union secure.

The ILWU's commitment to the war effort was embodied in a document titled "A Plan for Maximum Production in Maritime Transport of War Materials and Supplies." Known as the "Bridges Plan," it called for the creation of a tripartite industry council—composed of representatives from the waterfront employers, the union, and the government—for the purpose of "securing more efficient operation" on the waterfront. As part of its sweeping authority, the council would be empowered to recommend "changes in or suspensions of working rules that interfere with maximum production." The entire package was presented to San Francisco longshoremen at a special "stop work" meeting a few days after Pearl Harbor. Without a single voice raised in opposition, the membership voted unanimously to put the plan into effect at once.[14]

Longshoremen in the Northwest were less enthralled with the

plan, viewing with suspicion any arrangement predicated on union and employer collaboration. Following their deeply ingrained syndicalist inclinations, locals in Portland and Seattle, as well as in the smaller Washington ports of Aberdeen, Everett, and Bellingham, withheld their formal endorsement for three months. The employers, though responding favorably to the plan's emphasis on improving efficiency, also expressed reservations. They, too, objected to the council idea, characterizing it as an unnecessary "invasion of management" and accusing Bridges of "trying to socialize the industry." Pressure from the War Shipping Administration finally brought the shipowners around in March 1942 when, with the creation of the Pacific Coast Maritime Industry Board, the Bridges Plan became operative in all West Coast ports.[15]

Fears that the board might serve as a beachhead for socialism or as an instrument of class collaboration proved groundless. Neither the union nor the employers, after years of bitter struggle and deep mutual distrust, were prepared to concede any real ground. Steering away from the highly contentious issues of union job control and managerial prerogatives, the board confined itself to surveying port conditions, monitoring the labor supply, and generally working to eliminate any obvious bottlenecks in loading and discharging cargo. The result was a slight gain in productivity. In June, board chairman Paul Eliel, representing the government, reported that longshore output had increased at least 10 percent since March. One month later the *Pacific Shipper* placed the increase at between 10 and 15 percent.[16]

Much of this improvement, however, was a result of the board's rationalization of production, rather than any retreat by the union. "The bald fact is that the notorious inefficiency of cargo handling in our Pacific Coast ports continues almost unabated," reported employer spokesman Frank Foisie. Speaking before San Francisco's elite Commonwealth Club in July, he placed the blame on the union's refusal to lift its "restrictive practices":

> The board guarantees to restore any and all restrictive rules at the end of the war if the Union will abandon them for the duration. The responsibility for this refusal rests squarely on the Union leadership. The argument advanced is that the morale of the men will suffer.
>
> In addition to restrictive work rules, restrictive practices which are fastened on the industry by job-action of the last eight years

have also been continued in full vigor. These restrictive practices are evident on much if not most of the work and witnessed daily; feet still drag; loafing is widespread; leaving the job and the dock while on pay is common; early quitting and late starting is general; use of unnecessary men; the list is long. The facts are evident.[17]

Foisie's assessment was shared by a host of government officials assigned to the industry. Military officers in San Pedro attributed the port's "inefficient" loading operation to sling load restrictions imposed by the union. Following a War Shipping Administration report that was highly critical of the ILWU's sling load limits, the board retained Captain Joseph Tipp, an expert in maritime transportation, to conduct an on-site inspection of cargo-handling procedures on the West Coast. Tipp's final report, based on observations of 113 vessels, showed that as many as one-third were plagued by "bad operations" of various kinds.[18]

The union defended its efforts before a Congressional subcommittee formed in March 1943 to investigate Foisie's latest allegation that the ILWU was, as he put it, "practicing an organized slowdown." Bridges testified that the longshoremen were fully prepared "to tear up our trade union contract. Anything that will increase production we will do." He and other witnesses attributed any inefficiencies to employer mismanagement, citing numerous cases of improperly stowed and damaged cargo, inadequate loading gear, and unnecessary delays in sailing. After hearing several days of testimony from both sides, committee chairman Senator Sheridan Downey decided that Foisie's charge was without foundation.[19]

Yet if union leaders were not promoting a deliberate slowdown, they were not exactly tearing up the contract either. On paper, it is true, the longshoremen gave up far more than the employers: of the forty-one Orders issued by the board through 1943, all but five entailed some degree of sacrifice on the part of the union.[20] But, according to Eliel, the ILWU did not really concede very much in the end. "I have gone over the Orders issued by this board, one by one," he wrote,

and I fail to see how any of them, without exception, can be considered as entailing a real sacrifice on the part of the Union or of the longshoremen. It is true that some of them have been directed to-

ward practices which have accumulated over the years but which no
one can defend. In these instances . . . [union leaders] have merely
carried out what the Union was already obligated to carry out under
the terms of its contract with the employers.[21]

At the same time, Eliel acknowledged that many longshoremen
had shouldered great personal sacrifices as part of their patriotic
obligation. Though not required to work more than ten hours in
any one stretch, many gangs routinely worked shifts of twelve
hours or more for days on end. "You could refuse to work overtime," recalls San Francisco longshoreman Asher Harer, a member
of the Socialist Workers Party, a Trotskyist organization that opposed the war, but "there was such pressure to win this war, to get
those supplies going, that if you had raised any hell about it, you
would have been sort of a half-way traitor."[22]

The patriotic consensus was overpowering at times. When the
situation demanded it, longshoremen turned in nearly superhuman
efforts. Numerous ship turnaround records were set, as vessels
carrying urgently needed military supplies were discharged in about
half the normal time.[23] The ILWU's no-strike pledge, reflected in
popular slogans like "Keep It Moving," produced a marked de-
crease in work stoppages. In San Francisco, job actions declined
from an average of forty-three incidents a year before Pearl Harbor
to fewer than five each year during the war. And, unlike earlier
stoppages, most wartime job actions were small scale and defensive in nature, often directed at petty military regulations against
smoking on the job or bringing lunchboxes aboard ship.[24]

But wartime patriotism, though certainly powerful, was not omnipotent. When Bridges proposed an incentive pay scheme to the
membership of San Francisco's Local 10, reaction was decidedly
hostile. Jerry Cronin, a former Wobbly and a veteran of the 1934
strike, spoke in opposition. "I've listened very respectfully to everything you've said, President Bridges," he began, "but it boils down
to piecework, the very thing the trade union movement has always
fought. When I was a Wobbly we fought piecework . . . in 1934
we fought it. . . . We wouldn't take it then, and we're not going to
take it now." Whereupon Bridges quietly dropped his proposal
rather than engage the membership in a drawn-out and potentially
divisive fight.[25]

Bridges's flexibility on the issue of incentive pay contrasts sharply with the role of the left in other unions. In the UAW, for instance, the Communist Party and its allies waged a much more determined effort on behalf of incentives. Ignoring clear and mounting opposition from the rank and file, the Communist-supported left pushed its unpopular piecework proposal for more than four months. Finally, after being voted down by practically every governing body within the union, the issue of incentive pay died on the floor of the 1943 UAW convention—only to be resurrected a few years later by anti-communists who pointed to it as an example of the party's collaborationist posture during the war.[26]

If the ILWU's left-wing leadership showed greater sensitivity to the interests of the rank and file, it was partly because Communist marine workers on the West Coast were less determined in carrying out the CP's "national unity" line. Many seamen found Browder's argument for interclass cooperation difficult to accept. Bill Bailey, for one, refused to follow the new line. After reading the first three pages of *Teheran and America,* a widely distributed pamphlet in which Browder elaborated his vision of class collaboration, Bailey, an open Communist and official in the Marine Firemen's Union, had seen enough. "I was supposed to sell a hundred copies, but I couldn't sell a book," he recalls.

> I could see something was wrong here. Marx had said we are in a constant class struggle. And here we're coming up saying this struggle is being taken over by a group of so-called progressive capitalists, that the lamb is gonna lay down with the lion. Who are they talkin' to? Here you are, I'm getting my face beat in, kicked around, half dead for talking about class struggle, and now they're gonna say everything was all wrong. We got a beautiful society. Bullshit! It doesn't work that way.[27]

The seamen's gut-level militancy rubbed off on some of their comrades within the waterfront section of the party, creating a rift in some ILWU locals between hard-line followers of Browder and those who adopted a more flexible approach. In San Francisco this split surfaced in the fall of 1942 during a special union membership meeting called to discuss the Maritime Industry Board's recent action ordering the union to raise its sling load limit for cement from twenty-two to thirty 100-pound bags per load. Browderite John Schomaker, a highly respected veteran of the 1934 strike, announced that the Communist Party supported the proposed 3,000-pound limit as a means of aiding the war effort. Moreover, he argued, increasing the sling load was consistent with the union's own policy of doing everything within its power to maximize production. Archie Brown then jumped to his feet, demanding to be recognized. Turning to Schomaker, he insisted that the party had not yet reached a decision concerning load limits but that in his opinion the men should resolutely oppose any increase. "It simply ain't true," he said, "that that is what's gonna win the war." The membership agreed and voted to retain the existing 2,200-pound limit.[28]

Other locals followed suit. Union leaders in Seattle reported that the men were "up in arms" over the board's ruling and that "many of them have threatened to leave the industry if orders of this kind keep coming in." In San Pedro, defiant dockworkers continued building 2,200-pound loads, much to the dismay of local waterfront employers whose repeated threats of disciplinary action failed to bring compliance. Without the active support of union leaders for the thirty-bag limit, the board's order soon became a dead letter on the docks.[29]

The sling load controversy illustrates the complexity of working-class consciousness during the war. In objecting to heavier load limits for cement, union leaders cited safety concerns. But this was largely a smokescreen, for inexperienced army recruits had been building thirty-bag loads for some time without problems. What was really at stake was not so much a question of safety as it was a question of control. The longshoremen worked longer hours, put up with annoying military regulations, and even speeded up when they were convinced that doing so would aid the war effort—but they alone decided how, when, and to what degree such sacrifices were to be made. In contrast, the directive ordering the union to raise its sling load limits was seen as threatening the men's autonomy on the job and hence their ability, achieved through years of struggle, to control the terms of their own sacrifice. By resisting the board's order, the longshoremen were saying, in effect, that any sacrifices on their part would be made voluntarily and without coercion, or not at all.

In this way, the wartime ethic of personal sacrifice was held in check by the strong tradition of job control on the docks. Although certain contract provisions were watered down by the board's actions, the union's position was never seriously compromised. Even some of Bridges's most vocal left-wing critics, when pressed on the question of the union's wartime record, admit that the ILWU avoided many of the excesses commited in other "Stalinist unions." According to Asher Harer, the ILWU was one of the few Communist-led unions where, in his words, "working conditions didn't deteriorate too much. This is a union that had just come out of two strikes, had a very militant rank and file, and they just weren't about to work themselves to death."[30]

Comparison of labor productivity rates before and during the war also suggest that there was no widespread speed-up. Time-series data, available for both San Francisco and San Pedro, show little change in productivity between the two periods. From 1936 to 1939, San Francisco longshoremen loaded and discharged an average of 2.19 tons of cargo per work hour, compared to 2.21 tons from 1942 to 1945. In San Pedro, labor productivity actually declined from a prewar average of 2.44 tons per work hour to 2.18 tons during the war.[31]

In Portland, the pace of work slowed so much that newer workers "were spoiled" by their wartime experience, recalls veteran longshoreman Joe Werner. Younger men who secured work on the docks at that time "thought longshoring was a picnic." Indeed, one of the union's most restrictive work rules originated during the war. Known as "four on/four off," it grew out of the standard procedure of splitting the eight-man hold gang into two teams, each working its side of the hold, handling every other draft. Normally, this division of labor kept both teams constantly occupied, for as one was busy stowing, the other was finishing up and getting ready to catch the next load. But as the nature of cargo changed during the war from fairly uniform civilian commodities to more bulky and irregularly shaped military supplies such as jeeps, tanks, and planes, the work area beneath the hatch was no longer spacious enough to accommodate both teams working simultaneously. The necessity of working only one team at a time soon evolved into a full-blown system of "four on/four off," in which one team worked continuously for the first half of the shift, then rested while the other team worked the second half. With tacit approval from stevedoring operators who saw this arrangement as a way of padding their cost-plus contracts with the War Shipping Administration, "four on/four off" became an institutionalized practice in many ports, remaining one of the union's most potent work rules for years to come.[32]

On balance, then, the longshoremen surrendered very little while maintaining and in some cases increasing their control over the job. No amount of rhetoric calling on the longshoremen to sacrifice could change one simple but important fact: the workers, not the union or Bridges, "owned" their jobs, and they were the ones who, torn by the conflicting loyalties of nationalism and class, ultimately determined the proper mix of accommodation and resistance on the docks during the war.

On those rare occasions when union leaders veered too far in either direction, they paid for it. In May 1944 Bridges called on the membership to continue the no-strike pledge for the duration and "indefinitely thereafter," provided that the employers agreed to respect the union's security after the war. Arguing that such a "security preamble" belonged in every union contract, Bridges told the membership of Local 6, representing five thousand Bay Area warehouse workers, that "we reject any hostility of labor to capital as such, and any hostility to unions as such, knowing well that such approaches are luxuries that neither can now afford." The motion passed with only three dissenting votes.[33] Bridges had greater difficulty selling the security preamble to the more militant dockworkers, however, whose representatives, meeting in a coastwide longshore caucus that summer, voted 120 to 55 in favor. Less than a month later James Kearney, a leading anti-communist, defeated a Bridges-supported candidate for the presidency of Local 10. Although the security preamble was not a central issue in the campaign, Kearney's election was seen by many as a slap in the face of the pro-production left.[34]

Kearney's upset victory was a powerful statement of just how far the rank and file was willing to go to win the war. In weighing the nation's interests against their own as workers, the longshoremen were deeply influenced by the militant work culture of the waterfront, which exerted such pull on the men that few were willing to sacrifice their union's class struggle principles on the altar of national unity.

Restructuring the Wartime
Labor Force in the West

The wartime mobilization of American society created deep and lasting social dislocations in the civilian labor force. Within a year of the Japanese attack on Pearl Harbor, the number of men in uniform skyrocketed from a previous peacetime high of eight hundred thousand to more than six million. Despite the large number of former civilian employees entering the armed services during this period, the national labor force grew by more than five million workers. In 1943, as the war entered its decisive stages, a second wave of recruits was inducted into the military, creating gaping holes in the civilian work force. Their places were filled by putting the unemployed to work and redirecting hundreds of thousands of already employed workers, including many women, into more essential war industries. With workers coming and going in all directions by the end of the year, the resulting "structure of our labor force," noted the director of the War Manpower Commission, "represented a great transformation from what it was in 1940." [35]

This great transformation was mirrored in the changing membership base of the CIO. National mobilization removed from the shop floor many of the youthful insurgents who had participated in the mass social struggles that built the new unions. Some were among the eleven million draftees or volunteers who entered the armed services. Others followed the movement of capital rather than the flag, seeking occupational deferments and higher wages in the expanding defense sector. In certain "essential industries," it is true, the prewar labor force was frozen in place for the duration. But even where mobility was most restricted, many experienced workers moved out of their old jobs and into more skilled or supervisory positions. Each of these paths—whether leading to the armed forces, defense production, or occupational upgrading—drew many of the CIO's founding cadre out of their familiar workplaces and away from trusted co-workers, thus shattering the social combinations inside the shops which up to that point had provided much of the impetus and rank-and-file direction for the industrial union movement. [36]

In the wake of these departing CIO militants came a flood of less union-conscious workers. Recruited largely from among the urban unemployed, the surplus agricultural labor force, and other non-unionized sectors of the economy, most lacked even a rudimentary understanding of basic trade union principles. Compared to the veteran unionists they were replacing, these newer workers held more "negative or passive attitudes" toward the CIO's progressive social unionism, writes Joshua Freeman. "Some were still deeply immersed in rural, preindustrial cultures. Many had racial attitudes formed in the South." [37]

The membership turnover was greatest in the mass-production unions, especially those based in the defense sector. Consider the case of the UE. During the war more than two hundred thousand of its members, including many local officers, union organizers, and even an international official, left for the armed forces. At the same time, tens of thousands of incoming workers filled job vacancies as fast as they were being created by the mass exodus of military conscripts, on the one hand, and the war-stimulated demand for labor in electrical and machine-working plants, on the other. In 1943 the annual rate of turnover for UE workers was around 50 percent. By the end of the war more than four hundred thousand new members had passed through the UE's revolving doors. The turnover in leadership was so high that at the union's biennial convention in 1944 more than half of all voting delegates were attending for the first time. [38]

This wartime disruption of the labor force undermined the political base of the UE's left-wing leadership. Newer workers, in particular, proved to be unstable allies of the left. Unlike the union pioneers they replaced, the "war babies" lacked strong attachments to the older generation of radical leaders. [39] Hardly any were even aware, much less appreciative, of the Communists' role as militant founders of the UE. Of course, the party's own wartime policy of concealing its identity by hiding behind various patriotic "fronts" did little to counter this lapse in historical memory. But the characteristics of the "war babies" themselves—their comparatively weak ties to the left, their lack of union experience, and their generally more conservative outlook—also led them to side with the anti-communist International Union of Electrical Workers after the war.

The UE's experience was replicated in other large industrial unions. In the UAW, wartime mobilization radically altered the composition of the labor force. Figures are not available on the number of union members who left the industry during the war, but in Detroit, the center of auto production, almost 30 percent of the city's male workers entered the military.[40] This massive exodus, combined with countless voluntary withdrawals from the industry for personal reasons, set off a large countermigration. Between 1940 and 1943 an estimated half million migrants came to Detroit in search of work. Of this total, all but sixty thousand were white, and many were from the South and Appalachia. The wartime restructuring of the labor force in auto, as among electrical workers, was accompanied by a shift to the right in union politics, contributing in no small measure to Reuther's victory a few years later.[41]

The demographic convulsion that shook the social foundations of radicalism in basic industry was less of a destabilizing force on the West Coast waterfront. Unlike both the UE and the UAW, which lost many of their founding militants to the war effort, the ILWU emerged from the war with its original membership base fairly intact and solidly behind its left-wing leaders.

A good indication of the longshoremen's greater stability is the low rate of military withdrawals from the industry during the first several months of the war. According to labor turnover data compiled by the Bureau of Labor Statistics (BLS), roughly 15 percent of the nation's manufacturing labor force entered the armed services within a year of Pearl Harbor.[42] Although the BLS failed to collect equivalent data for the longshore industry, the available evidence, culled from union documents, suggests that the rate of military separations on the waterfront was well below the national average reported for manufacturing workers. The most complete information concerning labor turnover on the West Coast docks was compiled by union officers in San Pedro. Their records show that seventy-seven longshoremen were inducted into the armed forces during the first eleven months of the war. Given that the local's membership was around twenty-five hundred at the time, only about 3 percent of the work force had entered the military by the end of the year; this was about one-fifth the rate of induction for manufacturing workers.[43]

If the figure for San Pedro seems low—almost unbelievably so when compared to the tens of thousands of electrical, auto, and other manufacturing workers who were then entering the military—it was by no means unusual on the waterfront. Similarly low rates of military separation were reported elsewhere on the West Coast. In San Francisco, the only other port for which such data are available, 850 longshoremen served in the military between 1942 and 1945. At this rate of withdrawal, spread out over four years of war, fewer than 20 of the local's 9,500 members left the waterfront each month for military service. Overall, less than 10 percent of the port's longshoremen served in the armed forces [44]— compared to 30 percent of Detroit's auto labor force and what was probably an even higher proportion of inductees in electrical manufacturing.

The low rate of military separations on the docks was partly a consequence of the marine transport industry's strategic importance to the war effort. When longshoring was designated an "essential activity," most dockworkers became eligible for occupational deferments. But it was not only their draft-exempt status that held the longshoremen in place. An even more important source of stability was their intense occupational loyalty, which had been built on years of collective struggle and enduring generational bonds and conditioned by a high degree of job satisfaction. This sense of occupational identity was so developed among ILWU inductees that several hundred continued working together discharging military cargo as members of the army's "Longshore Battalions." Even as soldiers, many longshoremen managed to stay in close contact with the waterfront. [45]

Of course, military separations were neither the only nor the most important source of labor force instability during the war. What the BLS classified as "voluntary quits" were a far more frequent cause of turnover, representing anywhere from one-half to two-thirds of all wartime separations, depending on the industry. [46]

In the longshore industry, the quit rate soared during the first months of the war. The near total collapse of commercial shipping following Pearl Harbor and the consequent return of Depression-era levels of unemployment triggered a massive exodus from the waterfront. In San Pedro, where commercial activity was limited to one banana boat per week throughout the first half of 1942, almost 1,200 men left the docks in search of steadier work. Longshore employment in the Northwest also plummeted as the bulk of overseas shipments, consisting almost entirely of military cargo, was rerouted through the army's main port of embarcation in San Francisco.[47]

But the dispersal of the dockside labor force was limited in both time and space. In November, with fighting in the Pacific escalating, the army opened up San Pedro as a port of embarcation to handle the increasing overflow from San Francisco. Almost overnight, cargo began piling up on the docks. When the call went out for experienced longshoremen, hundreds of San Pedro dockworkers returned to the waterfront to claim their former jobs. Nearly 500 men came back from San Francisco, where they had been working as temporary "permit men." After the first of the year another group of 400 longshoremen began returning from the nearby shipyards with statements, signed by local waterfront employers, specifically requesting their services. By the middle of 1943, with all but 150 men back on the docks, San Pedro's prewar labor force had been largely reconstituted.[48]

Portland's labor force went through a similar cycle of disruption and reconstitution. After the initial drop-off in commercial shipping, many of the local's 800 members were forced to find work in the shipyards or to transfer to the busy San Francisco waterfront. Some were able to return from the shipyards after Portland was declared an auxiliary military port late in 1942. But most stayed put until the spring of 1944 when, with the revival of shipping in the Northwest, all the rest of the local's members were called back from the shipyards and San Francisco.[49]

As this information suggests, the high quit rate on the docks during the first months of the war paints a very misleading picture. Many longshoremen did leave the industry at that time, but the number of permanent quits represented only a small fraction of all separations. Most of what appeared as "voluntary quits" through the first half of 1942 were really short-term withdrawals; practically all were either intraunion transferees who never left the industry or men who, if they did venture from the waterfront, typically returned at the first possible opening.

Although the existing dockside labor force remained relatively stable, thousands of new workers entered the industry during the war. San Francisco's labor force more than doubled, growing from 4,400 men in 1938 to more than 9,000 by the end of the war. The rate of increase was even greater in San Pedro, where the number of registered longshoremen grew by 160 percent between June 1943 and January 1945. In Seattle, which supported a prewar labor force of 1,500, more than 5,000 new recruits were put to work during the last three years of the war.[50]

The political impact of this wartime influx varied somewhat from local to local, depending on the social backgrounds and ideological propensities of the new workers. In San Francisco, many of the earliest recruits were radicals of one type or another who had transferred into Local 10 from ILWU "sister locals" in the Bay Area. Attracted by the more congenial political climate on the docks, more than a few of the warehousemen, shipscalers, and cargo checkers who applied for membership in Local 10 early in 1942 did so out of personal political convictions. Several were products of the city's vital left-wing political movement. Many had been active for years on the fringes of the Communist Party, and some were members of the Socialist Workers Party, while others simply admired Bridges's courage and the militancy of the longshoremen. Far from depleting the left, these activist "war babies" infused the local with fresh radical blood.[51]

Outside of San Francisco, most early wartime recruits joined the union through its program of sponsorship in which current members nominated sons or close relatives for membership. Known as the "brother-in-law" system of hiring, this practice facilitated the transmission of dockside political culture from one generation to the next. Consequently, many of the younger men brought in during the initial phases of the war entered the union with a generally favorable view of Bridges and the left.[52]

But intraunion transfers and "hereditary recruitment" were stopgap measures at best. As the flow of military shipments out of San Francisco began picking up in the summer of 1942, the growing demand for labor soon outstripped available supplies. Later that year, the ILWU, led by Local 10, opened its doors for the first time to industry outsiders.

One of the largest and most politically important groups to enter the union at this time was made up of black longshoremen from the Gulf, who had been drawn to the West Coast after shipping in their home ports was sharply curtailed by German submarine activity. Many had belonged to dissident locals of the ILA, particularly around the ports of New Orleans and Houston, which had

long histories of opposing the Jim Crow and collaborationist policies of international union leaders. By the middle of 1943 several
hundred black dockworkers from Louisiana and southern Texas
were at work on the waterfront, mostly in the busy port of San
Francisco.[53]

The predominantly white work force did not roll out the red
carpet for these black workers, especially in the outlying ports. In
San Pedro, two union members, exercising the "choose your job"
clause, quit work when three blacks were dispatched to their gang.
Local leaders promptly investigated the incident and, after determining that the walkout constituted a violation of the union's no-
discrimination policy, threatened the two with immediate expulsion unless they made a full public apology for their actions and
returned to work at once. In Portland, where blacks had first been
hired as strikebreakers during the 1922 ILA strike, the reception
was colder still. Facing growing pressure from the international,
the local union agreed to accept blacks as probationary members
but refused to dispatch them from the hall or extend full union
voting rights to them. Bridges, in a letter to the President's Committee on Fair Employment Practice, promised to take "immediate
and drastic steps . . . to correct this situation." But despite continuing efforts by the international, Portland's membership remained lily-white throughout the war.[54]

Opposition to the international union was based mainly among
the large number of "Okies" and "rednecks" who had migrated to
the West Coast in search of work during the war. Still deeply influenced by their rural cultures, and guided at every turn by the
ideology of rugged individualism, traditional morality, and conservative religious beliefs, these white "war babies" fought the
union's left-wing leaders every bit as vigorously as they fought the
shipowners.[55] In San Pedro, where "rednecks" led the fight against
the ILWU's no-discrimination policy, their vocal opposition and
continuing harassment of blacks kept the port's racial cauldron
boiling, while in Portland, they, along with returning shipyard
workers, launched a vicious smear campaign against local progressives, denouncing them as "reds" and "commies" and threatening
to lead a mass defection from the "communistic" ILWU. Summing
up their case before the membership in 1943, a leading right-
winger declared that "when the local voted to keep out the 'nig-

gers' they should have voted to kick out the 'commies' also—and maybe they will."[56]

Blacks found the political climate more to their liking in San Francisco. Beginning with the 1934 strike, when two black longshoremen—both members of the Communist Party—had served on the San Francisco strike committee, the local had distinguished itself as a haven of racial equality.[57] By the time the 1936–1937 strike rolled around, fifteen black workers were serving on the local strike committee. That year, after three blacks were elected to its executive board, Local 10 instituted a special anti-discrimination committee to see that no worker was discriminated against because of race or color. Then in 1938 a black longshoreman was elected to the all-important post of job dispatcher. The local continued its color-blind policies throughout the war, clamping down hard and fast on anything that even remotely smacked of racism.[58]

Local 10's commendable civil rights record attracted the attention of minority workers in other West Coast industries. When the shipyards began laying off in mid-1944, many blacks headed for the docks, drawn by the promise of social equality and steady postwar employment. In San Pedro, nearly one-fifth of the 2,600 men added to the labor force between July 1944 and July 1945 were black. During the same period Seattle put 3,100 men to work, including a small number of blacks. Only Portland remained unaffected, taking in 557 men, most of them white former members of the local returning from other ports or the shipyards. But the racial composition of Local 10 was radically transformed. Of the 6,600 men added to the port's labor force during the last twelve months of the war, nearly half were blacks who had recently been released from the shipyards. By the end of 1945 the San Francisco local was almost one-third black.[59]

These later black arrivals, taking political direction from their predecessors, fell in with the left—a relationship that deepened with the growing political sophistication of the new recruits. In 1943 the union instituted a mandatory educational program designed to acquaint its newer members with the ILWU's progressive traditions. It proved to be an eye-opener for many "war babies," especially blacks whose earlier union experience had been in the shipyards. Cleophas Williams's response was in many ways typical. Describing his introduction to Local 10 in the fall of 1944 as "almost a religious experience," he recalls:

> I knew nothin' about trade unions before I went into the ILWU. As a child I read about the strikes on the West Coast, in the coal mines, auto, and steel. And I was in a right-to-work state, and the newspapers had everything slanted against unions, talkin' about the benevolence of Henry Ford and all that kind of stuff. I had no idea that the purpose of the union was to upgrade the way the ILWU did. The electrical union [in the shipyard] was inert, so far as moving you from one position to another. But the ILWU made you politically aware.[60]

As part of their political socialization, probationary members of Local 10 had to become registered voters and attend required classes at the city's left-wing California Labor School before being considered for full union membership. "Once you went to the California Labor School and were among other workers, hearing different talk, different rhetoric, you began to question, you began to see. It was a conversion," Williams explained, again using religious imagery to convey the depths of his personal transformation.

> It was "All this time I've been in the dark, and now I'm beginning to see the light. Why did you keep my eyes closed for so long?" It was a beautiful experience to see how you could be in concert with other workers to improve your lot, and not be out there saying "You gotta hustle, hustle, hustle, and you can get ahead, son." That's what I was taught—not to come together with the energies of other people and combine those energies for the cause of all.[61]

White radicals played a key role in winning over San Francisco's increasingly active black membership. As the war was winding down and cutbacks in the labor force became imminent, different factions within the local began jockeying for position. Conservatives called for restoring the work force to its prewar level by laying off workers on a strict seniority basis. The left, charging that this would eliminate most black newcomers, countered by advocating less severe cuts. Both plans were aired in the spring of 1945 at a special "stop work" meeting of the entire local. At a critical point in the discussion, a white worker rose and asked

Bridges to spell out exactly how he intended to deal with the "excessive number" of blacks once the war was over and work slacked off. Bridges replied evasively at first, saying that the real problem was not the apparent surplus of blacks but rather the capitalist system itself, which forced workers to compete with one another for jobs. Then, returning to the original question, he added that if work ever slowed to the point that there were only two workers left on the docks, he personally believed that one should be black. Williams, along with most other blacks in attendance, was taken aback. Bridges's statement, he remembers,

> was very shocking to me because there was no political gain for him by making this statement. There was no gain even among blacks at that particular time because many of the blacks were still on probation, so they couldn't vote. I considered it a statement of conviction. I was shocked. I had read and been exposed to some of the left-wing forces, but I had never heard anyone put his neck on the chopping block by making a public statement of this kind.[62]

Work remained plentiful for some time after V-J Day as troops and material still had to be brought home from across the Pacific. With the demand for labor running high, the union's "indefinite" no-strike pledge did not last very long. In the fall of 1946 the ILWU struck the West Coast for fifty-two days. A year of labor peace followed while the anti-union Taft-Hartley Act worked its way through Congress. Then in 1948 the longshoremen hit the bricks again in a protracted and often bitter walkout reminiscent of the union's prewar battles. The shipowners, armed with Taft-Hartley, demanded that Bridges "disavow communism" and sign the non-Communist affidavit as required by the act's Section 9(h) or step down from leadership. Bridges refused, and the longshoremen, registering their opinion in a coastwide referendum, supported their leader's decision by a twenty-to-one margin. The impasse was finally broken after ninety-eight days when the union agreed to accept a stricter system of arbitration and an unprecedented three-year contract in exchange for most of its other demands.[63]

The postwar strikes evidenced a widening breach between ILWU leaders and youthful strike activists for whom 1946 and 1948 were the "Big Strikes." Bridges, the militant leader of an earlier generation, was now seen by some as being too soft on the shipowners. During the 1946 walkout, Bridges and the left came under fire for agreeing to work military cargo, a policy insurgents denounced as "half a strike." In 1948, with young militants determined to conduct a tighter strike, the union extended mass picketing to the major military docks.[64]

Dissidents from 1946 and 1948 joined together with a few older syndicalists and the war-swollen ranks of ideological conservatives to form a viable right-wing opposition in many locals. For some, opposition to the Communist-supported left made good political sense in Cold War America, whereas for others it was more a matter of dollars and cents. Sometimes the two concerns overlapped, as in the spirited 1950 debate over U.S. policy in Korea, when rightists defended the government's actions both on patriotic grounds and because it would mean an increase in military shipments from the West Coast.[65]

When the postwar slump in shipping finally hit early in 1949, conservatives coalesced around a defensive strategy of job control unionism. In Local 10, leaders of a recently organized "Blue Slate"—so named to distinguish it from "reds" who were running in the upcoming local election—circulated petitions calling for sharp reductions in the number of workers. When black leaders voiced their concerns, a spokesman for the Blue Slate tersely replied: "We can work together, we can eat together, but we can't starve together." The left, as in the past, came out strongly against any system of layoffs that singled out blacks as its primary victims. The left-wing president of the local, Henry Schmidt, proposed cutting equally from "the top, middle, and bottom" of the seniority ladder. Both plans were eventually rejected by the rank and file, with the result that no cutbacks were made.[66]

The political factionalism that had been growing in many locals spilled out onto the floor of the ILWU convention a few months later. Meeting behind closed doors, delegates representing nearly one hundred thousand longshoremen, warehouse workers, and farm laborers from the West Coast, Alaska, and Hawaii engaged in what one correspondent described as "a masks off, no holds barred" exchange over Bridges's refusal to go along with national CIO policy that supported the Marshall Plan and favored withdrawing from the left-wing World Federation of Trade Unions, in which Bridges served as president of the maritime division. The showdown came on a resolution declaring that "the ILWU stands fast on its autonomy" in opposition to the national leadership of the CIO. "If they are right," Bridges said just before the vote, "you delegates had better reorganize this union and get a different set of officers because the ones that I am speaking for now are going to carry on as they have in the last couple of years." The delegates voted 632½ to 11½ in support of Bridges.[67]

The final tally was surprising only for its lopsidedness. Less than a year before, West Coast longshoremen had voted by a narrower margin against the Marshall Plan and for Henry Wallace's Progressive Party candidacy. Even in the politically pivotal San Francisco local, which was then headed by Kearney and other pro-CIO leaders working openly with the anti-communist Association of Catholic Trade Unionists, the rank and file ended up supporting the international's position on both issues.[68]

As the Cold War descended on the waterfront, the interracial progressive coalition in Local 10 solidified. Increasingly, black "war babies" and veteran white radicals found themselves in the same camp, both victimized by the growing anti-communist hysteria sweeping the country. In May 1950 the Coast Guard began screening "security risks" off the waterfront. Of the 243 longshoremen in San Francisco who were eventually denied Coast Guard passes to work on military docks, fully two-thirds were black, according to a survey conducted by the union.[69] The screening of individual subversives turned out to be a dress rehearsal for the screening of entire unions. A few weeks later the national CIO expelled the ILWU, along with ten other Communist-influenced unions.

The CIO's actions provided an opportunity for anti-communist forces to more openly challenge the ILWU's political direction. In July, a resolution was introduced in Local 10 pledging unconditional support for Truman's invasion of Korea and promising "not to join in, condone, or recognize any phony Communist demonstrations . . . to halt or . . . sabotage shipments of war materials." Bridges then introduced an alternative resolution in support of the United Nations–ordered cease-fire. In the emotional discussion that followed, punches were thrown and the police had to be brought in to restore order. Bridges, who was out on bail pending appeal in his latest deportation case, was promptly whisked off to jail as a threat to national security. In his absence, the coastwide longshore caucus voted 63 to 9 to sever relations with the World Federation of Trade Unions for its stand against U.S. intervention in Korea.[70]

Bridges, languishing in jail, appeared to be on his last legs, headed for the same fate as the rest of the left. His incarceration, noted an observer, was the latest in a series of events all pointing to "the possibility of a drastic debilitation of leftist leadership in the ILWU." But it was not to be. The more Bridges came under attack, the more his traditional allies rallied in defense of their embattled leader. "I felt like he was being abused same as I was," explained black longshoreman Odell Franklin. "The only thing different about it was he was a white man gettin' it."[71] With support from the large wartime influx of blacks, from his allies among the '34 men, and from the political left, Bridges was able to ride out the Cold War turbulence that toppled so many of his contemporaries in the American labor movement.

"Everything For Victory" in New York

World War II was a time of unparalleled opportunity for anti-Ryan insurgents in New York. With ILA leaders directed to do everything within their power to "solidly support" the war effort, conditions on the docks went from bad to worse after Pearl Harbor. The few union protections that existed against speed-up were either ignored or temporarily lifted by local ILA officers. Sling load limits, for example, crept upward with the increased strength of cargo nets and the improved weight-handling capabilities of winches. By the end of the war, loads of six thousand pounds were not uncommon. What little relief there was from the speed-up was a result not of union protection but of the port's antiquated and congested facilities, which slowed loading operations at many piers.[72]

Despite deteriorating working conditions, the ILA rank and file found itself in a stronger bargaining position, owing to the wartime contraction of the labor market. As better-paying defense jobs opened up, the city's dockworkers, lacking much sense of occupational loyalty, left the waterfront in droves. Countless others entered the military. Nearly half of the members of one large Manhattan local entered the armed services. By the end of 1942, with the normally large surplus of men nearly depleted and military shipments to Europe rising sharply, the longshoremen suddenly found themselves in a favorable bargaining position for the first time in years.[73]

Their capacity for collective action was also greatly enhanced by wartime changes in hiring. Under the traditional shape-up, job assignments for casual workers ranged anywhere from a few hours to no more than three or four days—however long it took to discharge a vessel. At the end of each job, individuals drifted back to the "shape," where they were eventually reassigned, often to another pier and usually working alongside different men. This constant circulation of labor prevented on-the-job solidarity from forming among the port's many casual workers.[74]

During the war, however, the individuation caused by the shape-up was mitigated by the limited regularization of hiring in New York. In an attempt to allocate longshore labor more efficiently, the Brooklyn army base pioneered a system of "steady gangs" early in the war, which cut down considerably on the movement into and out of work groups. Instead of working with a different group every day or two as was common under the shape-up, Brooklyn's longshoremen were assigned to the same gang every day and dispatched to the same pier, where they were given first crack at any work.[75] This system of regularized employment spread throughout the port following a 1943 Congressional investigation that condemned the shape-up as "wasteful and inefficient." By the end of the war approximately two-thirds of the port's longshoremen belonged to some form of steady gang.[76]

The wartime "decasualization" of hiring transformed the nature of social relationships on the job. Industrial anomie gave way to emerging informal work groups and the faint beginnings of a more solidaristic culture. Working together on a more regular basis, the men developed a sense of cohesion and a deeper awareness of their capacity for self-organization.[77]

All of these factors—deteriorating working conditions, labor's enhanced bargaining power, and the crystalization of on-the-job solidarity—combined to tilt the balance of power toward the rank and file. Insurgents boldly seized the initiative in a series of wildcat strikes in 1942. When a Hoboken longshoreman was dismissed for insubordination in March, 250 of his co-workers walked off the job in protest.[78] Wildcat fever spread to other areas of the port until by the end of the year thousands of longshoremen were in motion, openly defying Ryan by working without ILA buttons and disregarding union orders.

Early in 1943 a small group of insurgents from Brooklyn approached the Communist Party for help. Complaining of the corrupt, racket-ridden Ryan dictatorship, they asked for the party's assistance in establishing a centralized system of hiring modeled after the ILWU. "The authority of Ryan is breaking down all over the port," Roy Hudson wrote Browder after meeting with the Brooklyn delegation. "The men are in an independent mood," he continued,

> because there is plenty of work and they are anxious to shake off the racketeering bureaucratic officials in the ILA. To the men, the hiring hall is not purely an economic issue since there is plenty of work, but they recognize that without a hiring hall they can't stand the pace of working. They also see an opportunity to even the score with Ryan. There are frequent occurrances [*sic*] of whole gangs walking off the job when asked to work night shifts. It is a common practice for longshoremen to quit work after making what they consider a decent week's pay. Their actions are not in any way guided by the needs of the war.[79]

But New York's hard-line Communist leaders had no intention of fighting Ryan and the war at the same time. Assuring Browder of his priorities, Hudson wrote, "We have tried to direct the movement purely on the war issues and have laid off any open attacks on Ryan and the ILA." With the party dragging its feet on the anti-Ryan struggle, insurgents went ahead on their own and opened a hiring hall in Brooklyn. The self-proclaimed vanguard of the working class was in a quandary. "We have up until now been quite clear in directing the work," Hudson wrote, "but with the opening of the hall by these men a decision as to how far we are willing to go with them must be made." He decided to "go along" with the insurgents, at least until they openly declared a break with the ILA. Conceding that "the pressure upon us and the men is very strong for a break," Hudson refused to knuckle under. In the end, he advised the rebellious longshoremen to remain within the ILA, stick to war-related problems, and direct their anger at the slowness of ship turnaround times in New York.[80]

The anti-Ryan vacuum that the party had refused to fill in 1943 was occupied after the war by returning soldiers. "They were carrying with them certain ideas," recalls Jim Longhi. "You can't fight a war against fascism and not come back with some change in your understanding of what democracy is. The war was the great teacher." Mitchell Berenson, a left-wing organizer in Brooklyn for many years, attributes the change in attitude to Mussolini's defeat. Many older Italians, he insists, "felt a sense of liberation," which carried over into their struggle against Ryan after the war.[81]

Chelsea's Irish war veterans also came back from the war "ready to fight at the drop of a hat," recalls longshoreman Tom Connolly, a veteran of World War II. The experience of combat, he explained, "did something to these people. They had seen death, taken so much crap from officers and non-coms, and they just couldn't take any more." Returning to the waterfront after the war, these men pumped new life into the dormant insurgent movement within the ILA. Connolly, who himself became active in a dissident Manhattan local in 1945, remembers that most of their support came from "guys who had just come back from the war. And they just didn't give a damn. They didn't care who the boss was. They'd just say, 'Tools down,' and everybody would walk out. . . . The ones who had been in the union before—I'd say 75 percent—came over to our side immediately."[82]

Led by these returning soldiers, the rank-and-file longshoremen took matters into their own hands. On October 1, 1945, when Ryan announced the signing of a "fine new contract," fifteen hundred members of Local 791 in Manhattan voted with their feet by walking off the job. As in 1919, the spontaneous walkout spread like wildfire. Within three days thirty-five thousand workers were out and the port was shut down. Meeting in vacant lots and church buildings, the strikers formulated demands and elected a committee to negotiate with the shipowners. "At first," an insurgent leader recalled, "everyone wanted the moon—regular wages, rest periods—but then we got down to figuring what had a chance." They settled on a one-ton sling load limit, larger gangs, a minimum pay guarantee, and a reduction in the number of daily shapes from three to two.[83]

When Ryan was unable to talk the men back to work, he went on the offensive. Following the example of former ILA President T. V. O'Connor, who had blamed the 1919 strike on the "IWW and Bolsheviki," he began charging that "outside influences are fostering the strike"—a pointed reference to a statement of support offered to strikers by the NMU. A few days later Gene Sampson, business agent for Local 791 and one of Ryan's chief rivals, asserted that the unnamed influences were in fact Communists.[84]

To be sure, Communists did play a role in the strike. Only a few months before, party leaders in New York had targeted the docks as a major "concentration point." But Communist organizer Sam Madell, one of the principals in this campaign, was removed in the early stages of the strike when he refused to take over the leadership of the rank-and-file committee. With their leading functionary out of the picture, the Communists' role was limited to providing publicity, moral support, and legal assistance for the insurgents. According to Vernon Jensen, who studied the 1945 strike in some detail, the walkout was never anything more than a rank-and-file "revolt against [Ryan's] leadership" with "no Communist impetus at all."[85]

Red-baiting made good copy, however, so the press continued hammering away at the Communist issue. Confronted almost daily with lurid exposés of "CIO-red" plots and banner headlines screaming about "Soviet beachheads" on the waterfront, weary strikers began drifting back to work. "I've been fighting Ryan's gang since the last war," one dejected striker said, "so now they say I'm a Communist. Will it take another war to get him out?" Not this time, for Ryan, who had been elected president for life only two years before, now found himself fighting for survival. And the longshoremen were not about to make it easy for "King Joe." In 1947 they wildcatted again, then again in 1948 and 1951—incredibly, four portwide walkouts in six years. In all, there were eighteen recorded work stoppages between 1945 and 1951, accounting for a staggering total of more than half a million work days lost.[86]

Ryan's inability to maintain labor peace made him a growing liability to shippers, exporters, and other powerful commercial interests. After the 1951 wildcat, the New York State Crime Commission launched an exhaustive investigation of conditions on the waterfront. The commission's final report documented for the first time the full extent of corruption on the docks, as witness after witness described cases of kickbacks to union officers, bribery of steamship companies, and exploitation of longshoremen by underworld figures. Forced into action by the commission's findings, the national AFL decided it was time to clean its own house. After a year of strained negotiations and unfulfilled promises by ILA leaders to institute sweeping reforms, the AFL took the unprecedented action of expelling the union in the fall of 1953. Ryan resigned from office two months later.[87]

The rank-and-file insurgency that drove Ryan from office represented both a break and a continuity with the past. In their degree of militancy, the postwar strikes were certainly a radical departure from the preceding twenty-five years of labor peace. Politically, however, the insurgents were practically indistinguishable from the ILA's conservative anti-communist leadership. In fact, many of the same locals that led the postwar strikes were the most supportive of the ILA's policy against loading war materials bound for the Soviet Union or China. Local 791, for example, which spearheaded the anti-Ryan insurgency, was the first to extend the union's limited boycott of military cargo to include all shipments to the Soviet Union. As a member of the local told a reporter in 1951 when asked about charges of Communist influence in the local: "Strange breed of commies who never miss Mass in the morning and who'll give up a day's pay before they'll work a Russian ship."[88]

The conservative political culture in the East proved highly durable over the years, surviving not only Ryan but also the longshoremen out of whose experiences and culture it had emerged in the first place. Today, while dockworkers in New York endorse "new right" conservatives for office and periodically slap boycotts on vessels from offending Marxist governments, dockworkers in the West support progressive candidates and just as often refuse to handle military cargo bound for anti-communist regimes. The political contrast between the two coasts, despite changes in union leadership at the top, remains as striking as ever.[89]

Conclusion

The social and political forces unleashed by World War II posed the first serious challenge to the established leadership of longshore unionism on both coasts. While radical leaders in the West faced the formidable task of integrating several thousand new and, for the most part, less politically experienced workers into the union, their conservative counterparts in the East confronted a growing and highly volatile oppositional movement on the docks. The strength of insurgents on each coast, as well as the political direction they headed in after the war, was largely a product of the wartime transformation of the union membership together with the specific labor policies of local left-wing activists.

On the West Coast the relative stability of the prewar labor force, combined with the political neutralization of the more conservative workers who entered the union during the war, contributed to the resiliency of radical leadership. In most locals, the pro-Bridges generation of '34 men remained fairly intact, thus avoiding the mass disruption and social decomposition that occurred in the auto and electrical industries, where the left sustained heavy political losses after the war. Like many industrial unions, the ILWU also took in a large number of ideologically conservative "war babies." But their political impact was partially offset, particularly in San Francisco, by the early recruitment of radical activists from other ILWU locals and by the large wave of sympathetic blacks who came onto the docks in the later stages of the war.

The wartime transformation in union membership was no less significant in New York. There, however, disruption of the existing labor force was the spark that ignited the postwar insurgent movement. The release of many older workers to defense industries eroded Ryan's traditional base of support within the union, and military conscription siphoned off many younger workers who, transformed by the experience of combat, returned to the waterfront in a more belligerent and defiant mood.

What happened on the New York waterfront thus runs counter to the received interpretation of the war's disintegrating impact on the working class. The high rate of labor turnover did indeed atomize the rank and file, but it did so selectively by allowing older, more conservative workers to leave the industry. For those who remained behind, the war was a time of growing solidarity, thanks to the limited regularization of hiring and the sudden scarcity of labor. Even the large exodus of men into the military, while temporarily disrupting the labor force, had the long-term effect of transforming many younger men into battle-hardened veterans who were psychologically better prepared to take on Ryan when the war ended.

Yet the left in New York was unable to fully capitalize on the postwar surge in militancy, in part because of its own record of class collaboration during the war. Like their comrades in the UAW, the ILA's struggling Communist forces hewed closely to the official party line on labor sacrifice. In 1943, when dissidents rebelled against worsening conditions and threatened to defect from the ILA, party leaders counseled moderation, urging the militants to remain within the union and push instead for greater productivity. After watching over the wartime deterioration of working conditions, the left was in no position to play anything other than an ancillary role in the postwar struggle that swept Ryan from office.

In contrast, the Communist-supported left on the West Coast pursued a more flexible and balanced policy during the war. Despite the rhetoric of labor sacrifice emanating from union headquarters, the union stubbornly "refused to give up a single provision of its contracts," as Bridges himself admitted years later.[90] To the extent that the dockworkers relaxed certain conditions, they did so voluntarily out of a genuine desire to aid the war effort, not because Bridges or some other leader forced them to sacrifice.

The left's more balanced approach on the West Coast was partly a matter of conscious choice and partly a reflection of the militant work culture on the docks. Having just emerged from a decade of protracted and often violent struggles against the shipowners, the rank-and-file longshoremen were not about to surrender anything without good reason. It was their uncompromising militancy that kept Bridges honest during the war. Without it, he no doubt would have strayed closer to the position of all-out sacrifice advocated by Communist leaders on the New York waterfront.

The ILWU's refusal to give up basic contract conditions significantly narrowed the parameters of postwar union factionalism to a more limited range of issues. By delivering the goods, the ILWU's pro-production leaders managed to escape the charge of "red company unionism" that proved so damaging to the left in the UAW and elsewhere. Consequently, when anti-communists began organizing in the ILWU after the war, they were unable to fault Bridges for his handling of trade union matters. Focusing instead on the union's alleged un-Americanism, the right was forced to confine its attack to the political terrain of foreign policy and domestic anti-communism, where Bridges and his supporters were on firm enough ground to repel its advances.

Chapter Seven

Conclusion: Unions
in the Making

"In the last war, we joined the Communists to fight the fascists," James Carey, national CIO officer, told an American Legion—sponsored anti-communist conference in 1950. "In another war," he predicted, "we will join the fascists to fight the Communists."[1] In a manner of speaking, this other war had already begun. The political realignment Carey envisioned was being felt in his own organization, as centrist forces broke away from the dominant progressive coalition, leaving the Communists and their allies to face an emerging alliance of Cold War liberals and hard-boiled reactionaries. With battle lines sharply drawn, the CIO's war against communism claimed its first victims a few months later when the national office expelled its "Communist-dominated" affiliates.

The expulsions sent repercussions throughout the labor movement. Losing nearly one million trade unionists was damaging enough, but the interunion raids, jurisdictional battles, and internecine feuding that followed were far more destructive. The CIO's three-year campaign to repeal the "slave labor" Taft-Hartley Act stalled. Organizing ground to a halt. "Operation Dixie," the much-heralded master plan for bringing industrial unionism to the open-shop South, bogged down. For the first time since the founding of the CIO, major industrial unions reported little or no membership growth. Stagnating, hamstrung by political bickering, the CIO's crusading days were over, its ideological fervor spent. "By the time the CIO threw in the towel and merged with the AFL in 1955," historian David Caute observes, "the American trade union movement had become the most conservative and ideologically acquiescent among the capitalist democracies."[2]

Whether it could have been otherwise we can never say for sure. But it is clear that capitulation was only one of several possible routes leading out of the Cold War morass. Indeed, a bolder, more politically independent course had suggested itself to many union leaders, including non-Communists who were fed up with the growing indifference of the Truman administration. Late in 1946, locals all across the country, from Connecticut to California, had adopted third-party resolutions. Months later Henry Wallace launched his bid for the presidency. A victim of bad timing, Wallace nevertheless attracted well over a million votes. And at the state and local level, where labor took a more active interest in politics, third-party initiatives fared better still.[3]

But this flirtation with political independence was short-lived, killed off not so much by labor's sworn enemies as by its own leadership, particularly the CIO's decision to cleanse itself of "Communist" influence. After driving out the organized left, the industrial union movement drifted unchecked to the right, abandoning independent political action before finally collapsing into the waiting arms of the Democratic Party. Looking back, we can only ponder how different labor's postwar trajectory might have been had a majority of the expelled unions been anything like the ILWU—tough, politically committed, and, above all, resilient.

What was it about the ILWU? Returning to our original question, what accounts for its radical, aggressively left-wing politics, its durable socialist-oriented leaders? Were they products of historical contingency or the result of deeper sociological determinants? In the final analysis, was it human agency or social structure that formed the ILWU? The answer is that both were important, with structural conditions providing a sociological context or field—admitting several degrees of freedom—on which real social actors exercised their historically given options.

Social structure and human agency reciprocally conditioned each other in the emergence and consolidation of radical leadership on the West Coast. The early syndicalist inclinations of the labor force, heightened by years of employer hostility, created an opening for radical insurgency during the early 1930s. It was at this historical conjuncture, formed by intersecting patterns of occupational recruitment and industry structure, that the role of human agency became decisive. If in the spring of 1933 Communist organizers in the West had decided to follow their New York comrades in building the "revolutionary" marine workers' union instead of the ILA, the pivotal coastwide walkout that erupted the following year might never have happened. And if the walkout had occurred anyway, it is likely that without radical leadership pushing the strike forward, the level of repression would have been lower and the historical significance of the conflict—and possibly even its outcome—would have been different. In later years, the ILWU might not have survived the Cold War had Bridges insisted on following the self-destructive policy of class collaboration pursued by New York's Communist-supported insurgents during the war.

To attach such importance to the role of agency, however, is not to reduce history to mere intentions or to imply that all things were possible, subject only to the resolve and determination of key individuals and groups. The way in which real social actors were able to intervene in the historical process was itself influenced and circumscribed by their sociological inheritance. The final outcome, in other words, was neither predetermined by some primordial structural imperative nor left simply to the vagaries of history. Rather, the causal relationship more closely resembles Weber's historical analogy of throwing "loaded dice," where each toss is partly contingent on the one before it and where a particular outcome, in the presence of a prior "concrete determinant"—such as shifting the center of gravity in a die—becomes more favorable.[4]

On the docks, these prior determinants consisted of early patterns of occupational recruitment and industry structure. Their combined effect, giving rise to radically different political cultures, made certain outcomes in the form of organizing strategies, modes of industrial conflict, and leadership policies more likely, though by no means certain. By initially loading the historical dice in this manner, and then subsequently reloading them at each critical choice point, the element of pure chance, of so-called historical accident, was progressively diminished over time. Although it is true that the longshoremen made their own history, they did so, to paraphrase Marx, not under conditions of their own choosing.

Once we see the process of class formation in this light, as possessing, in Maurice Zeitlin's words, "an inherent relatively contingent historicity,"[5] we are forced, I would argue, to reconsider the way most scholars have approached the problem of American exceptionalism: closing their eyes to the real historical alternatives that may have existed at various points, choosing instead to view the past through the lens of the present and thereby reading into the failure of socialism an undeserved inevitability.

Just as it is ahistorical to assume that what was is what had to be, there is no reason to believe that, in the case of organized labor, the eventual triumph of conservatism somehow proves that radical insurgents never stood a chance. Clearly, the ILWU offers proof that they did, that alternatives to business unionism were not only possible but practical, and that socialist leadership remained a viable option well into the twentieth century for at least some American workers.

This is not to say that the ILWU was, in any strong sense of the word, a "socialist" union. It is true that Bridges and his supporters often espoused socialist beliefs and ideology, but the organization they led did not. Unlike its socialist ancestors from the turn of the century, the ILWU never articulated an alternative vision of the future. Its constitution contained no reference to "ultimate goals," no support for the time-honored principle of "collective ownership." Societal transformation was simply never on the agenda, for either the union or its members, few of whom were won over to the socialism of their leaders. Most longshoremen identified with the progressive social legislation of the New Deal. When voting, they rarely strayed from a straight Democratic ticket. Above all, they were practical.

Practicality, however, did not mean that the longshoremen accepted the world as it was. They may not have been revolutionary, or even visionary, but neither were they uncritical of "the system." The ILWU's leadership saw to that, constantly hammering away at capitalism's connection to unemployment, war, and racism. As a result, many longshoremen were willing to entertain ideas and support causes that most other American workers regarded as dangerous or subversive. If the majority did not think of themselves as socialists, it is nonetheless true that "socialism," as one longtime observer noted, "was never a dirty word on the waterfront."[6]

But recognizing that the system is flawed is one thing, and actively seeking its overthrow is something else. Few longshoremen, it seems, were prepared to take that second step. Perhaps they were cynical, apathetic, or just scared. For whatever combination of reasons, active opposition to capitalism was the exception rather than the rule. Only a fraction of the nearly fifteen thousand dock-workers in the ILWU, for example, ever joined the Communist Party. In 1945, the high-water mark of American communism, only 237 West Coast longshoremen were officially enrolled in the party. Subscriptions to the *Daily Worker* never exceeded five hundred.[7] Even allowing for a high turnover of readers and recognizing that the paper's influence extended well beyond its limited circulation, it is doubtful that the number of "fellow travelers" ever represented more than 20 percent of the longshoremen. That may seem like a significant number, and in some respects it is, especially in the American context. Yet the fact remains that committed radicals were a minority of the labor force, meaning that Bridges's more widespread support from the rank and file could not have rested entirely, even primarily, on ideological agreement.

Having thus dismissed political ideology as the sole basis of Bridges's popular support, it would be equally erroneous to reduce his success to "delivering the goods," for there is no evidence that Bridges was a more effective bargainer than any of the half-dozen or so Communist-supported union leaders who were driven from office during the Cold War. That Bridges survived suggests that the strength and resiliency of radical leadership, particularly when faced with a serious challenge, cannot be adduced from economic performance alone. Indeed, I would argue that Bridges held on as long as he did precisely because his ties to the rank and file were stronger than bonds based simply on a few more cents per hour, a few more pork chops.

Bridges's syndicalist vision provided such a strong link to the membership, especially to the old-timers, many of whom, like Bridges, were drawn to the IWW after World War I. In 1921 Bridges himself had joined the New Orleans local of the MTW, although he left it a short time later, complaining of the Wobblies' disregard for organization and their refusal to sign contracts. "All they succeed in doing," he said at his 1939 deportation hearing, "is creating a lot of general disruption and bogging down the advance of labor generally." Critical of the Wobblies' "extreme rank and file-ism," Bridges nevertheless remained sympathetic to their trade union program of industrial organization, direct action, and workers' control.[8] In later years as he drifted closer to the Communist Party, the pressure to shed his syndicalist beliefs intensified. But Bridges, acting partly on his own instincts and partly in response to the membership, was unable to do so. "Anyone who knew Bridges well during the fifties," remarked Joseph Starobin, a key figure in the Communist Party, "knew how deeply he was affected by syndicalist conceptions."[9]

It was Bridges the syndicalist who so forcefully articulated the concerns of the older men. Like Bridges, they remembered what it meant to work on the docks before the union. Having lived through the open-shop 1920s and suffered at the hands of the employers, they knew full well what they were up against. Higher wages, better conditions, even union recognition provided little comfort so long as the shipowners were free to treat the workers like so much human flotsam, discharging them without cause or pushing them to the limits of their endurance through long hours or speed-up. Not pork chops but control—that is what fired the imagination of Bridges and his contemporaries, and what later stamped the ILWU with its unmistakable syndicalist imprint.

Bridges was also a leader. He emerged from the 1934 strike as something of a heroic figure, one of those rare individuals who throughout history seem to come forward, risking personal security and safety, to lead a disadvantaged group into battle against a more powerful adversary. To the '34 men who fought alongside him, Bridges appeared larger than life. Stories of his courage and accomplishments abounded, some of them real, others imagined. "Harry had what it takes," as many old-timers put it; he was a "natural," a man seemingly destined for leadership.

Every union has a founder. The point is that Bridges was much more than that. In a very real sense, he was the union; attacking him was like attacking the ILWU. At least that is how the membership saw it: when the media referred to Bridges as a Communist, they were also red-baiting the longshoremen; when the shipowners broke off negotiations with Bridges, they were really trying to "bust up" the union; when various government agencies attempted to deport Bridges, they were simply out to "get" the dockworkers' leader. The ILWU's expulsion from the CIO in 1950 was seen in much the same light, as another in a long string of externally based attacks on the integrity of their union, a threat that was no more successful than the others. If anything, it reinforced the '34 men's identification with Bridges at a crucial time when anti-communist forces were closing in on visible left-wingers in other industries.[10]

Surviving the Cold War also depended on winning over the newest generation of workers for whom neither syndicalism nor the 1934 strike had special significance. What they saw of Bridges and the left was mostly wartime productivity campaigns and no-strike pledges. But that was not the whole story. Those looking more closely, especially many blacks, also saw a firm commitment to racial equality and justice. For them, the ILWU was not just another dues-collecting agency, but rather a place where they felt they belonged, where the leadership certainly, if not every member, welcomed them with open arms.

Bridges, then, delivered a lot more than just pork chops. To the old-timers he was, as the Wobblies used to say, a "fellow worker" who kept the syndicalist dream alive. To the '34 men he was a heroic figure, a veteran of the "Big Strike," a trusted member of their generation, and the founding father of the union. To most blacks, he was a man of deep personal convictions, one of the few white leaders in postwar America who attempted to make good on his promise of racial equality. Bridges's strength, in short, resided in what might be termed the "extraeconomic" basis of his support within the union—whether it was his vision of syndicalism, his close personal identification with the union, or his support for racial equality. Each of these stands made him appear indispensable to different generational and racial blocs among the membership—so much so that even if someone else had been capable of delivering the goods or preaching politics, Bridges himself still would not have been replaceable.

To argue that extraeconomic processes were at work in the ILWU is to question one of the central assumptions underlying much of the existing research on the dynamics of trade union loyalty. From the seminal studies of John Commons on the nature of unionism to Mancur Olson's more recent work on collective action, the primacy of economic self-interest has rarely been questioned. Uncritically accepting the basic tenets of Selig Perlman's influential theory of "job consciousness," industrial sociologists, institutional historians, labor economists, and even many union leaders contend that manual workers, particularly in America, are narrowly concerned with employment security, wages, conditions, and the like. It is often asserted that, in the two great ideological showdowns of this century—the AFL versus the socialists, and the CIO versus the Communists—conservative forces came out on top largely because they were more attentive to the immediate bread-and-butter concerns of their members.[11]

But a close reading of the historical evidence does not offer much support for this economistic interpretation of working-class consciousness. The socialists delivered the goods every bit as effectively as their victorious craft union rivals. Similarly, Communist successes and failures do not correlate in any simple way with the relative efficacy of individual union leaders. The vulnerability of the left cannot be understood primarily in terms of economic performance.[12]

Economic theorists of human behavior might better follow the lead of the new social historians in exploring the actual lived experiences of ordinary men and women. Older, institutional approaches looked down at "labor" and saw only an abstract mass of wage earners driven by the single-minded pursuit of self-interest. But the new history, looking up, sees an infinitely more complex social reality in which human beings are torn in different, often conflicting, directions by loyalties rooted in union, class, ethnic, gender, ideological, regional, and generational identifications. Their economic interests as wage earners constitute only one of several possible bases of group formation and mobilization.

Recognizing that economic interests are merely "one of several" sources of working-class organization is not to argue that all interests are therefore equally important. As everyone from Marx to Commons points out, unions are fundamentally economic institutions. Although they may dabble in politics, agitating among their members about certain pieces of legislation or particular candidates, such activities are rarely more than means to what are essentially economic ends: higher wages, better conditions, greater job security.[13] It is with the promise of delivering these goods that unions are born. Whether they endure, however, depends not only on how well they deliver on their economic promise but also on the socially constructed meanings that in the course of history come to be attached to the union, its mission, and its leadership.

This noneconomic dimension of union durability is evident in the case of the ILWU. The argument that Bridges survived by delivering the goods is obviously inadequate unless it can be demonstrated that those leaders who were driven from office during the Cold War were somehow less effective on the economic front. So far, no such case has been made. Nor is it likely to be made, given the consensus among both pro- and anti-communist labor historians that the expelled unions were, in David Saposs's words, "superlatively successful . . . in securing better wages and working conditions for their members."[14]

If, as the record seems to indicate, Bridges cannot be distinguished from his less resilient contemporaries by economic performance, then the answer to his remarkable durability must lie elsewhere—perhaps in his more enduring ties to the rank and file, ties that went beyond immediate economic self-interest. Contrary to conventional wisdom, then, it was not the practice of economism but rather its transcendence that may best account for the "Bridges phenomenon."

The lesson for the left in all of this is the supreme importance of developing more than an instrumental relationship to the rank and file. Particularly in times of political challenge, simply delivering the goods may not be enough. During the Cold War, for example, radical leaders appear to have been most vulnerable where their support rested on little more than economic self-interest. In the UE, the UAW, the NMU, and other leftist strongholds, anti-communist rivals had only to demonstrate that they were equally able to win at the bargaining table. By doing so they effectively disarmed many left-wing leaders, severing the leftists' one link to the membership and leaving them with nothing to fall back on except their increasingly unpopular politics.[15]

The left was most resilient where its relationship to the rank and file involved more than economics. Consider the remarkable loyalty displayed by the UE's machinists. Whereas workers in both the radio and the electrical divisions wavered in their support for the union's left-wing leaders, the machinists rarely did. James Matles, the UE's organizational director, had personally organized many of these same machine shops years before and had a long-standing relationship with the machinists. Over the years, they remained grateful to Matles, following him out of the AFL's International Association of Machinists in 1929 and into the Sheet Metal Workers Industrial Union, a TUUL affiliate. Then, when the TUUL was dissolved in 1935, they returned briefly to the IAM before finally moving on with Matles into the UE when it was founded two years later. That kind of loyalty cannot be purchased with a fatter paycheck. Obviously, the machinists saw something appealing in Matles over and above his ability to deliver the goods.[16]

The extraeconomic basis of support for the left was also evident wherever there were large concentrations of blacks and other minority workers. In the West Coast Marine Cooks and Stewards Union, the predominantly nonwhite membership remained loyal to President Hugh Bryson even after the union was expelled from the CIO and Bryson himself was indicted by the federal government for falsely signing the Taft-Hartley noncommunist affidavit. "Sure, the union leaders follow the party line," a black rank and filer explained in 1956. "But I let white folks worry about communism. Bryson has given us colored guys a real fair shake." Echoing these sentiments, a black miner in the South defended Bob Travis, the Communist leader of Mine, Mill, another of the expelled unions. "I've never known a Communist in the labor movement to mob a man outside city hall, lynch him, castrate him, and everything else, even shoot him on sight," he said. "It's the good white man who does that, you see. So, why am I going to go out and fight somebody who doesn't do the things that the good white folks have done?"[17]

In each of these cases, left-wing leaders retained rank-and-file support to the extent that they were able to provide something that the opposition could not. For the machinists, it was Matles's prestige as the founding father of unionization, while for black marine stewards on the West Coast and miners in the South, it was the left's principled commitment to racial equality. Bridges's strength was that he managed to offer something of value to practically everyone in the union. To some he was a militant syndicalist, or a Communist, or a champion of civil rights. Others saw him in a less political light, as a "fellow worker" whose stewardship of the ILWU symbolized their generation's lasting contribution to waterfront unionism. To be sure, Bridges gave the membership a great deal to admire, even those who might have disagreed with his radical political vision. "He may be Red Harry," the longshoremen used to say, "but he's *our* Red Harry." And he remained so for nearly half a century.

At first blush this may appear to be a warmed-over "great man" theory of history. It is not. Bridges's greatness—his courage to grasp at something more than "pork chops"—reflected the history, the struggles, and the social composition of the dockside labor force on the West Coast. The explosive combination of syndicalism, shipowner hostility, working-class resistance, and communism molded Bridges even as he, in turn, molded the union. The relationship was dialectical. Bridges no more made the ILWU than the ILWU made him. In the end, he was as great a leader as the rank and file allowed.

Notes

Chapter One

1. Karl Marx, "American Pauperism and the Working Class," in *On America and the Civil War*, vol. 2 of *The Karl Marx Library*, ed. Saul K. Padover (New York: McGraw-Hill, 1972), p. 7; Karl Marx, "The Possibility of Non-Violent Revolution," in *The Marx-Engels Reader*, 2d ed., ed. Robert C. Tucker (New York: W. W. Norton, 1978), p. 523.

2. Gerald N. Grob, in *Workers and Utopia: A Study of Ideological Conflict in the American Labor Movement, 1865–1900* (Chicago: Quadrangle Books, 1969), pp. 74–78, places the eight-hour movement in its historical perspective. Also see Richard O. Boyer and Herbert M. Morais, *Labor's Untold Story* (New York: United Electrical, Radio and Machine Workers of America, 1955), pp. 87–91.

3. Friedrich Engels, "Engels to Florence Kelley Wischnewetsky, London, June 3, 1886," in *The Correspondence of Marx and Engels*, ed. Dona Torr (New York: International Publishers, 1935), pp. 448–449.

4. Grob, *Workers and Utopia*, pp. 78, 176–179.

5. Werner Sombart, *Why Is There No Socialism in the United States?* ed. C. T. Husbands, trans. Patricia M. Hocking and C. T. Husbands (White Plains, N.Y.: International Arts and Sciences Press, 1976).

6. The literature on the failure of socialism is already voluminous and still growing. A good overview can be found in John H. M. Laslett and Seymour Martin Lipset, eds., *Failure of a Dream? Essays in the History of American Socialism*, rev. ed. (Berkeley and Los Angeles: University of California Press, 1984). For a more unified statement of the problem, see Seymour Martin Lipset, "Why No Socialism in the United States?" in *Radicalism in the Contemporary Age*, vol. 1 of *Sources of Contemporary Radicalism*, ed. Seweryn Bialer and Sophia Sluzar (Boulder: Westview

Press, 1977), pp. 31–149. Recent worthwhile contributions to the debate on exceptionalism include Michael Shalev and Walter Korpi, "Working Class Mobilization and American Exceptionalism," *Economic and Industrial Democracy* 1 (February 1980): 31–61; Theodore J. Lowi, "Why Is There No Socialism in the United States? A Federal Analysis," *International Political Science Review* 5, no. 4 (1984): 369–380; Eric Foner, "Why Is There No Socialism in the United States?" *History Workshop* 17 (Spring 1984): 57–80; and Mike Davis, "Why the U.S. Working Class Is Different," *New Left Review* 123 (September–October 1980): 3–44.

7. Wilbert E. Moore, "Sociological Aspects of American Socialist Theory and Practice," in *Socialism and American Life,* ed. Donald Drew Egbert and Stow Persons (Princeton: Princeton University Press, 1952), vol. 1, p. 553.

8. The logic of analyzing "deviant cases"—cases that operate in ways not anticipated by an established body of social theory—is not to refute the theory in question, but to refine it through a more precise specification of its parameters. Rather than treating unexpected outcomes as a source of embarrassment or, worse still, as something to be tidied up and explained away, deviant case analysis can "play a positive role" in theory construction by focusing on why the received explanation is inadequate; see Patricia L. Kendall and Katherine M. Wolf, "The Two Purposes of Deviant Case Analysis," in *The Language of Social Research: A Reader in the Methodology of Social Research,* ed. Paul F. Lazarsfeld and Morris Rosenberg (Glencoe, Ill.: Free Press, 1955), p. 167. Unfortunately, the social sciences have been slow to appreciate the advantages of deviant case analysis. For students of American exceptionalism, this has meant that deviations from the anti-socialist rule either go unnoticed or are dismissed as inconsequential. As a result, theories concerning the *absence* of socialism have rarely had to contend with the stubborn reality of its *presence* among certain segments of the population.

9. Sombart's way of posing the problem has recently come under fire from several writers, mostly American historians, who argue that the anti-socialist trajectory of the U.S. labor movement was not so exceptional after all. There are two versions of this argument—one "hard," the other "soft." The "hard" version maintains that "the European model," far from representing a coherent pattern of class formation against which all other industrialized countries can be compared, was itself characterized by a high degree of national diversity; see Aristide R. Zolberg, "How Many Exceptionalisms?" in *Working-Class Formation: Nineteenth-Century Patterns in Western Europe and the United States,* ed. Ira Katznelson and Aristide R. Zolberg (Princeton: Princeton University Press, 1986), pp. 397–455. The "soft" version of the same argument faults the excep-

tionalist school for exaggerating the differences between American and European working-class experiences, pointing out that Western European workers, despite their more flamboyant rhetoric, were animated by many of the same concerns as their American counterparts. Thus, although the language and strategies available to both groups differed along several critical dimensions, the workers' basic objectives did not; see Sean Wilentz, "Against Exceptionalism: Class Consciousness and the American Labor Movement, 1790–1920," *International Labor and Working-Class History* 26 (Fall 1984): 1–24. But arguing that working-class consciousness was comparable on both sides of the Atlantic—if indeed it was—does not change the historical fact that only in America did a socialist party based in the working class fail to survive. As a nation, the United States is still paying for this failure through the underdevelopment of the American welfare state; see John D. Stephens, *The Transition from Capitalism to Socialism* (Urbana: University of Illinois Press, 1979).

10. Recent studies of Communist trade union activity include Bert Cochran, *Labor and Communism: The Conflict That Shaped American Unions* (Princeton: Princeton University Press, 1977); Harvey A. Levenstein, *Communism, Anti-Communism, and the* CIO (Westport, Conn.: Greenwood Press, 1981); and volume 4 of the research annual *Political Power and Social Theory* (1984), which is devoted to historical sociological studies of American labor and the left. The assessment of Communist strength is from Bernard Karsh and Phillips L. Garmen, "The Impact of the Political Left," in *Labor and the New Deal,* ed. Milton Derber and Edwin Young (Madison: University of Wisconsin Press, 1961), p. 111.

11. Lincoln Fairley, *Facing Mechanization: The West Coast Longshore Plan*, Monograph no. 23 (Los Angeles: Institute of Industrial Relations, University of California, Los Angeles, 1979), pp. 2–4. Also see Paul T. Hartman, *Collective Bargaining and Productivity: The Longshore Mechanization Agreement* (Berkeley and Los Angeles: University of California Press, 1969), chap. 2, for a discussion of how the ILWU acquired job control.

12. Paul Eliel ("Industrial Peace and Conflict: A Study of Two Pacific Coast Industries," *Industrial and Labor Relations Review* 2 [July 1949]: 499) writes of the ILWU's unique brand of political unionism: "While left-wing officers of some other unions may hold similar views, some of them effectively divorce their economic beliefs from their union activity, so that, as to the latter, they are hardly to be distinguished from business unionists. From 1934 to 1948 this was not the case as to the officers of the Longshoremen's Union."

13. Wallace's 1948 campaign caught many left-wing unionists off guard. ILWU leaders, while stopping short of formally endorsing the Pro-

gressive Party, did speak out against "the evils of the two-party system"; see Joseph R. Starobin, *American Communism in Crisis, 1943–1957* (Berkeley and Los Angeles: University of California Press, 1972), pp. 166, 167. The rank and file got the message, and in a coastwide referendum they narrowly voted to support Wallace's candidacy; see Eliel, "Industrial Peace and Conflict," p. 497. On the ILWU's successful efforts to overturn federal legislation barring Communists from holding union office, see Philip Bart, Theodore Bassett, William W. Weinstone, and Arthur Zipser, eds., *Highlights of a Fighting History: 60 Years of the Communist Party, USA* (New York: International Publishers, 1979), pp. 379, 380.

14. Estimates of Communist strength on the docks are from "Comparative Absolute Figures of Basic Industry," on microfilm, reel 3, series 2–47, p. 3, Earl Browder Papers, University Research Library, University of California, Los Angeles; and Archie Brown, interview with author, San Francisco, September 12, 1981. For a sampling of opinion regarding the ILWU's left-wing credentials, see especially Nathan Glazer, *The Social Basis of American Communism* (New York: Harcourt, Brace & World, 1961), pp. 111, 117; David J. Saposs, *Communism in American Unions* (New York: McGraw-Hill, 1959), pp. 208, 212; and Starobin, *American Communism in Crisis,* p. 286n.

15. The American Communication Association, a white-collar union representing about seven thousand radio and television engineers and technicians—most of them employed at the New York Metropolitan Western Union offices—also survived the Cold War anti-communist offensive. F. S. O'Brien, in "The 'Communist-Dominated' Unions in the United States Since 1950," *Labor History* 9 (Spring 1968): 184–209, surveys the post-expulsion performance of the left-wing unions. In the case of the ILWU, the Teamsters reportedly spent more than a quarter of a million dollars on a series of raids against the union's warehouse stronghold in San Francisco, netting a total of 250 members. But the longshore division, which is the focus of this analysis, was never pierced; see Robert E. Randolph, "History of the International Longshoremen's and Warehousemen's Union" (M.A. thesis, University of California, Berkeley, 1952).

16. Richard L. Neuberger, "Labor's Overlords," *American Magazine* 125 (March 1938): 17.

17. Richard L. Neuberger, "Bad-Man Bridges," *Forum* 101 (April 1939): 195.

18. The views of the West Coast shipowners are quoted in Neuberger, "Labor's Overlords," p. 169. Bridges's legal difficulties with immigration are covered in Charles P. Larrowe, *Harry Bridges: The Rise and Fall of Radical Labor in the United States,* 2d ed. (Westport, Conn.: Lawrence Hill, 1977), chaps. 5–7; and Harvey Schwartz, "Harry Bridges and the

Scholars: Looking at History's Verdict," *California History* 59 (Spring 1980): 66–78.

The presiding judge at the 1939 deportation hearing concluded that "Bridges' aims [were] energetically radical" but did not conflict with the Constitution; see Estolv Ward, *Harry Bridges on Trial* (New York: Modern Age Books, 1940), p. 230. Coverage of the trial is found in *Time,* August 14, 1939, pp. 15–16. The Seattle banker is quoted in Neuberger, "Labor's Overlords," p. 170.

19. David A. Shannon, *The Decline of American Communism: A History of the Communist Party of the United States Since 1945* (New York: Harcourt, Brace, 1959), p. 217; *Business Week,* July 29, 1950, p. 64. The classic theoretical statement about the importance of delivering the goods is Selig Perlman, *A Theory of the Labor Movement* (New York: Augustus M. Kelley, 1949). For elaborations of Perlman's thesis, see Arthur Max Ross, *Trade Union Wage Policy* (Berkeley and Los Angeles: University of California Press, 1948), p. 110; Philip Taft, "Theories of the Labor Movement," in *Interpreting the Labor Movement,* Industrial Relations Research Association, Publication no. 9 (Champaign, Ill.: Industrial Relations Research Association, 1952), p. 34; Irving Bernstein, *Turbulent Years: A History of American Workers, 1933–1941* (Boston: Houghton Mifflin, 1970), p. 783; and Saposs, *Communism in American Unions,* pp. 184–185. In the case of Bridges, those who attribute his durability, in the main, to economic performance include Randolph, "International Longshoremen's and Warehousemen's Union," p. 227; Larrowe, *Harry Bridges,* p. 377; and Robert S. Keitel, "The Merger of the International Union of Mine, Mill and Smelter Workers into the United Steelworkers of America," *Labor History* 15 (Winter 1974): 36.

20. Eliel, "Industrial Peace and Conflict," pp. 480, 500.

21. John H. M. Laslett, "Socialism and the American Labor Movement: Some New Reflections," *Labor History* 8 (Spring 1967): 136–155; David A. Levinson, "Left-Wing Labor and the Taft-Hartley Act," *Labor Law Journal* 1 (November 1950): 1086; Robert W. Ozanne, "The Effects of Communist Leadership on American Trade Unions" (Ph.D. diss., University of Wisconsin, 1954), p. 321; James R. Prickett, "Some Aspects of the Communist Controversy in the CIO," *Science & Society* 33 (Summer–Fall 1969): 319.

22. For similar critiques of economic instrumentalism as it applies more generally to problems of union loyalty and strike activity, see Douglas E. Booth, "Collective Action, Marx's Class Theory, and the Union Movement," *Journal of Economic Issues* 12 (March 1978): 163–185; and Michael Mann, *Consciousness and Action Among the Western Working Class* (London: Macmillan, 1977), pp. 50, 51.

23. Jack Barbash, *Labor Unions in Action* (New York: Harper & Brothers, 1948), p. 217; Max M. Kampelman, *The Communist Party vs. the CIO: A Study in Power Politics* (New York: Praeger, 1957), p. 251; Saposs, *Communism in American Unions*, p. 221. Organizational factors also figure prominently in the analyses of Glazer, *Social Basis of American Communism*, pp. 120–121; Albert Epstein and Nathaniel Goldfinger, "Communist Tactics in American Unions," *Labor and Nation* 6 (Fall 1950): 36; Henry Pelling, *American Labor* (Chicago: University of Chicago Press, 1960), p. 192; and Philip Selznick, *The Organizational Weapon: A Study of Bolshevik Strategy and Tactics* (Glencoe, Ill.: Free Press, 1960), pp. 195–215. The passage of time has apparently done little to calm the political passions that are aroused whenever the issue of union democracy and communist leadership is raised; see James R. Prickett, "Anti-Communism and Labor History," *Industrial Relations* 13 (October 1974): 219–227; and Walter Galenson, "Communists and Trade Union Democracy," *Industrial Relations* 13 (October 1974): 228–236.

24. John H. M. Laslett, "Giving Superman a Human Face: American Communism and the Automobile Workers in the 1930s," *Reviews in American History* 9 (March 1981): 113. Regarding the charge of organizational domination, British socialist Harold Laski, an uncompromising critic of communists, writes that such arguments do "not go more than a little way to explain the volume of their influence in the trade unions. The fact still remains that the Communist Party secures from its members an energetic loyalty that is far and away greater than anything the ordinary member of the rank and file is likely to display"; see Harold Laski, *Trade Unions in a New Society* (New York: Viking Press, 1949), p. 167.

25. Ozanne, "Effects of Communist Leadership," pp. 47, 103, 104.

26. Fairley, *Facing Mechanization*, pp. 3–4; Larrowe, *Harry Bridges*, p. 127. For a more general and critical discussion of such practices as they influence leadership accountability within unions, see the classic study by Robert Michels, *Political Parties: A Sociological Study of the Oligarchical Tendencies of Modern Democracy* (New York: Free Press, 1962), esp. pt. 5.

27. Wayne Wilbur Hield, "Democracy and Oligarchy in the International Longshoremen's and Warehousemen's Union" (M.A. thesis, University of California, Berkeley, 1949); Jay Selwyn Goodman, "One-Party Union Government: The I.L.W.U. Case" (M.A. thesis, Stanford University, 1963); Seymour Martin Lipset, Martin A. Trow, and James S. Coleman, *Union Democracy: The Internal Politics of the International Typographical Union* (New York: Free Press, 1956), p. 132n.

28. Bridges is quoted in Lipset, Trow, and Coleman, *Union Democracy*, p. 5.

29. In the early 1960s, Bridges was accused of not respecting due process in the dismissal of 82 "B-men." The classification "B-men" had been created in 1959 when 743 workers were added to the labor force as probationary members of the union. Four years later a joint union-management committee evaluated the work records of the 561 remaining "B-men" and found 82 of them lacking. Stan Weir, one of the aggrieved longshoremen, lays out their case in "The ILWU: A Case Study in Bureaucracy," in *Autocracy and Insurgency in Organized Labor,* ed. Burton Hall (New Brunswick, N.J.: Transaction Books, 1972), pp. 80–92. Bridges vigorously denied allegations of any wrongdoing.

30. Congress of Industrial Organizations, *Proceedings of the Eleventh Constitutional Convention,* Cleveland, Ohio, October 31–November 4, 1949, pp. 252, 258.

31. Paul Jacobs, *The State of the Unions* (New York: Atheneum, 1963), p. 90.

32. Kampelman, *Communist Party vs. the CIO,* p. 251.

33. Much of this research is summarized in Albert Szymanski, *The Capitalist State and the Politics of Class* (Cambridge, Mass.: Winthrop, 1977), chap. 3. Indicative of the growing concern with industry at the time, Robert Blauner, in his classic study *Alienation and Freedom: The Factory Worker and His Industry* (Chicago: University of Chicago Press, 1964), argues for a "systematic, self-conscious sensitivity to the diversity of industrial environments" as a prelude to developing a genuine "sociology of industries" (pp. 186, 187).

34. Seymour Martin Lipset, *Political Man: The Social Bases of Politics* (Garden City, N.Y.: Anchor Books, 1963), chap. 7, esp. pp. 263–267; Clark Kerr and Abraham J. Siegel, "The Interindustry Propensity to Strike—An International Comparison," in *Labor and Management in Industrial Society,* ed. Clark Kerr (Garden City, N.Y.: Doubleday, 1964), pp. 105–147. For critical examinations of the Kerr-Siegel thesis, see P. K. Edwards, "A Critique of the Kerr-Siegel Hypothesis of Strikes and the Isolated Mass: A Study of the Falsification of Sociological Knowledge," *Sociological Review* 25 (August 1977): 551–574; Edward Shorter and Charles Tilly, *Strikes in France, 1830–1968* (Cambridge: Cambridge University Press, 1974); Harold Berenson, "The Community and Family Bases of U.S. Working-Class Protest, 1880–1920: A Critique of the 'Skill Degradation' and 'Ecological' Perspectives," *Research in Social Movements, Conflicts, and Change* 8 (1985): 109–132; and Joel I. Nelson and Robert Grams, "Union Militancy and Occupational Communities," *Industrial Relations* 17 (October 1978): 342–346.

35. In the Chilean countryside, for example, the radicalism of agrarian communities varies inversely with their degree of contact with the Communist-led miners; see James Petras and Maurice Zeitlin, "Miners

and Agrarian Radicalism," *American Sociological Review* 32 (August 1967): 578–586.

36. Stanley Weir, interview with author, San Pedro, California, April 22, 1981.

37. On the isolation of New York's dockworkers, see Elizabeth Ogg, *Longshoremen and Their Homes* (New York: Greenwich, 1939), p. 48; and Glazer, *Social Basis of American Communism*, p. 120.

38. Ryan's obsessive anti-communism is readily admitted—in fact, celebrated—by a sympathetic historian of the ILA: see Maud Russell, *Men Along the Shore* (New York: Brussel & Brussel, 1966), esp. pp. 122–124, 137–138. Ryan's support for European fascism is mentioned in Maurice Rosenblatt, "Joe Ryan and His Kingdom," *The Nation* 161 (November 24, 1945): 550. The secret anti-communist fund is discussed in George Morris, *A Tale of Two Waterfronts* (New York, 1953), p. 29. Lundberg is quoted in Edward Rosenbaum, "The Expulsion of the International Longshoremen's Association from the American Federation of Labor" (Ph.D. diss., University of Wisconsin, 1954), p. 397.

39. Daniel Bell, *The End of Ideology: On the Exhaustion of Political Ideas in the Fifties* (Glencoe, Ill.: Free Press, 1960), p. 165.

40. Mathew Josephson, "Red Skies over the Water Front," *Colliers* 118 (October 5, 1946): 17; Morris, *Tale of Two Waterfronts*, p. 21.

41. Guided by what is essentially an industry-based analysis, Raymond Charles Miller, in "The Dockworker Subculture and Some Problems in Cross-Cultural and Cross-Time Generalizations" (*Comparative Studies in Society and History* 11 [June 1969]: 310), concludes with Lipset and others that "dockworkers are generally liberal or leftist in their political views." The ILA stands as a powerful rejoinder to this kind of industrial reductionism. For similar critiques of industry as a determinant of working-class politics, see the provocative comparative studies by Duncan Gallie, *Social Inequality and Class Radicalism in France and Britain* (Cambridge: Cambridge University Press, 1983); and Scott Lash, *The Militant Worker: Class and Radicalism in France and America* (London: Heinemann, 1984).

42. Developments on both coasts since the 1950s are covered in Larrowe, *Harry Bridges;* and Vernon H. Jensen, *Strife on the Waterfront: The Port of New York Since 1945* (Ithaca: Cornell University Press, 1974). The major challenge of this period—containerization—is thoroughly discussed in Fairley, *Facing Mechanization*. A comparison of how both unions responded to containerization can be found in Philip Ross, "Distribution of Power Within the ILWU and the ILA," *Monthly Labor Review* 91 (January 1968): 1–7.

43. Herbert G. Gutman, *Work, Culture, and Society in Industrializ-*

ing America: Essays in American Working-Class and Social History (New York: Vintage Books, 1977); Herbert G. Gutman, *Power and Culture: Essays on the American Working Class,* ed. Ira Berlin (New York: Pantheon, 1987); David Montgomery, *Workers' Control in America: Studies in the History of Work, Technology, and Labor Struggles* (Cambridge: Cambridge University Press, 1979); David Montgomery, *The Fall of the House of Labor: The Workplace, the State, and American Labor Activism, 1865–1925* (Cambridge: Cambridge University Press, 1987). For an insightful criticism of Gutman's and Montgomery's work, see Lawrence T. McDonnell, "'You Are Too Sentimental': Problems and Suggestions for a New Labor History," *Journal of Social History* 17 (Summer 1984): 629–654.

The other major figure in working-class historiography is of course E. P. Thompson, whose *The Making of the English Working Class* (New York: Vintage Books, 1963) spans the "culturalist"–"syndicalist" divide. William Sewell, Jr. ("Classes and Their Historical Formation: Critical Reflections on E. P. Thompson's Theory of Working-Class Formation," in *E. P. Thompson: Critical Debates,* ed. Harvey J. Kaye and Keith McClelland [Oxford: Basil Blackwell, forthcoming]) argues that *The Making of the English Working Class* actually represents a third camp, which he terms "experientialist."

Chapter Two

1. David J. Saposs, *Left Wing Unionism* (New York: International Publishers, 1926), p. 185.

2. Communists, often working through the Trade Union Unity League, were instrumental in forming the American Communication Association; the Food, Tobacco, Agricultural and Allied Workers' Union; the United Electrical, Radio and Machine Workers Union; the United Office and Professional Workers of America; and the United Public Workers. The five remaining unions within the Communist orbit that were expelled also had an early exposure to radical leadership: the Fur and Leather Workers Union, which had a strong socialist presence at its founding; the International Mine, Mill and Smelter Workers, an offshoot of the radical Western Federation of Miners; and three West Coast maritime unions—the ILWU, the National Marine Cooks and Stewards, and the International Union of Fishermen and Allied Workers—all of which were influenced early on by the syndicalist perspective of the Industrial Workers of the World; see O'Brien, "'Communist-Dominated' Unions"; and Karsh and Gorman, "Impact of the Political Left," pp. 104–105.

3. Richard F. Hamilton, *Affluence and the French Worker in the*

Fourth Republic (Princeton: Princeton University Press, 1964), p. 185. Also see Glazer, *Social Basis of American Communism*, p. 111; Szymanski, *The Capitalist State*, p. 72.

4. Founded as the National Industrial Union of Marine Transport Workers in 1913, the MTW grew into one of the most powerful unions ever built by the IWW. Its six thousand card-carrying members in 1920 accounted for fully one-seventh of the IWW's national membership. Conducting increasingly successful forays into the guarded preserves of craft unionism, the MTW siphoned off growing numbers of disaffected maritime workers. During the last half of 1921, the MTW issued almost fifteen hundred membership cards to former AFL members. While conservative craft unions were suffering mass defections, the MTW absorbed more than twenty-four thousand new members over the next two years, making it the most viable organization in many ports. See "Minutes of the First Convention of the Marine Transport Workers Industrial Union 510, IWW," Box 70, folder 3, p. 4; and "Minutes of the Second Annual Convention of the Marine Transport Workers I. U. 510, IWW," Box 70, folder 10, p. 16; both found in Industrial Workers of the World Papers, Archives of Labor and Urban Affairs, Wayne State University, Detroit, Michigan.

5. Bill Bailey, interview with author, San Francisco, September 15, 1981.

6. Max Weber, *Economy and Society,* ed. Guenther Roth and Claus Wittich (Berkeley and Los Angeles: University of California Press, 1968), p. 929.

7. Bridges is quoted in Larrowe, *Harry Bridges,* p. 5.

8. The 1913 survey is cited in Carlton H. Parker, *The Casual Laborer and Other Essays* (Seattle: University of Washington Press, 1972), p. 79. Labor turnover data are from Cloice R. Howd, *Industrial Relations in the West Coast Lumber Industry,* Bureau of Labor Statistics Bulletin no. 349 (Washington, D.C.: Government Printing Office, 1924), p. 53.

9. Eric Hobsbawm, *Labouring Men* (London: Wiedenfeld and Nicolson, 1964), p. 52. The 1923 study is cited in Howd, *Industrial Relations,* p. 53.

10. The relationship between geographic mobility and radicalism is also suggested, at least indirectly, by numerous empirical studies showing a correlation between economic insecurity and leftist politics among manual workers. Most analysts treat the radicalizing effects of unemployment and underemployment as a response to unfulfilled needs for secure income or as a reaction to felt deprivation; see, for example, Lipset, *Political Man,* pp. 243–248; Hamilton, *Affluence and the French Worker,* chap. 9; Maurice Zeitlin, *Revolutionary Politics and the Cuban Working*

Class (Princeton: Princeton University Press, 1967), chap. 2; and John C. Leggett, *Class, Race, and Labor: Working-Class Consciousness in Detroit* (Oxford: Oxford University Press, 1968), chap. 5. Although such psychological orientations may incline economically insecure workers toward radicalism, their leftism may also in part be a product of greater "uprootedness," reflected not only in higher rates of labor turnover but in accelerated geographic mobility as well.

11. Living conditions aboard ship are described in James C. Healey, *Foc's'le and Glory Hole: A Study of the Merchant Seaman and His Occupation* (New York: Merchant Marine Publishers Association, 1936), pp. 47–53.

12. Bruce Nelson, "'Pentecost' on the Pacific: Maritime Workers and Working-Class Consciousness in the 1930s," *Political Power and Social Theory* 4 (1984): 141–182.

13. Ralph Winstead, "Enter a Logger: An I.W.W. Reply to the Four L's," *Survey* 44 (July 3, 1920): 475, 476.

14. Industrial Workers of the World, *The Lumber Industry and Its Workers* (Chicago: Industrial Workers of the World, n.d.), p. 50.

15. The Department of Labor official is quoted in Howd, *Industrial Relations*, p. 43.

16. William Preston, Jr., *Aliens and Dissenters: Federal Suppression of Radicals, 1903–1933* (Cambridge: Harvard University Press, 1963), pp. 157–161.

17. William W. Pilcher, *The Portland Longshoremen: A Dispersed Urban Community* (New York: Holt, Rinehart & Winston, 1972), p. 17; Oscar Hagan, interview with author, San Pedro, California, June 2, 1982.

18. Rosco Craycraft, interview with author, Seattle, Washington, December 16, 1981.

19. Thomas G. Plant, transcript of interview with Corinne L. Gilb, 1956, Oral History Collection, Social Science Library, University of California, Berkeley.

20. Stanley Weir, *Informal Workers' Control: The West Coast Longshoremen,* Reprint series no. 247 (Urbana-Champaign: Institute of Industrial Relations, University of Illinois, 1975), p. 57.

21. Eliot Grinnell Mears, *Maritime Trade of the Western United States* (Stanford: Stanford University Press, 1935), appendix, table IV.

22. Correspondence from E. Nichols, undated; and "Office of the General Manager of Employment Service Bureau," report dated January 15, 1924; both found in United States Shipping Board Papers, Record Group 32, General File 1920–1936, National Archives, Washington, D.C.

23. Montgomery, *Workers' Control,* p. 94.

24. Ibid., pp. 104, 96. American syndicalism has also been examined

in Melvyn Dubofsky, *Industrialism and the American Worker, 1865–1920* (Arlington Heights, Ill.: AHM Publishing, 1975), chap. 4; and Mike Davis, "The Stop Watch and the Wooden Shoe: Scientific Management and the Industrial Workers of the World," *Radical America* 9 (January–February 1975): 69–95.

25. Joe Dorfman, "The Longshoremen Strikes of 1922 and After" (B.A. thesis, Reed College, 1924).

26. For more on the economics of shipping, see Hartman, *Collective Bargaining and Productivity*, chap. 1.

27. Other industrial unionists were involved in the dockside struggles of 1919–1923, but their influence was far less than that of the IWW. The One Big Union Movement, Canada's equivalent of the IWW, had a following in the Pacific Northwest, while the Federation of Marine Transport Workers, an independent body with mild syndicalist leanings, was active in the Puget Sound area and in California, particularly San Pedro; see [Joseph] Bruce Nelson, "Maritime Unionism and Working-Class Consciousness in the 1930s" (Ph.D. diss., University of California, Berkeley, 1982), pp. 102–107.

28. The longshoremen's role in the Seattle general strike is discussed in Robert L. Friedmann, *The Seattle General Strike* (Seattle: University of Washington Press, 1964), pp. 17, 18; and Harvey O'Connor, *Revolution in Seattle: A Memoir* (New York: Monthly Review Press, 1964), pp. 158, 159.

29. Report of Agent 106, dated July 16, 1919, Broussais Beck Papers on Industrial Espionage, Suzzallo Library, University of Washington, Seattle (hereafter cited as Beck Papers). This collection contains two sets of labor-spy reports furnishing daily accounts of Seattle's labor movement during 1919 and 1920. Agent 17 submitted highly sensationalized reports, whereas those of Agent 106, the source of this information, were considerably more detailed and objective.

30. *Seattle Times,* May 4, 1920, p. 15.

31. *Seattle Union Record,* September 19, 1919, p. 1; O'Connor, *Revolution in Seattle,* p. 276; Report of Agent 106, dated September 18, 1919, Beck Papers.

32. Dorfman, "The Longshoremen Strikes," pp. 2–7; Dwight L. Palmer, "Pacific Coast Maritime Labor" (Ph.D. diss., Stanford University, 1935), p. 178.

33. *Seattle Times,* May 4, 1920, p. 15.

34. *Seattle Union Record,* May 8, 1920, p. 1.

35. Head of Labor Council quoted in ibid.; information from reliable informant found in report from S. B. McKenzie, executive secretary, dated May 7, 1920, Northwest Waterfront Employers Union Papers,

International Longshoremen's and Warehousemen's Union Library, San Francisco (hereafter cited as Northwest Papers).

36. Report of S. B. McKenzie, executive secretary, dated June 24, 1920, Northwest Papers; Frank P. Foisie, "Stabilizing Seattle's Longshore Labor" (Statement presented at the National Conference of Social Work, Denver, Colorado, June 11, 1925, typescript, Labor Collection, Social Science Library, University of California, Berkeley).

37. *Industrial Solidarity,* January 6, 1923, pp. 1, 2.

38. *Portland Oregonian,* June 14, 1922, p. 14.

39. Jack Mowrey, interview with author, Portland, Oregon, December 21, 1981.

40. *Industrial Solidarity,* January 6, 1923, p. 5; report titled "Joint Organization. Outlined by O. S. Swenson, Secretary for Portland Longshore Work," n.d., Northwest Papers.

41. *Portland Oregonian,* October 19, 1922, p. 1, and October 20, 1922, p. 1.

42. Art Shields, "The San Pedro Strike," *Industrial Pioneer* 1 (June 1923): 15.

43. *Industrial Solidarity,* May 19, 1923, p. 1, and May 12, 1923, p. 1.

44. *Long Beach Daily Press,* May 11, 1923, p. 1.

45. Hyman Weintraub, "The I.W.W. in California, 1905–1931" (M.A. thesis, University of California, Los Angeles, 1947), p. 229.

46. *Long Beach Daily Press,* May 15, 1923, p. 1.

47. Louis B. Perry and Richard S. Perry, *A History of the Los Angeles Labor Movement, 1911–1941* (Berkeley and Los Angeles: University of California Press, 1963), pp. 188–191.

48. William Martin Camp, *San Francisco: Port of Gold* (Garden City, N.Y.: Doubleday, 1947), pp. 443, 444.

49. Herb Mills and David Wellman, in "Contractually Sanctioned Job Action and Workers' Control: The Case of San Francisco Longshoremen" (*Labor History* 28 [Spring 1987]: 167–195), demonstrate the close connection between sling load limits, size of gangs, and job control.

50. *San Francisco Chronicle,* September 20, 1919, p. 3. Sam Kagel (*A Right Wing Dual Union,* 1930, typescript) argues that rumors circulated on the waterfront after the strike claiming that the union's final demand was inspired by agents of the shipowners in an attempt to discredit the union.

51. *San Francisco Chronicle,* October 14, 1919, p. 2.

52. *San Francisco Chronicle,* October 4, 1919, pp. 1, 2, and October 14, 1919, p. 2; *San Francisco Daily News,* October 13, 1919, p. 1, and October 14, 1919, p. 5.

53. *San Francisco Daily News,* October 15, 1919, p. 1, and October

21, 1919, p. 1. Quote is from correspondence signed by executive secretary, dated October 25, 1919, Northwest Papers.

54. Correspondence from executive secretary O. S. Swensen, dated February 2, 1920, Northwest Papers; Bernstein, *Turbulent Years*, p. 225.

55. Paul Ware, interview with author, Palm Desert, California, January 23, 1982; Pilcher, *Portland Longshoremen*, pp. 38–42.

56. Craycraft interview, December 16, 1981.

57. Joseph P. Goldberg, *The Maritime Story: A Study in Labor-Management Relations* (Cambridge: Harvard University Press, 1958), pp. 118–129.

58. Charles P. Larrowe, *Shape-Up and Hiring Hall: A Comparison of Hiring Methods and Labor Relations on the New York and Seattle Waterfronts* (Berkeley and Los Angeles: University of California Press, 1955), p. 9.

59. Bailey interview, September 15, 1981.

60. United States Bureau of the Census, *Population 1920. Fourteenth Census of the United States* (Washington, D.C.: Government Printing Office, 1923), vol. 4, pp. 884, 983, 1002, 1036.

61. Weir interview, April 22, 1981.

62. Larrowe, *Shape-Up and Hiring Hall*, pp. 2, 85; National Adjustment Commission, *Longshore Labor: An Investigation in Hours, Earnings, Labor Cost, and Output in the Longshore Industry in the Port of New York* (New York: National Adjustment Commission, 1920), p. 27. This same report estimates that only about twenty-one thousand out of New York's nearly forty thousand longshoremen were able to find regular employment.

63. For a discussion of the shape-up and how it operated in New York, see Vernon H. Jensen, *Hiring of Dock Workers and Employment Practices in the Ports of New York, Liverpool, London, Rotterdam, and Marseilles* (Cambridge: Harvard University Press, 1969), chap 2. Unsavory hiring practices and the resulting corruption are detailed in Malcolm Johnson, *Crime on the Labor Front* (New York: McGraw-Hill, 1950).

64. National Adjustment Commission, *Longshore Labor*, p. 131.

65. Ibid.; Charles B. Barnes, *The Longshoremen* (New York: Russell Sage Foundation, 1915), pp. 88, 92.

66. "Dock Employment in New York City," *Monthly Labor Review* 4 (February 1917): 292.

67. Louis I. Dublin and Robert J. Vane, "Shifting of Occupations Among Wage Earners as Determined by Occupational History of Industrial Policyholders," *Monthly Labor Review* 18 (April 1924): 37, 38.

68. United States Bureau of the Census, *Population 1910. Thirteenth Census of the United States* (Washington, D.C.: Government Printing Office, 1914), vol. 4, pp. 573, 592, 601, 603; United States Bureau of the Census, *Population 1920. Fourteenth Census of the United States,* vol. 4, pp. 884, 1002, 1036, 1159.

69. Plant interview, 1956, p. 30; Weir interview, April 22, 1981; Ware interview, January 23, 1982.

70. Barnes, *Longshoremen,* p. 5.

71. Perlman, *Theory of the Labor Movement,* p. 169. On the conservative, anti-socialist influence of Catholicism, see William V. Shannon, *The American Irish* (London: Macmillan, 1966), pp. 140, 141; Marc Karson, "Catholic Anti-Socialism," in Laslett and Lipset, *Failure of a Dream?* pp. 82–102; Montgomery, *Workers' Control,* pp. 76–82; and Jack Barbash, "Ethnic Factors in the Development of the American Labor Movement," in *Interpreting the Labor Movement,* Industrial Relations Research Association, Publication no. 9 (Champaign, Ill.: Industrial Relations Research Association, 1952), p. 876.

72. Charles Leinenweber, "The Class and Ethnic Bases of New York City Socialism, 1904–1915," *Labor History* 22 (Winter 1981): 47, 49n.

73. The impact of Irish immigration on another group of New York City workers is discussed by Joshua Freeman in "Catholics, Communists, and Republicans: Irish Workers and the Organization of the Transport Workers Union," in *Working-Class America: Essays on Labor, Community, and American Society,* ed. Michael H. Frisch and Daniel J. Walkowitz (Urbana: University of Illinois Press, 1983), esp. p. 262.

74. Barnes, *Longshoremen,* p. 5; Leonard Covello, "The Influence of Southern Italian Family Mores upon the School Situation in America," in *The Italians: Social Background of an American Group,* ed. Francesco Cordasco and Eugene Bucchioni (Clifton, N.J.: Augustus M. Kelley, 1974), p. 513.

75. The padrone system is described in Humbert Nelli, "The Italian Padrone System in the United States," *Labor History* 5 (Spring 1964): 153–167; Rudolph J. Vecoli, "Contadini in Chicago: A Critique of the Uprooted," in *Many Pasts: Readings in American Social History, 1865–the Present,* ed. Herbert G. Gutman and Gregory S. Kealy (Englewood Cliffs, N.J.: Prentice-Hall, 1973), vol. 2, pp. 164–194.

76. Barnes, *Longshoremen,* pp. 7, 8.

77. Russell, *Men Along the Shore,* p. 39.

78. Barnes, *Longshoremen,* pp. 6, 100.

79. Hobsbawm, *Labouring Men,* p. 206.

80. *New York Times,* October 10, 1919, p. 1.

81. Ibid., pp. 1, 7.

82. Ibid.

83. Ibid., p. 1; see also *New York Times,* October 28, 1919, p. 3, and October 19, 1919, p. 1.

84. *Industrial Solidarity,* November 15, 1919, p. 1.

85. Richard J. Butler and Joseph Driscoll, *Dock Walloper: The Story of 'Big Dick' Butler* (New York: Putnam, 1933), pp. 205–221.

86. Vacarelli is quoted in Larrowe, *Shape-Up and Hiring Hall,* p. 14.

87. *New York Times,* October 18, 1919, p. 1, and November 2, 1919, p. 3.

88. *Industrial Solidarity,* August 19, 1922, p. 8.

Chapter Three

1. Jack Barbash, *The Practice of Unionism* (New York: Harper & Brothers, 1956), p. 342. On the relationship between employer intransigence and labor radicalism, see Seymour Martin Lipset, "Radicalism or Reformism: The Sources of Working-Class Politics," *American Political Science Review* 77 (March 1983): 1–18; Mann, *Consciousness and Action,* p. 42; and James Holt, "Trade Unionism in the British and U.S. Steel Industries, 1888–1912: A Comparative Study," *Labor History* 18 (Winter 1977): 5–35.

2. Eliel ("Industrial Peace and Conflict") examines the impact of employer responses on unionization in the maritime and the wood products industries.

3. Ryan is quoted in the ILA's national publication, *Longshoremen's Journal,* December 1930, p. 3. On contrasting employer responses, see Ross, "Distribution of Power," pp. 2, 3.

4. Wytze Gorter and George H. Hildebrand, *The Pacific Coast Maritime Shipping Industry, 1930–1948* (Berkeley and Los Angeles: University of California Press, 1954), vol. 2, *An Analysis of Performance,* p. 261. For a similar view, see Betty V. H. Schneider and Abraham Siegel, *Industrial Relations in the Pacific Coast Longshore Industry* (Berkeley: Institute of Industrial Relations, University of California, 1956), p. 34.

5. Henry Schmidt, interview with author, Sonoma, California, January 25, 1984; Bjourne Halling, transcript of interview with Herb Mills and David Wellman, Grass Valley, California, October 16 and 17, 1979, p. 21.

6. Clinton Golden and Harold Ruttenberg, *Dynamics of Industrial Democracy* (New York: Harper & Brothers, 1942), p. 58. The impact of employer ideologies on industrial relations is clearly demonstrated in Philip Taft, "Ideologies and Industrial Conflict," in *Industrial Conflict,*

ed. Arthur Kornhauser, Robert Dubin, and Arthur M. Ross (New York: McGraw-Hill, 1954), pp. 257–265; and Reinhard Bendix, *Work and Authority in Industry: Ideologies of Management in the Course of Industrialization* (Berkeley and Los Angeles: University of California Press, 1956). The term "strict parallelism" is from Clarence E. Bonnett, *History of Employers' Associations in the United States* (New York: Vintage Books, 1956).

7. The "mirror analogy" is critiqued in Kerr and Siegel, "The Interindustry Propensity to Strike."

8. Cross-industry variations in conflict are demonstrated in ibid.; and in Dirk Kruijt and Menno Vellinga, "On Strike and Strike Propensity," *The Netherlands Journal of Sociology* 12 (December 1976): 137–151. The relationship between product markets and unionization is argued at some length by Robert T. Averitt, *The Dual Economy: The Dynamics of American Industry Structure* (New York: W. W. Norton, 1968); and by James O'Connor, *The Fiscal Crisis of the State* (New York: St. Martin's Press, 1973). Empirical support for this position can be found in Martin Segal, "Union Wage Impact and Market Structure," *Quarterly Journal of Economics* 78 (February 1964): 96–114; John E. Kwoka, Jr., "Monopoly, Plant, and Union Effects on Worker Wages," *Industrial and Labor Relations Review* 36 (January 1983): 251–257; and Richard B. Freeman, "Effects of Unions on the Economy," in *Unions in Transition: Entering the Second Century*, ed. Seymour Martin Lipset (San Francisco: Institute for Contemporary Studies, 1986), pp. 177–200.

9. For statements of the corporate liberal thesis, see Gabriel Kolko, *The Triumph of Conservatism: A Reinterpretation of American History, 1900–1916* (New York: Free Press, 1963); William Appleman Williams, *The Contours of American History* (Chicago: Quadrangle Books, 1966), esp. pp. 390–413; Ronald Radosh, "The Corporate Ideology of American Labor Leaders from Gompers to Hillman," *Studies on the Left* 6 (November–December 1966): 66–88; and James Weinstein, *The Corporate Ideal in the Liberal State: 1900–1918* (Boston: Beacon Press, 1968). One of the few empirical studies of firm behavior determined that large corporations were typically the most anti-union and that they responded like corporate liberals only when fearing retaliation from labor; see Richard E. Ratcliff and David Jaffe, "Capitalists vs. Unions: An Analysis of Anti-Union Political Mobilization Among Business Leaders," *Research in Social Movements, Conflicts, and Change* 4 (1981): 95–121.

10. Randy Hodson, *Workers' Earnings and Corporate Economic Structure* (New York: Academic Press, 1983), p. 16. Harold Levinson ("Unionism, Concentration, and Wage Changes: Toward a Unified Theory," *Industrial and Labor Relations Review* 20 [January 1967]: 205)

argues that sheltered producers frequently pursue strategies of co-optation and resistance, often simultaneously.

11. Almarin Phillips, "A Theory of Interfirm Organization," in *Interorganizational Relations,* ed. William M. Evan (Philadelphia: University of Pennsylvania Press, 1978), pp. 17–26. Levinson ("Unionism, Concentration, and Wage Changes") attributes employer accommodation in coal, construction, and trucking to spatial restrictions on production that limit capital mobility.

12. See, for example, Donald Palmer, Roger Friedland, and Jitendra V. Singh, "The Ties That Bind: Organizational and Class Bases of Stability in a Corporate Interlock Network," *American Sociological Review* 51 (December 1986): 781–796; Beth Mintz and Michael Schwartz, *The Power Structure of American Business* (Chicago: University of Chicago Press, 1985); and Michael Useem, "Business and Politics in the United States and United Kingdom: The Origins of Heightened Political Activity of Large Corporations During the 1970s and Early 1980s," *Theory and Society* 12 (March 1983): 281–300.

13. "Analysis of Results of Operation of Ocean-Going Shipping Services Owned by American Companies," dated August 19, 1932, General File 1920–1936, United States Shipping Board Papers.

14. Paul Eliel, "Labor Problems in Our Steamship Business," *Yale Review* 26 (March 1937): 513.

15. James C. Marony, "The International Longshoremen's Association in the Gulf States During the Progressive Era," *Southern Studies* 16, no. 2 (1977): 232.

16. Russell, *Men Along the Shore,* p. 70; Charles P. Larrowe, *Maritime Labor Relations on the Great Lakes* (East Lansing: Labor and Industrial Relations Center, Michigan State University, 1959), pp. 17–18.

17. Russell, *Men Along the Shore,* p. 63.

18. Hobsbawm, *Labouring Men,* p. 220.

19. On U.S. Steel's domination of the Lake Carriers Association, see Larrowe, *Maritime Labor Relations,* chap. 3. For the Gulf Coast, see Marony, "International Longshoremen's Association."

20. Camp, *San Francisco,* p. 413.

21. Plant interview, 1956, p. 33.

22. Mike Quin, *The Big Strike* (New York: International Publishers, 1979), pp. 45, 54.

23. Joyce Clements, "The San Francisco Maritime and General Strikes of 1934 and the Dynamics of Repression" (Ph.D. diss., University of California, Berkeley, 1975), p. 113.

24. The estimate of coastwise cargo is from *Business Week,* July 14, 1934, p. 7. San Pedro's strikebreaking expenses are reported in William F.

Dunne, *The Great San Francisco General Strike* (New York: Workers' Library [1934], p. 41.

25. *San Francisco Chronicle*, May 12, 1934, p. 1.

26. The La Follette Committee is quoted in George E. Lucy, "Group Employer-Employee Industrial Relations in the San Francisco Maritime Industry, 1888–1947" (Ph.D. diss., St. Louis University, 1948), p. 211. Lapham's Washington visit is mentioned in Larrowe, *Harry Bridges*, p. 100.

27. Plant expounded his views in a private letter reprinted in United States Congress, Senate Subcommittee of the Committee on Education and Labor, *Hearings on Violations of Free Speech and Rights of Labor*, 78th Cong., 1st sess., 1943, S. Rept. 398, pt. 1, p. 1055 (hereafter cited as La Follette Committee Hearings).

28. Lapham is quoted in ibid., p. 1056. The position of dissenting lines is documented in ibid., p. 1066. The *New York Times* article is cited in Louis Adamic, "Harry Bridges: Rank-and-File Leader," *The Nation* 142 (May 6, 1936): 579.

29. La Follette Committee Hearings, pp. 1068, 1069.

30. Nelson, "Maritime Unionism," p. 373; Casey is quoted in Larrowe, *Harry Bridges*, p. 108.

31. The *Pacific Shipper* quoted in International Longshoremen's Association, Local 38–79, *The Maritime Crisis: What It Is and What It Isn't* (San Francisco: International Longshoremen's Association [1937]), p. 15; *Oregon Daily Journal*, October 24, 1936.

32. Editorial from the *Pacific Shipper*, September 28, 1936, p. 15; International Longshoremen's Association, Local 38–79, *Maritime Crisis*, p. 7; *Pacific Shipper*, December 14, 1936, p. 7.

33. *Business Week*, October 24, 1938, p. 32.

34. Clark Kerr and Lloyd Fisher, "Multiple Employer Bargaining: The S.F. Experience," in *Insights into Labor Issues*, ed. Richard A. Lester and Joseph Shister (New York: Macmillan, 1948), p. 33.

35. *Pacific Marine Review*, April 1937, p. 17 (emphasis added).

36. Despite "conference agreements," "pooling arrangements," and other attempts at economic self-regulation, rate wars were an accepted, if disliked, form of competition in the maritime industry. Underbidding, in particular, was an effective weapon in the hands of larger operators who could more easily afford a temporary loss in income in order to capture a bigger share of the market; see United States Office of the Federal Coordinator of Transportation, *Hours, Wages, and Working Conditions in Domestic Water Transportation* (Washington, D.C.: Government Printing Office, 1936), vol. 1, pp. 7–10.

37. *Moody's Manual of Investments. American and Foreign Industrial*

Securities (New York: Moody's Investors Service, 1931), pp. 304, 2762.

38. On the 1907 strike, see Barnes, *Longshoremen*, pp. 118, 119. The Labor Department study is by Benjamin M. Squires, "Associations of Harbor Boat Owners and Employees in the Port of New York," *Monthly Labor Review* 7 (August 1918): 47.

39. Benjamin M. Squires, "The Strike of the Longshoremen at the Port of New York," *Monthly Labor Review* 9 (December 1919): 100, 114.

40. On the government's role in the maritime industry, see Darrell Hevenor Smith and Paul V. Betters, *The United States Shipping Board: Its History, Activities, and Organization* (Washington, D.C.: Brookings Institution, 1931).

41. The Shipping Board's more extensive involvement in the East was largely a result of the greater number of overseas mail routes connecting New York with major population and commercial centers in Europe, Africa, and the Near East. Given this larger volume of mail, the Shipping Board found it economically feasible to maintain its own fleet in New York well into the 1930s. On the Pacific Coast, where there were fewer mail routes, the government liquidated its fleet in 1928, thereafter paying commercial shippers a small subsidy to carry mail overseas.

42. Cargo statistics for 1929 are from United States Department of Commerce, Bureau of Foreign and Domestic Commerce, *Statistical Abstract of the United States, 1932* (Washington, D.C.: Government Printing Office, 1932), p. 413. Information on the extent of government service to New York is in Smith and Betters, *United States Shipping Board,* pp. 92, 93.

43. The history of New York's Foreign Commerce Club is related in *Marine Progress,* June 1934, pp. 15, 30. The estimate of cargo carried in foreign vessels is from Frederick J. Lang, *Maritime: A Historical Sketch and a Workers' Program* (New York: Pioneer Publishers, 1943), p. 11. Hebermann's resignation and statement are reported in the *New York Times,* August 19, 1927, p. 25.

44. These figures fail to reflect the full economic significance of foreign trade for commercial shipping. First, they refer to volume, rather than to dollar values of cargo. Yet shipowners are compensated not only on the basis of volume but also according to the distance a shipment is carried. In comparing categories of shipping, then, it is important to bear in mind that although the volume of coastwise shipments is larger, owing to the shorter distance and greater frequency of sailings, the rate per cargo unit is considerably less than in intercoastal and, particularly, long-distance overseas trade. Consequently, the dollar value of foreign trade, and thus its significance for commercial shipping, far exceeds its relative

importance as measured by tonnage. Second, cargo figures, of course, do not reflect revenue earned from passenger traffic. This was a far more important source of income in the East than in the West. In 1929, for example, transatlantic tourists outnumbered transpacific tourists by a ratio of 19 to 1. See Walter A. Radius, *United States Shipping in Transpacific Trade, 1922–1938* (Stanford: Stanford University Press, 1944), p. 12. In short, foreign commerce was an even more vital part of New York's maritime industry than tonnage figures alone might indicate.

45. *Business Week,* January 21, 1931, p. 6.

46. *Pacific Shipper,* June 22, 1931, p. 6.

47. Paul J. St. Sure, transcript of interview with Corinne L. Gilb, 1957, Oral History Collection, Social Science Library, University of California, Berkeley, pp. 609, 610. In 1948, the PMA replaced the WEA as the main employers' association on the West Coast.

48. On the more compliant posture of foreign operators, see Harold M. Levinson, *Determining Forces in Collective Bargaining* (New York: Wiley, 1966), p. 154.

49. *New York Times,* September 29, 1931, p. 51, and January 28, 1932, p. 17.

50. John J. Collins, "Longshoremen of the Port of New York" (M.A. thesis, New School for Social Research, 1955), p. 28.

51. The internal procedures of the NYSA are outlined in "New York Shipping Association," dated January 24, 1939, United States Maritime Commission Papers, Record Group 157, File 095, 1938–1942, National Archives, Washington, D.C.

52. "Report of Interview" with Mr. J. E. Craig, and with E. Lyon, both dated June 1939, United States Maritime Commission Papers, Record Group 157, File 055.2, 1938–1942.

53. Bell, *End of Ideology,* p. 167.

54. The contractor is quoted in Larrowe, *Shape-Up and Hiring Hall,* p. 64.

55. Mowrey interview, December 21, 1981.

56. "Minutes of General Meeting," signed by H. H. Lawson, Executive Secretary, dated July 23, 1921, pp. 6, 2, 3, Northwest Papers.

Chapter Four

1. Earl Browder interview with W. Goldsmith, August 1955, Box 9 Closed, Daniel Bell Papers, Tamiment Institute, New York University. Levenstein argues that "in general, the Communists were almost always better off the more remote they were from the control of Browder and his

theorists, who were obsessive in applying 'the line'" (*Communism, Anti-Communism, and the CIO,* p. 84).

2. The quote on scientific management is taken from David W. Mabon, "The West Coast Waterfront and Sympathy Strikes of 1934" (Ph.D. diss., University of California, Berkeley, 1966), p. 11. Cargo figures are cited in Clements, "San Francisco Maritime and General Strikes," p. 36.

3. Al Langley, interview with author, San Pedro, California, February 4, 1982.

4. Conditions in San Francisco are described in N. Sparks, *The Struggle of the Marine Workers* (New York: International Pamphlets, 1930), p. 40. Bridges described the shape-up in his 1950 deportation hearing; see United States District Court, Northern District of California, Southern Division, Case no. 32117-H, *United States v. Harry Renton Bridges, Henry Schmidt, and J. R. Robertson,* 1950, typescript (trial transcript), International Longshoremen's and Warehousemen's Union Library, San Francisco, p. 4782 (hereafter cited as 1950 Deportation Hearing).

5. Bulcke is quoted in Frederick Chiles, "General Strike: San Francisco, 1934—An Historical Compilation Film Storyboard," *Labor History* 22 (Summer 1981): 437. *Marine Workers' Voice,* June 1933, p. 2, describes the speed-up.

6. For a closer analysis of the Third Period as it pertains to Communist trade union work, see James R. Prickett, "New Perspectives on American Communism and the Labor Movement," *Political Power and Social Theory* 4 (1984): 3–36. Harvey Klehr, in *The Heyday of American Communism: The Depression Decade* (New York: Basic Books, 1984), pp. 12–17, discusses the doctrine of social fascism.

7. Cochran, *Labor and Communism,* pp. 43, 357n.

8. The MWIU's preamble is reproduced in Sparks, *Struggle of the Marine Workers,* pp. 59–60.

9. Bridges is quoted in United States Department of Labor, *Official Report of Proceedings Before the Immigration and Naturalization Service of the Department of Labor,* Docket no. 55073/217, In the Matter of Harry Bridges, Deportation Hearing, 1939, typescript (trial transcript), International Longshoremen's and Warehousemen's Union Library, San Francisco, p. 2602 (hereafter cited as 1939 Deportation Hearing); Orrick Johns, *Time of Our Lives: The Story of My Father and Myself* (New York: Stackpole, 1937), p. 325.

10. Sam Darcy, "The Great West Coast Maritime Strike," *Communist* 13 (July 1934): 665.

11. Sam Darcy, "San Francisco General Strike—1934," *Hawsepipe: Newsletter of the Marine Workers Historical Association* 1 (Septem-

ber–October 1982): 7. Slobodek is quoted in Larrowe, *Harry Bridges,* p. 13.

12. *Party Organizer* 6 (January 1933): 26; *Waterfront Worker,* April 1933, p. 2.

13. Darcy, "San Francisco General Strike," p. 7.

14. Klehr, *Heyday of American Communism,* p. 124; Levenstein, *Communism, Anti-Communism, and the CIO,* p. 24.

15. Nelson, "Maritime Unionism," pp. 188–193; Ben B. Jones, interview with author, Mill Valley, California, January 26, 1984.

16. *Waterfront Worker,* May 1933, p. 5.

17. *Western Worker,* July 10, 1933, pp. 1, 3.

18. Sam Darcy, interview with author, Fort Lauderdale, Florida, May 10, 1986. Testimony from former CP members indicates that Albion Hall was never conceived as "the beginnings of the CP's dual union for longshoremen," as Andrew Bonthius asserts in "Origins of the International Longshoremen's and Warehousemen's Union," *Southern California Quarterly* 59, no. 4 (1977): 423n.

19. Darcy, "Great West Coast Maritime Strike," p. 666; Darcy interview, May 10, 1986.

20. This estimate of Communist strength inside Albion Hall is based on the testimony of former member Eugene Dietrich, who testified against Bridges in 1939; see 1939 Deportation Hearing, p. 1468. Jones is quoted in Larrowe, *Harry Bridges,* p. 16.

21. Quoted in Chiles, "General Strike," p. 443.

22. Larrowe, *Harry Bridges,* p. 17.

23. Certain details of the Matson walkout are still in dispute. The book-burning incident, which has become a part of waterfront lore, appears in a number of historical accounts, including Larrowe's authoritative work (*Harry Bridges,* p. 19). Yet there are no reports of any such book-burning in the available contemporary sources.

24. Bridges is quoted in Larrowe, *Harry Bridges,* pp. 19–21; see also Mabon, "West Coast Waterfront and Sympathy Strikes," pp. 18, 19.

25. Radical Albion Hall members led the convention in adopting resolutions against loading Nazi vessels and in support of imprisoned labor leader Tom Mooney and the Scottsboro boys; see Darcy, "Great West Coast Maritime Strike," p. 667.

26. Ibid.

27. The scene in San Francisco is reported in the *Los Angeles Times,* March 23, 1934, p. 1; Paul Eliel, *The Waterfront and General Strike* (San Francisco: Hooper, 1934), p. 11.

28. Bernstein, *Turbulent Years,* p. 263; Darcy, "Great West Coast Maritime Strike," pp. 672, 673.

29. *Marine Workers' Voice,* November 1933, p. 1; Walter Stack, interview with author, San Francisco, May 28, 1982.

30. Mabon, "West Coast Waterfront and Sympathy Strikes," pp. 8, 9, 16; Meyer Baylin, interview with author, Mill Valley, California, January 23, 1984.

31. Personal correspondence from Sam Darcy to author, dated September 22, 1982.

32. On the party's earlier condemnation of working inside the ILA, see Mabon, "West Coast Waterfront and Sympathy Strikes," p. 202. Browder is quoted in the *Western Worker,* August 30, 1934, p. 3.

33. "Longshore Labor Conditions in the United States—Part I," *Monthly Labor Review* 31 (October 1930): 7, 8.

34. Johnnie Dwyer, interview with Debra Bernhardt, November 21, 1980, Immigrant Labor History Collection, Tamiment Institute, New York University.

35. Sam Madell, interview with author, New York, October 6, 1981.

36. Roy Hudson, "The Work of the Marine Union," *Party Organizer* 7 (May–June 1934): 30.

37. Madell interview, October 6, 1981.

38. One of Darcy's successors, Steve Nelson, who was assigned to District 13 in 1939, offered a similar explanation for the independence of his West Coast comrades. "The California Party," he wrote years later, ". . . enjoyed more autonomy than most districts because the national leadership was over three thousand miles away, in New York City. . . . In many ways we set our own course. There was a lively internal life to the organization, due in part to an iconoclastic Western mood. It was the healthiest Party district I'd been in. People talked back to you— they argued their points and did it in plain language, freer of leftist jargon than in most places." See Steve Nelson, James R. Barrett, and Rob Ruck, *Steve Nelson: American Radical* (Pittsburgh: University of Pittsburgh Press, 1981), p. 255.

39. Sam Madell, interview with author, New York, May 6, 1986.

40. *Party Organizer* 6 (November 1933): 17.

41. *Daily Worker,* January 12, 1934, p. 3.

42. Hudson, "Work of the Marine Union," pp. 29, 28.

43. Madell interview, May 6, 1986; Jones interview, January 26, 1984.

44. Roy Hudson, "Rooting the Party on the Waterfront," *Party Organizer* 14 (December 1934): 1164.

45. Kenneth Waltzer, in "The New History of American Communism," *Reviews in American History* 11 (June 1983): 259, writes that "while affiliated with and obedient to the Comintern, American communism was also shaped by national experience." Prickett, in "New Perspec-

tives on American Communism," also emphasizes the indigenous sources of organizing strategies and tactics. The same point about the role of Communists on the waterfront is made by Bruce Nelson in "Unions and the Popular Front: The West Coast Waterfront in the 1930s," *International Labor and Working-Class History* 30 (Fall 1986): 59–78.

46. Staughton Lynd, "The Possibility of Radicalism in the Early 1930s: The Case of Steel," *Radical America* 6 (November–December 1972): 37–64; Frank Emspak, "The Breakup of the CIO," *Political Power and Social Theory* 4 (1984): 122, 123. The argument being made here—that the choice of which organizing tactics to follow during the 1930s had a significant impact on Communist success—has its critics; see David Brody, "Radical Labor History and Rank-and-File Militancy," *Labor History* 16 (Winter 1975): 121–122; and Harvey Levenstein, "Economism, Anti-Economism, and the History of the Communist Party," *Political Power and Social Theory* 4 (1984): 289–295.

47. Putting the importance of strategy bluntly, William Overholt writes: "Had Mao been a better sociologist and a worse military strategist he probably would have lived a short life" ("Sources of Radicalism and Revolution: A Survey of the Literature," in Bialer and Sluzar, *Radicalism in the Contemporary Age,* p. 334). On the importance of tactical innovation to movement success, see also David R. Cameron, "Toward a Theory of Political Mobilization," *Journal of Politics* 136 (February 1974), esp. pp. 147–153; Doug McAdam, "Tactical Innovation and the Pace of Insurgency," *American Sociological Review* 48 (December 1983): 735–754; and Jo Freeman, ed., *Social Movements of the Sixties and Seventies* (New York: Longman, 1983), esp. pt. 4. Along with discovering the importance of strategy, movement theorists have come to appreciate the significance of activists; see Richard F. Hamilton and James Wright, *New Directions in Political Sociology* (Indianapolis: Bobbs-Merrill, 1975), pp. 40, 41; Richard E. Ratcliff, "Introduction," *Research in Social Movements, Conflicts, and Change* 6 (1984): xii; David Montgomery, "Spontaneity and Organization: Some Comments," *Radical America* 7 (November–December 1973): 70–80; and Aldon D. Morris, *The Origins of the Civil Rights Movement: Black Communities Organizing for Change* (New York: Free Press, 1984).

Chapter Five

1. The concept of political generations derives from Karl Mannheim, "The Problem of Generations," in *The New Pilgrims: Youth Protest in Transition,* ed. Philip G. Altbach and Robert S. Laufer (New York: David McKay, 1972), pp. 101–138; and Rudolf Heberle, *Social Movements:*

An Introduction to Political Sociology (New York: Appleton-Century-Crofts, 1951), chap. 6. Also see T. Allen Lambert, "Generations and Change: Toward a Theory of Generations as a Force in Historical Process," *Youth & Society* 4 (September 1972): 21–45; and Maurice Zeitlin, "Political Generations in the Cuban Working Class," *American Journal of Sociology* 71 (March 1966): 493–508.

2. Bernstein, *Turbulent Years;* Art Preis, *Labor's Giant Step: Twenty Years of the CIO* (New York: Pathfinder Press, 1964), chap. 4.

3. The doctor is quoted in Chiles, "General Strike," p. 449. Bridges placed the number of deaths at nine (1950 Deportation Hearing, p. 4842). Arrest records in San Francisco were compiled by Herbert Resner in "The Law in Action During the San Francisco Longshore and Maritime Strike of 1934" (Works Progress Administration Project, Alameda County, California, 1936, typescript), p. 23.

4. Pilcher, *Portland Longshoremen,* p. 46.

5. *San Francisco Chronicle,* May 10, 1934, p. 1; *Portland Oregonian,* May 12, 1934, p. 1; *Seattle Times,* May 13, 1934, p. 36.

6. Langley interview, February 4, 1982.

7. *San Pedro News Pilot,* May 15, 1934, p. 3.

8. Quin, *Big Strike,* pp. 58, 59.

9. *San Francisco Chronicle,* May 29, 1934, p. 1.

10. Bernstein, *Turbulent Years,* p. 271; Quin, *Big Strike,* p. 85.

11. George Morris, interview with author, Los Angeles, September 2, 1980. Internal party documents are contained in United States Congress, Senate Subcommittee of the Committee on Education and Labor, *Hearings on Violations of Free Speech and Rights of Labor,* 76th Cong., 2d sess., December 16, 18, 1939, p. 18182.

12. Mabon, "West Coast Waterfront and Sympathy Strikes," p. 66; *Seattle Times,* June 21, 1934, pp. 1, 9.

13. *Seattle Times,* June 23, 1934, p. 1. Seattle's police chief is quoted in Larrowe, *Shape-Up and Hiring Hall,* pp. 100, 101.

14. *Seattle Times,* July 1, 1934, p. 1; Fred Richardson, interview with author, Seattle, Washington, December 18, 1981.

15. *Voice of Action,* July 6, 1934, pp. 1, 4; *Seattle Times,* July 6, 1934, pp. 1, 9.

16. Quin, *Big Strike,* p. 110; Larrowe, *Harry Bridges,* pp. 66–68.

17. *San Francisco Chronicle,* July 6, 1934, p. 1; Bridges is quoted in ibid., July 11, 1934, p. 4.

18. The organizer's report appears in Grace Mettee, "Zero Hour on the Coast," *The Nation* 139 (July 25, 1934): 102.

19. Paul S. Taylor and Norman Leon Gold, "San Francisco and the

General Strike," *Survey Graphic* 23 (September 1934): 407; Mettee, "Zero Hour on the Coast," p. 102.

20. *San Francisco Chronicle,* July 10, 1934, pp. 1, 5. For more information on the general strike, see Wilfred H. Crook, *Communism and the General Strike* (Hamden, Conn.: Shoe String Press, 1960), chaps. 8, 9; and Richard T. LaPiere, "The General Strike in San Francisco: A Study of the Revolutionary Pattern," *Sociology and Social Research* 19 (March–April 1935): 355–363.

21. *Seattle Times,* July 3, 1934, p. 1, and July 5, 1934, p. 1.

22. Mowrey interview, December 21, 1981; *Portland Oregonian,* July 6, 1934, p. 1.

23. *Portland Oregonian,* July 7, 1934, p. 9.

24. Roger B. Buchanan, *Dock Strike: History of the 1934 Waterfront Strike in Portland, Oregon* (Everett, Wash.: Working Press, 1975), pp. 78, 79.

25. Joe Werner, interview with author, Portland, Oregon, July 15, 1985.

26. *Seattle Times,* July 20, 1934, p. 9; Richardson interview, December 18, 1981.

27. The transformative or liberating effect of collective violence and "disruptive events" has been noted by a number of scholars, including Charles F. Sabel, *Work and Politics: The Division of Labor in Industry* (Cambridge: Cambridge University Press, 1982), pp. 128–132; Frances Fox Piven and Richard A. Cloward, *Poor People's Movements: Why They Succeed, How They Fail* (New York: Vintage Books, 1979), p. 14; and Jeremy Brecher, *Strike!* (Greenwich, Conn.: Fawcett, 1972), chap. 7. More general discussions of collective violence and its relationship to movement success can be found in Charles Tilly, *From Mobilization to Revolution* (Reading, Mass.: Addison-Wesley, 1978), chap. 6; and William A. Gamson, *The Strategy of Social Protest* (Homewood, Ill.: Dorsey, 1975), chap. 6.

28. Mabon, "West Coast Waterfront and Sympathy Strikes," p. 120; *Longshoremen's Bulletin,* March 31, 1942; Nelson, "'Pentecost' on the Pacific," p. 161.

29. Asher Harer, interview with author, San Francisco, May 25, 1982.

30. Werner interview, July 15, 1985; *Waterfront Worker,* May 21, 1934, p. 4.

31. Schmidt is quoted in Chiles, "General Strike," p. 461; see also Eliel, "Industrial Peace and Conflict," p. 487.

32. *Western Worker,* September 17, 1934, pp. 1, 3, and September 30, 1934, pp. 1, 3.

33. Schneider and Siegel, *Industrial Relations,* p. 58.

34. For a discussion of the "choose your job" clause, see Quin, *Big Strike,* pp. 196–199.

35. The employer is quoted in Weir, *Informal Workers' Control,* p. 51.

36. See Mills and Wellman, "Contractually Sanctioned Job Action," for a more thorough discussion of the setting in which this control evolved.

37. Clark Kerr and Lloyd Fisher, "Conflict on the Waterfront," *Atlantic Monthly* 184 (September 1949): 18.

38. Camp (*San Francisco,* p. 471) reports that 561 work stoppages took place between October 1934 and November 1936.

39. *Marine Workers' Voice,* December 1934, p. 2. Figures on productivity and work stoppages are from Richard A. Liebes, "Longshore Labor Relations on the Pacific Coast, 1934–1942" (Ph.D. diss., University of California, Berkeley, 1943), p. 95; Leo Espy, "An Examination of the 1934 Waterfront Strike as a Turning-Point for West Coast Longshore Labor" (B.A. thesis, Reed College, 1952), p. 54.

40. Fred Nau, interview with Herb Mills and David Wellman, Sausalito, California, November 15, 1979; *Waterfront Worker,* October 22, 1934, p. 4; Langley interview, February 4, 1982.

41. Nelson, "'Pentecost' on the Pacific," pp. 150, 151.

42. For a brief history of the march inland, see Harvey Schwartz, "Union Expansion and Labor Solidarity: Longshoremen, Warehousemen, and Teamsters, 1933–1937," *New Labor Review* 2 (Fall 1978): 6–21.

43. For background on the Maritime Federation of the Pacific, see Robert J. Lampman, "The Rise and Fall of the Maritime Federation of the Pacific, 1935–1941," in *Proceedings of the Twenty-Fifth Annual Convention of the Pacific Coast Economic Association* (Corvallis, Ore.: Pacific Coast Economic Association, 1950), pp. 64–67. Bridges is quoted in Neuberger, "Bad-Man Bridges," p. 196.

44. Quin, *Big Strike,* p. 199; Nelson, "'Pentecost' on the Pacific," p. 162. Bridges is quoted in *Voice of the Federation,* October 24, 1935, p. 1.

45. Bridges's opposition to Roosevelt is reported in Theodore Dreiser, "The Story of Harry Bridges," *Friday* 1 (October 4, 1940): 8.

46. Irving Howe and Lewis Coser, *The American Communist Party: A Critical History (1919–1957)* (Boston: Beacon Press, 1957), pp. 184–186.

47. *New York Times,* February 16, 1936, sec. IV, p. 7.

48. *Voice of the Federation,* December 24, 1936, p. 4. The split that surfaced within the Maritime Federation between the Communists and the syndicalist-influenced left opposition was only partly ideological. It was also rooted in ongoing disagreements between the seamen and the

longshoremen about the scope and propriety of direct action tactics; see Nelson, "Maritime Unionism," chap. 7.

49. Archie Brown, interview with author, San Francisco, September 7, 1982; *Waterfront Worker,* February 24, 1936, p. 1. See Richard Alan Cushman, "The Communist Party and the Waterfront Strike of 1936–1937: The San Francisco Story" (M.A. thesis, San Francisco State College, 1970), for a more critical assessment of the Popular Front line on the waterfront.

50. Quin, *Big Strike,* pp. 218–236.

51. The *Marine Worker* is quoted in Cushman, "Communist Party and Waterfront Strike," p. 97. California's statewide recruitment totals are taken from William Schneiderman, *The Pacific Coast Maritime Strike* (San Francisco: Western Worker Publishers, 1937), p. 30. The breakdown by port and occupation is from the *Party Organizer* 10 (March–April 1937): 22, 23.

52. Roth is quoted in Liebes, "Longshore Labor Relations," p. 183.

53. Information on San Francisco's scrap iron incident is from Germain Bulcke, interview with author, San Francisco, September 4, 1981; Schmidt is quoted in Larrowe, *Harry Bridges,* p. 131.

54. *Voice of the Federation,* March 16, 1939, p. 1, and July 7, 1939, p. 1. An extensive discussion of the scrap iron protests can be found in Liebes, "Longshore Labor Relations," pp. 183–191.

55. Al Lannon, *The Maritime Workers and the Imperialist War* (New York: Communist Party, USA, 1939), p. 3. See Levenstein, *Communism, Anti-Communism, and the CIO,* pp. 84–87, for a discussion of the pact's consequences for labor.

56. The *New Republic* is quoted in Maurice Isserman, *Which Side Were You On? The American Communist Party During the Second World War* (Middletown, Conn.: Wesleyan University Press, 1982), p. 37.

57. Elmer Mevert, interview with author, San Pedro, California, June 2, 1981; Nelson, Barrett, and Ruck, *Steve Nelson,* p. 248.

58. Walter Galenson, *The CIO Challenge to the AFL: A History of the American Labor Movement, 1935–1941* (Cambridge: Harvard University Press, 1960), p. 448.

59. Baylin interview, January 23, 1984. Budd Schulberg, in "Joe Docks, Forgotten Man of the Waterfront" (*New York Times Magazine,* December 28, 1952, p. 29), describes the politics of New York's dockworkers: "Traditionally Democratic, as befits good New York Irish and Italians, but you might say their universal party is cynicism."

60. Vincent "Jim" Longhi, interview with author, New York, May 7, 1986.

61. The New York Crime Commission findings are reported in John

Hutchinson, *The Imperfect Union: A History of Corruption in American Trade Unions* (New York: E. P. Dutton, 1970), p. 103. Ryan is quoted in Mary Heaton Vorse, "The Pirates Nest of New York," *Harpers Magazine* 204 (April 1952): 33.

62. Larrowe, *Shape-Up and Hiring Hall,* p. 19; Hutchinson, *Imperfect Union,* p. 99.

63. Hutchinson, *Imperfect Union,* p. 98.

64. *Daily Worker,* May 27, 1933, p. 5; Vorse, "Pirates Nest," p. 28.

65. Bell, *End of Ideology,* p. 169; Hutchinson, *Imperfect Union,* p. 98.

66. For discussions of the effect of union decentralization and port size on industrial racketeering, see Robert Lamson, "The 1951 New York Wildcat Dock Strike: Some Consequences of Union Structure for Management-Labor Relations," *Southwestern Social Science Quarterly* 34 (March 1954): 37; and Larrowe, *Shape-Up and Hiring Hall,* p. 1.

67. Testifying in 1953 before the New York State Crime Commission, Bridges pointed out that "the same evils" found in New York "flourished in San Francisco" before 1934: "There was oversupply of labor, speed-up, irregularity of work, great inequality of earnings, with the majority earning less than enough to support themselves and their families. There was discrimination and favoritism. There was blacklisting, bribery, extortion, loan-sharking and kickbacks. The accident rate was high. . . . While conditions never became as bad as they are in New York, the seeds of corruption had begun to sprout and would without a doubt have produced full-fledged mobsters and racketeering had the sprouts not been cut off by the revolt of the men in 1934"; see Harry Bridges, President, "Statement on Behalf of the International Longshoremen's and Warehousemen's Union Before the New York State Crime Commission," 1953, typed transcript, p. 3, International Longshoremen's and Warehousemen's Union Papers, ILWU Library, San Francisco (hereafter cited as ILWU Papers). The reporter cited is Josephson ("Red Skies over the Water Front," p. 90).

68. Madell interview, May 6, 1986. For a more general analysis of the factors contributing to union racketeering in New York, see Philip Taft, *Corruption and Racketeering in the Labor Movement,* Bulletin no. 38 (Ithaca: New York State School of Industrial and Labor Relations, Cornell University, 1970), pp. 13–15.

69. Madell interview, October 6, 1981. Circulation figures for the *Shape-Up* are found in the August 24, 1936, issue. Anti-Ryan candidates were also elected in Boston and Philadelphia; see *Shape-Up,* January 7, 1937, p. 4.

70. Bridges's encounter with Ryan was reported by Louis Adamic in

"Harry Bridges Comes East," *The Nation* 143 (December 26, 1936): 753. Bridges's speech is quoted in *Shape-Up*, December 19, 1936, p. 4.

71. Endorsement of the CIO principles is reported in unsigned correspondence to Bridges, dated August 2, 1937, East Coast file, ILWU Papers. Jones's report appeared in the *ILWU Bulletin*, February 5, 1938, p. 3.

72. Felice Swados, "Waterfront," *New Republic* 93 (February 2, 1938): 362; Edward Levinson, "Waterfront East and West," *New Republic* 96 (September 14, 1938): 152. The delegate is quoted in *Shape-Up*, July 30, 1938, p. 1.

73. Madell interview, October 6, 1981.

74. Correspondence from Madell to Joe Curran, dated August 30, 1940, p. 1, East Coast file, ILWU Papers.

75. Correspondence from Curran to Bridges, dated August 10, 1940, p. 1; Curran to Bridges, dated October 1, 1940, p. 2; and Sam Kovnat to Matt [Meehan], dated July 5, 1939(?); all found in East Coast file, ILWU Papers.

76. Correspondence from Kovnat to Bob [Robertson], dated August 1939, East Coast file, ILWU Papers; Longhi interview, May 7, 1986. Subsequent investigations disclosed that Panto's murder had been ordered by Anthony Anastasia, chief executioner for the syndicate's "Murder, Inc.," and brother of Albert Anastasia, kingpin of the Brooklyn ILA; see Morris, *Tale of Two Waterfronts*, pp. 12, 13.

77. Madell interview, October 6, 1981; Bailey interview, September 15, 1981; Lew Amster, "Waterfront Gangsters," *Sunday Worker,* July 26, 1936, p. 1; the Reverend Philip Carey, interview with author, New York, October 6, 1981.

78. The solidarity that emerged out of the '34 men's historical experiences was reinforced in later years by their strong sense of community on the job; see Herb Mills, "The San Francisco Waterfront: The Social Consequences of Industrial Modernization," *Urban Life* 5 (July 1976): 221–250.

79. Sociology's ahistoricism is not without its critics. C. Wright Mills (in *The Sociological Imagination* [New York: Oxford University Press, 1954], chap. 8) long ago condemned the ahistorical bias of modern sociology. Objections have also been raised by Reinhard Bendix, whose work emphasizes not just the importance of history but also the variability and particularity of historical processes; see Dietrich Rueschemeyer, "Theoretical Generalization and Historical Particularity in the Comparative Sociology of Reinhard Bendix," in *Vision and Method in Historical Sociology*, ed. Theda Skocpol (Cambridge: Cambridge University Press, 1984), pp. 129–169. Also see Hamilton and Wright, *New Directions in Political Sociology*, pp. 32–39, on the significance of exceptional events.

Chapter Six

1. David Milton ("Class Struggle American Style," *Political Power and Social Theory* 4 [1984]: 265, 269) dates the left's decline from 1940, when Sidney Hillman and Philip Murray seized the reins of the CIO from John L. Lewis and the left. In the UE, the war stalled James Carey's bid to unseat the left; see Ronald L. Filippelli, "UE: An Uncertain Legacy," *Political Power and Social Theory* 4 (1984): 232–236. Harold Pritchett, Communist leader of the International Woodworkers of America, was not so lucky. In the forests of the Pacific Northwest the war came too late to deflect the right; see Jerry Lembcke and William M. Tatam, *One Union in Wood: A Political History of the International Woodworkers of America* (New York: International Publishers, 1984).

2. For an overview of the left's postwar decline, see Levenstein, *Communism, Anti-Communism, and the CIO,* chaps. 9–17; Cochran, *Labor and Communism,* chaps. 10–12; and George Lipsitz, *Class and Culture in Cold War America: "A Rainbow at Midnight"* (South Hadley, Mass.: J. F. Bergin, 1982), chaps. 7, 8. The 1948 NMU election results are reported in the *New York Times,* July 27, 1948, p. 45.

3. See, for example, Joshua Freeman, "Delivering the Goods: Industrial Unionism During World War II," *Labor History* 19 (Fall 1978): 587, 588; Stanley Weir, "U.S.A.: The Labor Revolt," in *American Society Inc.: Studies of the Social Structure and Political Economy of the United States,* 2d ed., ed. Maurice Zeitlin (Chicago: Rand McNally, 1977), pp. 487–524; and James Green, "Fighting on Two Fronts: Working-Class Militancy in the 1940s," *Radical America* 9 (July–August 1975): 38, 39.

4. See, for example, Preis, *Labor's Giant Step;* Joel Seidman, *American Labor from Defense to Reconversion* (Chicago: University of Chicago Press, 1953); Nelson Lichtenstein, "Defending the No-Strike Pledge: CIO Politics During World War II," *Radical America* 9 (July–August 1975): 49–75; Martin Glaberman, "Vanguard to Rearguard," *Political Power and Social Theory* 4 (1984): 37–62; and Stanley Aronowitz, *False Promises: The Shaping of American Working Class Consciousness* (New York: McGraw-Hill, 1973), p. 348.

5. Cochran, *Labor and Communism,* pp. 209, 211.

6. Levenstein, *Communism, Anti-Communism, and the CIO,* p. 163.

7. James West, "Communists in World War II," *Political Affairs* 48 (September–October 1969): 94. Party clubs or "cells" were dissolved in many industries by 1943; see Ozanne, "Effects of Communist Leadership," p. 136; and Isserman, *Which Side Were You On?* pp. 187–192.

8. See sources in note 4, above.

9. Ganley is quoted in Cochran, *Labor and Communism,* p. 220. The party's denunciations of wartime strikes are taken from Roger Keeran, *The Communist Party and the Auto Workers Union* (Bloomington: Indiana University Press, 1980), p. 243.

10. The NMU's wartime record is mentioned in Henry Spira, "The Unambiguity of Labor History," in *Autocracy and Insurgency in Organized Labor,* ed. Burton Hall (New Brunswick, N.J.: Transaction Books, 1972), p. 251. On the UE's "Speed-Up Committees," see Hugh G. Cleland, "The Political History of a Local Union: Local 601 of the CIO Electrical Workers Union" (Ph.D. diss., Western Reserve, 1957), p. 202.

11. Emspak is quoted in Epstein and Goldfinger, "Communist Tactics in American Unions," p. 41; Bridges is quoted in Larrowe, *Harry Bridges,* p. 255.

12. It is significant that Reuther, Quill, and Curran all consolidated their positions by attacking the Communist Party for its wartime lack of militancy, not by red-baiting per se; see James R. Prickett, "Communists and the Communist Issue in the American Labor Movement, 1920–1950" (Ph.D. diss., University of California, Los Angeles, 1975).

13. Bridges's speech to the group of civic leaders is quoted in William Davis Waring, "Harry Renton Bridges and the International Longshoremen's and Warehousemen's Union" (M.A. thesis, University of Washington, 1966), p. 67; Bridges's comments before the CIO council are taken from Preis, *Labor's Giant Step,* p. 185.

14. The Bridges Plan is briefly outlined in Richard P. Boyden, "The West Coast Longshoremen, the Communist Party, and the Second World War" (Department of History, University of California, Berkeley, 1967, typescript). San Francisco's endorsement of the plan is reported in *Longshoremen's Bulletin,* December 16, 1941. Minutes from the "stop work" meeting show no sign of any opposition.

15. The position of the Northwest locals is reported in *Longshoremen's Bulletin,* April 14, 1942; employers are quoted in ibid., January 13, 1942.

16. Productivity data are from C. Thomas, *West Coast Longshoremen and the "Bridges Plan"* (1943), p. 13.

17. Foisie is quoted in ibid., p. 14.

18. Correspondence from Abbott Boone to Brehon Somervell, dated August 25, 1943, Army Service Forces Papers, Record Group 160, Port of Embarcation 1942–1944, National Archives, Washington, D.C.; correspondence from Hugh Fulton to Maxwell Brandwen, dated July 27, 1943, War Shipping Administration Papers, Record Group 248, National Archives, Washington, D.C. Tipp's report is found in "Analysis of Captain Tipp's Reports," Box 8, MS. 1438, Francis Murnane Papers, Oregon

Historical Society, Portland, Oregon (hereafter cited as Captain Tipp's Reports).

19. Foisie's statement appeared in the *New York Times*, March 12, 1943, p. 22. The union's reply is in "Notes on Downey Hearing," dated April 23, 1943, p. 5, World War II file, ILWU Papers.

20. "The Union's War Record," dated February 1947, p. 6, World War II file, ILWU Papers.

21. "Statement of Chairman to Pacific Coast Maritime Industry Board, February 4, 1943," pp. 5, 6, Maxwell Brandwen Papers, Record Group 248, Box 12, Records of Maxwell Brandwen October 1942–April 1944, National Archives, Washington, D.C.

22. Harer interview, May 25, 1982.

23. Ship turnaround times are reported in "Wartime Shipping: A Plan and a Memorandum," Prepared and Submitted by Maritime Unions Affiliated with the Congress of Industrial Organizations, dated February 1943, p. 24, World War II file, ILWU Papers.

24. Work stoppages are recorded in "Chronological Index of Work Stoppages," compiled March 4, 1948, Pacific Maritime Association Papers, Pacific Maritime Association, San Francisco. Minutes from the joint union-employer Labor Relations Committee indicate that most disciplinary cases involved single individuals who were accused of violating military regulations or slacking off on the job. In 1942, for example, Portland's LRC heard eight cases involving a total of only eleven men. Six of these cases, involving nine men, concerned either drunkenness or smoking aboard ship. See Labor Relations Committee Minutes, Index to Local 8 Minutes, 1942, ILWU Papers.

25. Cronin's words were reconstructed in an interview included in Boyden, "West Coast Longshoremen," p. 34.

26. Keeran, *Communist Party and the Auto Workers Union*, p. 238.

27. Bailey interview, September 15, 1981.

28. Archie Brown, interview with author, San Francisco, September 7, 1982.

29. Seattle's position is reported in T. R. Richardson et al. to Labor Relations Committee, dated October 26, 1942, Local 19 file, Correspondence—General, 1936–1944 folder, ILWU Papers. Information on San Pedro is found in correspondence from N. Miller to Mr. McGowen, dated October 28, 1942, Labor Relations Committee Minutes, Local 13 file, ILWU Papers. When Bridges initially tried to sell the idea of a thirty-bag limit in San Pedro, he met with little success; see Larrowe, *Harry Bridges*, pp. 255, 256.

30. Harer interview, May 25, 1982. Another left critic of Bridges, Ed

Harris ("The Trouble with Harry Bridges," *International Socialist Review* 34 [September 1973]: 10), conceded that the longshoremen "maintained job control and working conditions" during the war.

31. Productivity data are from James Chester Armstrong, "A Critical Analysis of Cargo Handling Cost in the Steamship Industry" (M.A. thesis, University of California, Berkeley, 1947), pp. 133–135.

32. Joe Werner, interview with author, Portland, Oregon, December 14, 1981. "Four on/four off" evolved for different reasons in different ports. This account is based on a conversation with five retirees from the San Pedro local. In San Francisco the practice was already widespread by 1942; see Captain Tipp's Reports. Employer support for redundant labor is discussed in Bulcke interview, September 4, 1981.

33. "Excerpt from William Winter Broadcast—CBS—10:15 P.M. Friday May 26, '44," World War II file, ILWU Papers. Bridges's security preamble was denounced as "un-American" and worse by scores of union leaders; see *PM Magazine*, May 31, 1944. Even Communist leaders were reluctant to go along with an indefinite no-strike pledge; see Starobin, *American Communism in Crisis,* pp. 59, 77, 91.

34. *ILWU Dispatcher,* August 11, 1944, p. 6, and October 6, 1944, p. 7.

35. "Can We Allot Manpower by Voluntary Methods?" by William Haber, Director, Bureau of Program Planning, 1943, p. 1, War Production Board Papers, Record Group 179, Log no. 775, Class. no. 832. 2, Manpower Distribution, National Archives, Washington, D.C.

36. Stanley Weir, "American Labor on the Defensive: A 1940s Odyssey," *Radical America* 9 (July–August 1975): 167–169. The dynamics of union membership growth during the war are examined in Judith Stepan-Norris, "The War Labor Board: The Political Conformity and Bureaucratization of Organized Labor," in *How Mighty a Force? Studies of Workers' Consciousness and Organization in the United States,* ed. Maurice Zeitlin (Los Angeles: Institute of Industrial Relations, University of California, 1983), pp. 198–230.

37. "Can We Allot Manpower by Voluntary Methods?" by William Haber, 1943, p. 1, War Production Board Papers; Freeman, "Delivering the Goods," p. 587.

38. James J. Matles and James Higgins, *Them and Us: Struggles of a Rank and File Union* (Boston: Beacon Press, 1974), p. 137. The UE's rate of turnover is based on industry rates reported for the electrical, radio, and machine-working complex in United States Department of Labor, Bureau of Labor Statistics, *Handbook of Labor Statistics,* 1947 ed., Bulletin no. 916 (Washington, D.C.: Government Printing Office, 1948),

pp. 43–46 (hereafter cited as *Handbook of Labor Statistics 1947*). The description of convention delegates is reported in Cleland, "Political History of a Local Union," p. 218.

39. This conclusion is based on Ronald Schatz, *The Electrical Workers: A History of Labor at General Electric and Westinghouse, 1923–1960* (Urbana: University of Illinois Press, 1983), esp. pp. 195–197. Analyzing the bases of factionalism in the UE, Schatz finds that supporters of the anti-communist IUE were "comparatively young workers," whereas the UE's support came from "considerably older" men and women belonging "to that generation of workers born about 1900 who had founded local unions during the Great Depression."

40. Martin Glaberman, *Wartime Strikes: The Struggle Against the No-Strike Pledge in the UAW During World War II* (Detroit: Bedwick Editions, 1980), p. 17.

41. The demographics of Detroit's war population are reported in Keeran, *Communist Party and the Auto Workers Union*, p. 231. Communist leaders in the UAW, according to Levenstein, also traced their defeat to "wartime changes in the auto industry's work force, especially the influx of new workers from the South and Appalachia and the failure of many prewar militants to return to the industry after their mobilization" (*Communism, Anti-Communism, and the CIO*, p. 204).

42. The 15 percent figure, representing the combined monthly totals for 1942, includes a small number of nonmilitary withdrawals from the labor force, which are reported as "miscellaneous separations" in *Handbook of Labor Statistics 1947*, p. 42.

43. "Local 13 Members in U.S. Army," dated November 9, 1942, Local 13 file, ILWU Papers.

44. *ILWU Dispatcher*, November 2, 1945, p. 7.

45. "Essential activities" are identified in "List of Essential Activities," 1944, Document 7, Class. no. 832.11, Manpower Requirements, p. 4, War Production Board Papers. The "Longshore Battalions" are covered in the *Daily Commercial News*, July 3, 1942, pp. 1, 6.

46. *Handbook of Labor Statistics 1947*, p. 42.

47. Mevert interview, June 2, 1982; Werner interview, December 14, 1981.

48. L. B. Thomas to Clarence R. Johnson, dated May 15, 1942, Local 13 file, Correspondence—General, 1936–1944 folder, ILWU Papers; Langley interview, February 4, 1982.

49. Werner interview, December 14, 1981; *Longshoremen's Bulletin*, May 25, 1944.

50. Waterfront Employers to Eliel et al., dated July 1, 1942, Pacific Coast Maritime Industry Board file, Manpower—General, ILWU Papers;

"Increase in Membership of ILWU Longshore Locals Pacific Coast States—1943–1946," Membership Statistics file, ILWU Exhibit, Fact Finding Panel, April 1946, ILWU Papers; "Number of New Men Recruited Each Month in San Francisco, Seattle, Portland, Los Angeles–Long Beach and Tacoma, June 1943–August 1945, Incl.," Pacific Coast Maritime Industry Board file, Manpower—General, ILWU Papers.

51. Harer interview, May 25, 1982.

52. Ibid.

53. Odell Franklin, interview with author, Berkeley, California, January 23, 1984. For background on the "maverick" reputation of ILA locals in New Orleans and Houston, see Russell, *Men Along the Shore*, pp. 88, 134, 144; and Herbert R. Northrup, "The New Orleans Longshoremen," *Political Science Quarterly* 57 (December 1942): 539, 540.

54. L. B. Thomas to Clarence R. Johnson, dated May 15, 1942, Local 13 file, Correspondence—General, 1936–1944 folder, ILWU Papers; Bridges to Malcolm Ross, dated December 20, 1943, Local 8 file, Correspondence—General, 1937–1943 folder, ILWU Papers.

55. This combination of militancy on the job and ideological conservatism was characteristic of white "war babies" in other industries, especially auto; see Nelson Lichtenstein, "Auto Worker Militancy and the Structure of Factory Life, 1937–1955," *Journal of American History* 67 (September 1980): 335–353.

56. Personal correspondence from Gus Rystad, retired Seattle longshoreman, to author, dated February 26, 1984; Langley interview, February 4, 1982; Matt Meehan to Harry [Bridges], dated January 1, 1944, Local 8 file, Correspondence—General, 1937–1943 folder, ILWU Papers.

57. Karl Yoneda, interview with author, San Francisco, January 26, 1984. Yoneda's own case is illustrative of the ILWU's commitment to fighting racism. A known Communist and San Francisco longshoreman of Japanese descent, he was sheltered by his co-workers when government officials came to the docks early in the war to take him into custody for internment in a relocation center. The Communist Party suspended Yoneda during the war, and the shipowners opposed his registration in the industry. Only the ILWU came to his defense, as they did for other persecuted Japanese-Americans; see Harvey Schwartz, "A Union Combats Racism: The ILWU's Japanese-American 'Stockton Incident' of 1945," *Southern California Quarterly* 62 (Summer 1980): 161–176. Also see Lester Rubin, *The Negro in the Longshore Industry* (Philadelphia: Industrial Research Unit, The Wharton School, University of Pennsylvania, 1974); and David E. Thompson, "The ILWU as a Force for Interracial Unity in Hawaii," *Social Processes in Hawaii* 15 (1951): 32–43.

58. Philip S. Foner, *Organized Labor and the Black Worker, 1619–*

1973 (New York: International Publishers, 1974), p. 225; Philip S. Foner and Ronald L. Lewis, eds., *The Black Worker: A Documentary History from Colonial Times to the Present* (Philadelphia: Temple University Press, 1983), vol. 7, *The Black Worker from the Founding of the CIO to the AFL-CIO Merger, 1936–1955*, pp. 129, 130; Bulcke interview, September 4, 1981.

59. The number of men recruited in each port is from "Number of New Men Recruited," Pacific Coast Maritime Industry Board file, Manpower—General, ILWU Papers. Information on racial composition is based on Langley interview, February 4, 1982; Werner interview, December 14, 1981; and Cleophas Williams, interview with author, Oakland, California, January 25, 1984.

60. Williams interview, January 25, 1984.

61. Ibid.

62. Ibid.

63. Pacific American Shipowners, *White Paper: West Coast Maritime Strike* (San Francisco: Waterfront Employers' Association of California, 1948), p. 14; Randolph, "International Longshoremen's and Warehousemen's Union," pp. 105, 106. The 1948 strike inaugurated the "new look" in maritime labor relations, ushering in an era of peaceful coexistence on the docks. For an analysis of the 1948 strike as a turning point in labor relations, see Bruce Dancis, "San Francisco Employers and Longshore Labor Relations, 1934–1949: A Reinterpretation" (Department of History, Stanford University, 1975, typescript); and Kerr and Fisher, "Conflict on the Waterfront."

64. Harer interview, May 25, 1982. The Cold War made strange bedfellows. In Local 10, for example, Trotskyists usually sided with their old nemesis, the pro-Soviet left, rather than allying with the anti-communist opposition.

65. Seldon Osborne, interview with author, San Francisco, September 11, 1981.

66. Franklin interview, January 23, 1984.

67. "Indestructible Bridges," *New Republic* 120 (April 18, 1949): 7. In his many Cold War skirmishes with the right, Bridges counted not only on the veteran longshoremen but also on the ILWU's warehouse division and the huge Hawaiian locals, where his support on certain issues was even stronger than on the docks; see Wayne Hield, "What Keeps Harry Bridges Going?" *Labor and Nation* (January–March 1952): 38–40, 55; Sanford Zalburg, *A Spark Is Struck: Jack Hall and the ILWU in Hawaii* (Honolulu: University of Hawaii Press, 1979).

68. Eliel, "Industrial Peace and Conflict," p. 497; *Longshoremen's Bulletin*, May 14, 1948, p. 1.

69. *ILWU Dispatcher,* July 20, 1951, p. 2, and August 17, 1951, p. 6. The waterfront screening program is discussed more extensively in David Caute, *The Great Fear: The Anti-Communist Purge Under Truman and Eisenhower* (New York: Simon and Schuster, 1978), chap. 21; and Peter Trimble, "Thought Control on the Waterfront," *The Nation* 173 (July 14, 1951): 27–29.

70. Randolph, "International Longshoremen's and Warehousemen's Union," p. 219.

71. Levinson, "Left-Wing Labor," p. 1088; Franklin interview, January 23, 1984.

72. Ryan's support for the war effort is outlined in American Merchant Marine Conference, *1945 Proceedings* (New York, 1945), p. 135. Sling load weights are reported in *Business Week,* October 20, 1945, p. 96.

73. Bill Hagen and Larry Sullivan, interview with author, New York, October 1981.

74. For a discussion of informal work groups, see Weir, *Informal Workers' Control.*

75. Wartime changes in hiring are covered in Bell, *End of Ideology,* p. 163.

76. United States Congress, Senate Subcommittee on War Mobilization of the Committee on Military Affairs, *Mobilization of Shipping Resources,* 78th Cong., 1st sess., October 7, 1943, S. Rept. 3, p. 13. Vernon H. Jensen has estimated that between 60 and 80 percent of New York's longshoremen were in regular gangs by the early 1950s (*Strife on the Waterfront,* pp. 32, 33). Eugene V. Lyons, head of the New York Shipping Association, testified in 1953 that 90 percent of the men were in regular gangs; see New York, *Record of the Public Hearings Held by Governor Thomas E. Dewey on the Recommendations of the New York State Crime Commission for Remedying Conditions on the Waterfront of the Port of New York,* June 8, 9, 1953, pp. 219, 220. Regardless of the exact figure, it is clear that the use of steady gangs—which before the war was limited to the port's regularly employed longshoremen—increased markedly during the war.

77. Bell, *End of Ideology,* pp. 163, 164.

78. *New York Times,* March 24, 1942, p. 19. Several of the larger wartime wildcats were reported in the media; see *New York Times,* February 25, 1943, p. 23, and July 1, 1943, p. 11; *ILWU Dispatcher,* August 13, 1943, p. 3.

79. Correspondence from Roy [Hudson] to Browder, dated May 28, 1943, C.P. Intensive Post-War Efforts—General file, Box 3, Daniel Bell Papers.

80. Ibid.

81. Longhi interview, May 7, 1986; Mitchell Berenson, interview with author, Chappaqua, New York, May 8, 1986.

82. Tom Connolly, interview with author, New York, October 18, 1981.

83. The insurgent leader is quoted in Maurice Rosenblatt, "The Scandal of the Waterfront," *The Nation* 161 (November 17, 1945): 518. See Rank and File Committee (New York ILA), *This Is Our Story* (New York, 1945), for the strikers' demands.

84. Larrowe, *Shape-Up and Hiring Hall,* pp. 27, 28.

85. United States Congress, Senate Committee on the Judiciary, Hearings Before the Subcommittee to Investigate the Administration of the Internal Security Act and Other Internal Security Laws, *Scope of Soviet Activity in the United States, Communism on the Waterfront,* 84th Cong., 2d sess., June 21 and July 12, 1956, pt. 30, pp. 1627, 1628; Jensen, *Strife on the Waterfront,* p. 52. The party's involvement in the strike is chronicled by Hal Simon, "The Rank and File Strike of the New York Longshoremen," *Political Affairs* 24 (December 1945): 1088–1096.

86. Rosenblatt, "Scandal of the Waterfront," p. 518. Work stoppages are reported in Russell, *Men Along the Shore,* p. 154.

87. Larrowe, *Shape-Up and Hiring Hall,* p. 46.

88. Newspaper clippings and leaflets concerning the ILA's anticommunist boycott are collected in the Waterfront file, Xavier Institute of Industrial Relations Papers, Xavier Institute of Industrial Relations, New York; longshoreman quoted in Schulberg, "Joe Docks," p. 30.

89. While dockworkers in New York were boycotting the Soviet Union for its invasion of Afghanistan and threatening to also boycott Poland for clamping down on Solidarity, West Coast dockworkers were refusing to handle cargo bound for the right-wing governments of South Africa and El Salvador; see *Washington Post,* January 10, 1980, p. 1; *Los Angeles Times,* December 23, 1980, p. 1, January 31, 1982, p. 14, and November 11, 1984, p. 2.

90. Bridges is quoted in "To All Longshore, Shipclerks and Bosses Locals," dated September 19, 1950, p. 2, World War II file, ILWU Papers.

Chapter Seven

1. Carey is quoted in Foner, *Organized Labor and the Black Worker,* p. 283.

2. Caute, *The Great Fear,* p. 352. The consequences of the expulsion are discussed in Emspak, "Breakup of the CIO," pp. 129–133; and Cochran, *Labor and Communism,* chap. 12.

3. Starobin, *American Communism in Crisis*, p. 109; John H. M. Laslett, "Why Is There Not More of a Socialist Movement in the United States?" *Reviews in American History* 5 (June 1977): 265. For a less sanguine assessment of labor's political capabilities after the war, see Robert H. Zieger, *American Workers, American Unions, 1920–1985* (Baltimore: Johns Hopkins University Press, 1986), pp. 114–123.

4. Max Weber, *The Methodology of the Social Sciences* (New York: Free Press, 1949), pp. 182–183.

5. Maurice Zeitlin, "On Classes, Class Conflict, and the State: An Introductory Note," in *Classes, Class Conflict, and the State: Empirical Studies in Class Analysis,* ed. Maurice Zeitlin (Cambridge, Mass.: Winthrop, 1980), p. 3. Also see Adam Przeworski's provocative essay "Proletariat into a Class: The Process of Class Formation from Karl Kautsky's *The Class Struggle* to Recent Controversies," *Politics & Society* 7, no. 4 (1977): 343–401.

6. Herb Mills, interview with author, San Francisco, California, September 4, 1981.

7. "Comparative Absolute Figures of Basic Industry," on microfilm, reel 3, series 2–47, p. 3, Earl Browder Papers; Brown interview, September 12, 1981.

8. Bridges's comments about the IWW are taken from Larrowe, *Harry Bridges*, pp. 6, 7.

9. Starobin, *American Communism in Crisis*, p. 286.

10. Repression was not just ineffective—it backfired, uniting the entire membership behind Bridges and making him "almost sacrosanct . . . within the ILWU"; see Jacobs, *State of the Unions*, p. 99.

11. John R. Commons, "American Shoemakers, 1648–1895: A Sketch of Industrial Evolution," *Quarterly Journal of Economics* 24 (November 1909): 39–84; Mancur Olson, Jr., *The Logic of Collective Action: Public Goods and the Theory of Groups* (Cambridge: Harvard University Press, 1965). In the contest between the AFL and the socialists, Perlman avers that the former flourished because its economism better "fitted" the "scarcity consciousness" of American workers. Adopting Perlman's reasoning, a number of authors have tied the fortunes of the Communists to their performance at the bargaining table. Thus, David Brody ("Labor and the Great Depression: The Interpretative Prospects," *Labor History* 13 [Spring 1972]: 241) argues that Communist leaders were thrown out of office when they subordinated economics to politics, while Bernstein (*Turbulent Years*, p. 783) attributes their isolated successes to delivering the goods. A similar form of economism figures prominently in the burgeoning literature on the determinants of union growth. Reviewing this research, Herbert G. Heneman III and Marcus H.

Sandver ("Predicting the Outcome of Union Certification Elections: A Review of the Literature," *Industrial and Labor Relations Review* 36 [July 1983]: 553) argue for a "stronger theoretical framework," one that incorporates such noneconomic variables as the social backgrounds of employees, their history of contact with unions, belief in the desirability of change, and peer group pressure.

12. See Laslett, "Socialism and the American Labor Movement."

13. The economic appeal of unionism is hardly a peculiarity of American labor. Among Europe's more "radical" workers, it seems, union loyalty is still based overwhelmingly on job-related issues; see William H. Form, "Job Unionism Versus Industrial Unionism in Four Countries," in *The American Working Class: Prospects for the 1980s,* ed. Irving Louis Horowitz, John C. Leggett, and Martin Oppenheimer (New Brunswick, N.J.: Transaction Books, 1979), pp. 214–230.

14. Saposs, *Communism in American Unions,* p. 185. The consensus on the economic effectiveness of Communist trade unionism is fairly remarkable, spanning the Communist Party's critics from left to right; see Prickett, "Communists and the Communist Issue"; and Ozanne, "Effects of Communist Leadership."

15. This interpretation runs counter to the contentions of many writers, especially leftists, that red-baiting was largely ineffective; see James R. Prickett, "Communism and Factionalism in the United Automobile Workers, 1939–1947," *Science & Society* 32 (Summer 1968): 271; Michael Harrington, "Catholics in the Labor Movement: A Case History," *Labor History* 1 (Fall 1960): 260. By itself, red-baiting seems to have been ineffective. But when combined with aggressive bargaining and militant rhetoric it gave anti-communist insurgents added, and often critical, leverage in their efforts to dislodge the left.

16. Franklin J. Anderson, "Behind the Matles Mask," *Plain Talk* (September 1947): 23–24. Aronowitz attributes the machinists' extraordinary loyalty to Matles's "close relationship with local leaders over the years" (*False Promises,* pp. 347, 348).

17. The worker from the Marine Cooks is quoted in Jane Cassels Record, "The Rise and Fall of a Maritime Union," *Industrial and Labor Relations Review* 10 (October 1956): 92. The black miner is quoted in Prickett, "Communists and the Communist Issue," p. 417. The Communists' responsiveness to racism was partly a product of ideology, but it varied somewhat depending on the racial composition of the unions they headed; see Donald T. Critchlow, "Communist Unions and Racism: A Comparative Study of the Responses of the United Electrical, Radio and Machine Workers and the National Maritime Union to the Black Question During World War II," *Labor History* 17 (Spring 1976): 230–244.

Bibliography

This bibliography is divided into three sections: general references (including books, articles, public documents, and unpublished manuscripts); archival sources; and oral histories (including transcripts and tape recordings). Various newspapers published in New York and West Coast cities, by labor organizations, and by the left also were widely consulted for this study; newspaper articles are cited in the notes.

General References

Adamic, Louis. "Harry Bridges: Rank-and-File Leader." *The Nation* 142 (May 6, 1936): 576–580.

———. "Harry Bridges Comes East." *The Nation* 143 (December 26, 1936): 753.

American Bureau of Shipping. *1930 Record of American and Foreign Shipping*. New York: American Bureau of Shipping, 1930.

American Merchant Marine Conference. *1945 Proceedings*. New York, 1945.

Amster, Lew. "Waterfront Gangsters." *Sunday Worker,* July 26, 1936, p. 1.

Anderson, Franklin J. "Behind the Matles Mask." *Plain Talk,* September 1947, pp. 23–24.

Armstrong, James Chester. "A Critical Analysis of Cargo Handling Cost in the Steamship Industry." M.A. thesis, University of California, Berkeley, 1947.

Aronowitz, Stanley. *False Promises: The Shaping of American Working Class Consciousness*. New York: McGraw-Hill, 1973.

Averitt, Robert T. *The Dual Economy: The Dynamics of American Industry Structure*. New York: W. W. Norton, 1968.

Barbash, Jack. "Ethnic Factors in the Development of the American Labor Movement." In *Interpreting the Labor Movement*, Industrial Relations Research Association, Publication no. 9, pp. 70–82. Champaign, Ill.: Industrial Relations Research Association, 1952.

———. *Labor Unions in Action*. New York: Harper & Brothers, 1948.

———. *The Practice of Unionism*. New York: Harper & Brothers, 1956.

Barnes, Charles B. *The Longshoremen*. New York: Russell Sage Foundation, 1915.

Bart, Philip, Theodore Bassett, William W. Weinstone, and Arthur Zipser, eds. *Highlights of a Fighting History: 60 Years of the Communist Party, USA*. New York: International Publishers, 1979.

Bell, Daniel. *The End of Ideology: On the Exhaustion of Political Ideas in the Fifties*. Glencoe, Ill.: Free Press, 1960.

Bendix, Reinhard. *Work and Authority in Industry: Ideologies of Management in the Course of Industrialization*. Berkeley and Los Angeles: University of California Press, 1956.

Berenson, Harold. "The Community and Family Bases of U.S. Working-Class Protest, 1880–1920: A Critique of the 'Skill Degradation' and 'Ecological' Perspectives." *Research in Social Movements, Conflicts, and Change* 8 (1985): 109–132.

Bernstein, Irving. *Turbulent Years: A History of American Workers, 1933–1941*. Boston: Houghton Mifflin, 1970.

Blauner, Robert. *Alienation and Freedom: The Factory Worker and His Industry*. Chicago: University of Chicago Press, 1964.

Bonnett, Clarence E. *History of Employers' Associations in the United States*. New York: Vintage Books, 1956.

Bonthius, Andrew. "Origins of the International Longshoremen's and Warehousemen's Union." *Southern California Quarterly* 59, no. 4 (1977): 379–426.

Booth, Douglas E. "Collective Action, Marx's Class Theory, and the Union Movement." *Journal of Economic Issues* 12 (March 1978): 163–185.

Boyden, Richard P. "The West Coast Longshoremen, the Communist Party, and the Second World War." Department of History, University of California, Berkeley, 1967. Typescript.

Boyer, Richard O., and Herbert M. Morais. *Labor's Untold Story*. New York: United Electrical, Radio and Machine Workers of America, 1955.

Brecher, Jeremy. *Strike!* Greenwich, Conn.: Fawcett, 1972.

Brody, David. "Labor and the Great Depression: The Interpretative Prospects." *Labor History* 13 (Spring 1972): 231–244.

————. "Radical Labor History and Rank-and-File Militancy." *Labor History* 16 (Winter 1975): 117–126.

Buchanan, Roger B. *Dock Strike: History of the 1934 Waterfront Strike in Portland, Oregon.* Everett, Wash.: Working Press, 1975.

Butler, Richard J., and Joseph Driscoll. *Dock Walloper: The Story of 'Big Dick' Butler.* New York: Putnam, 1933.

Cameron, David R. "Toward a Theory of Political Mobilization." *Journal of Politics* 36 (February 1974): 138–171.

Camp, William Martin. *San Francisco: Port of Gold.* Garden City, N.Y.: Doubleday, 1947.

Caute, David. *The Great Fear: The Anti-Communist Purge Under Truman and Eisenhower.* New York: Simon and Schuster, 1978.

Chiles, Frederick. "General Strike: San Francisco, 1934—An Historical Compilation Film Storyboard." *Labor History* 22 (Summer 1981): 430–463.

Cleland, Hugh G. "The Political History of a Local Union: Local 601 of the CIO Electrical Workers Union." Ph.D. dissertation, Western Reserve, 1957.

Clements, Joyce. "The San Francisco Maritime and General Strikes of 1934 and the Dynamics of Repression." Ph.D. dissertation, University of California, Berkeley, 1975.

Cochran, Bert. *Labor and Communism: The Conflict That Shaped American Unions.* Princeton: Princeton University Press, 1977.

Collins, John J. "Longshoremen of the Port of New York." M.A. thesis, New School for Social Research, 1955.

Commons, John R. "American Shoemakers, 1648–1895: A Sketch of Industrial Evolution." *Quarterly Journal of Economics* 24 (November 1909): 39–84.

Congress of Industrial Organizations. *Proceedings of the Eleventh Constitutional Convention,* Cleveland, Ohio, October 31–November 4, 1949.

Covello, Leonard. "The Influence of Southern Italian Family Mores upon the School Situation in America." In *The Italians: Social Background of an American Group,* edited by Francesco Cordasco and Eugene Bucchioni, pp. 511–565. Clifton, N.J.: Augustus M. Kelley, 1974.

Critchlow, Donald T. "Communist Unions and Racism: A Comparative Study of the Responses of the United Electrical, Radio and Machine Workers and the National Maritime Union to the Black Question During World War II." *Labor History* 17 (Spring 1976): 230–244.

Crook, Wilfred H. *Communism and the General Strike.* Hamden, Conn.: Shoe String Press, 1960.

Cushman, Richard Alan. "The Communist Party and the Waterfront Strike of 1936–1937: The San Francisco Story." M.A. thesis, San Francisco State College, 1970.

Dancis, Bruce. "San Francisco Employers and Longshore Labor Relations, 1934–1949: A Reinterpretation." Department of History, Stanford University, 1975. Typescript.

Darcy, Sam. "The Great West Coast Maritime Strike." *Communist* 13 (July 1934): 664–686.

———. "San Francisco General Strike—1934." *Hawsepipe: Newsletter of the Marine Workers Historical Association* 1 (September–October 1982): 1, 7, 8, 9.

Davis, Mike. "The Stop Watch and the Wooden Shoe: Scientific Management and the Industrial Workers of the World." *Radical America* 9 (January–February 1975): 69–95.

———. "Why the U.S. Working Class Is Different." *New Left Review* 123 (September–October 1980): 3–44.

"Dock Employment in New York City." *Monthly Labor Review* 4 (February 1917): 290–294.

Dorfman, Joe. "The Longshoremen Strikes of 1922 and After." B.A. thesis, Reed College, 1924.

Dreiser, Theodore. "The Story of Harry Bridges." *Friday* 1 (October 4, 1940): 2–8, 28.

Dublin, Louis I., and Robert J. Vane. "Shifting of Occupations Among Wage Earners as Determined by Occupational History of Industrial Policyholders." *Monthly Labor Review* 18 (April 1924): 34–43.

Dubofsky, Melvyn. *Industrialism and the American Worker, 1865–1920.* Arlington Heights, Ill.: AHM Publishing, 1975.

Dunne, William F. *The Great San Francisco General Strike.* New York: Workers' Library, [1934].

Edwards, P. K. "A Critique of the Kerr-Siegel Hypothesis of Strikes and the Isolated Mass: A Study of the Falsification of Sociological Knowledge." *Sociological Review* 25 (August 1977): 551–574.

Eliel, Paul. "Industrial Peace and Conflict: A Study of Two Pacific Coast Industries." *Industrial and Labor Relations Review* 2 (July 1949): 477–501.

———. "Labor Problems in Our Steamship Business." *Yale Review* 26 (March 1937): 510–532.

———. *The Waterfront and the General Strike.* San Francisco: Hooper, 1934.

Emspak, Frank. "The Breakup of the CIO." *Political Power and Social Theory* 4 (1984): 101–139.

Engels, Friedrich. "Engels to Florence Kelley Wischnewetsky, London,

June 3, 1886." In *The Correspondence of Marx and Engels,* edited by Dona Torr, pp. 448–449. New York: International Publishers, 1935.

Epstein, Albert, and Nathaniel Goldfinger. "Communist Tactics in American Unions." *Labor and Nation* 6 (Fall 1950): 36–43.

Espy, Leo. "An Examination of the 1934 Waterfront Strike as a Turning-Point for West Coast Longshore Labor." B.A. thesis, Reed College, 1952.

Fairley, Lincoln. *Facing Mechanization: The West Coast Longshore Plan.* Monograph no. 23. Los Angeles: Institute of Industrial Relations, University of California, Los Angeles, 1979.

Filippelli, Ronald L. "UE: An Uncertain Legacy." *Political Power and Social Theory* 4 (1984): 217–252.

Foisie, Frank P. "Stabilizing Seattle's Longshore Labor." Statement presented at the National Conference of Social Work, Denver, Colorado, June 11, 1925. Labor Collection, Social Science Library, University of California, Berkeley. Typescript.

Foner, Eric. "Why Is There No Socialism in the United States?" *History Workshop* 17 (Spring 1984): 57–80.

Foner, Philip S. *Organized Labor and the Black Worker, 1619–1973.* New York: International Publishers, 1974.

Foner, Philip S., and Ronald L. Lewis, eds. *The Black Worker: A Documentary History from Colonial Times to the Present.* Vol. 7, *The Black Worker from the Founding of the CIO to the AFL-CIO Merger, 1936–1955.* Philadelphia: Temple University Press, 1983.

Form, William H. "Job Unionism Versus Political Unionism in Four Countries." In *The American Working Class: Prospects for the 1980s,* edited by Irving Louis Horowitz, John C. Leggett, and Martin Oppenheimer, pp. 214–230. New Brunswick, N.J.: Transaction Books, 1979.

Freeman, Jo, ed. *Social Movements of the Sixties and Seventies.* New York: Longman, 1983.

Freeman, Joshua. "Catholics, Communists, and Republicans: Irish Workers and the Organization of the Transport Workers Union." In *Working-Class America: Essays on Labor, Community, and American Society,* edited by Michael H. Frisch and Daniel J. Walkowitz, pp. 256–283. Urbana: University of Illinois Press, 1983.

———. "Delivering the Goods: Industrial Unionism During World War II." *Labor History* 19 (Fall 1978): 570–593.

Freeman, Richard B. "Effects of Unions on the Economy." In *Unions in Transition: Entering the Second Century,* edited by Seymour Martin Lipset, pp. 177–200. San Francisco: Institute for Contemporary Studies, 1986.

Friedmann, Robert L. *The Seattle General Strike*. Seattle: University of Washington Press, 1964.

Galenson, Walter. *The CIO Challenge to the AFL: A History of the American Labor Movement, 1935–1941*. Cambridge: Harvard University Press, 1960.

———. "Communists and Trade Union Democracy." *Industrial Relations* 13 (October 1974): 228–236.

Gallie, Duncan. *Social Inequality and Class Radicalism in France and Britain*. Cambridge: Cambridge University Press, 1983.

Gamson, William A. *The Strategy of Social Protest*. Homewood, Ill.: Dorsey, 1975.

Glaberman, Martin. "Vanguard to Rearguard." *Political Power and Social Theory* 4 (1984): 37–62.

———. *Wartime Strikes: The Struggle Against the No-Strike Pledge in the UAW During World War II*. Detroit: Bedwick Editions, 1980.

Glazer, Nathan. *The Social Basis of American Communism*. New York: Harcourt, Brace & World, 1961.

Goldberg, Joseph P. *The Maritime Story: A Study in Labor-Management Relations*. Cambridge: Harvard University Press, 1958.

Golden, Clinton, and Harold Ruttenberg. *Dynamics of Industrial Democracy*. New York: Harper & Brothers, 1942.

Goodman, Jay Selwyn. "One-Party Union Government: The I.L.W.U. Case." M.A. thesis, Stanford University, 1963.

Gorter, Wytze, and George H. Hildebrand. *The Pacific Coast Maritime Shipping Industry, 1930–1948*. Vol. 2, *An Analysis of Performance*. Berkeley and Los Angeles: University of California Press, 1954.

Green, James. "Fighting on Two Fronts: Working-Class Militancy in the 1940s." *Radical America* 9 (July–August 1975): 7–47.

Grob, Gerald N. *Workers and Utopia: A Study of Ideological Conflict in the American Labor Movement, 1865–1900*. Chicago: Quadrangle Books, 1969.

Gutman, Herbert G. *Power and Culture: Essays on the American Working Class*. Edited by Ira Berlin. New York: Pantheon, 1987.

———. *Work, Culture, and Society in Industrializing America: Essays in American Working-Class and Social History*. New York: Vintage Books, 1977.

Hamilton, Richard F. *Affluence and the French Worker in the Fourth Republic*. Princeton: Princeton University Press, 1964.

Hamilton, Richard F., and James Wright. *New Directions in Political Sociology*. Indianapolis: Bobbs-Merrill, 1975.

Harrington, Michael. "Catholics in the Labor Movement: A Case History." *Labor History* 1 (Fall 1960): 231–263.

Harris, Ed. "The Trouble with Harry Bridges." *International Socialist Review* 34 (September 1973): 6–11, 39.

Hartman, Paul T. *Collective Bargaining and Productivity: The Longshore Mechanization Agreement.* Berkeley and Los Angeles: University of California Press, 1969.

Healey, James C. *Foc's'le and Glory Hole: A Study of the Merchant Seaman and His Occupation.* New York: Merchant Marine Publishers Association, 1936.

Heberle, Rudolf. *Social Movements: An Introduction to Political Sociology.* New York: Appleton-Century-Crofts, 1951.

Heneman, Herbert G., III, and Marcus H. Sandver. "Predicting the Outcome of Union Certification Elections: A Review of the Literature." *Industrial and Labor Relations Review* 36 (July 1983): 537–559.

Hield, Wayne Wilbur. "Democracy and Oligarchy in the International Longshoremen's and Warehousemen's Union." M.A. thesis, University of California, Berkeley, 1949.

———. "What Keeps Harry Bridges Going?" *Labor and Nation* (January–March 1952): 38–40, 55.

Hobsbawm, Eric. *Labouring Men.* London: Wiedenfeld and Nicolson, 1964.

Hodson, Randy. *Workers' Earnings and Corporate Economic Structure.* New York: Academic Press, 1983.

Holt, James. "Trade Unionism in the British and U.S. Steel Industries, 1888–1912: A Comparative Study." *Labor History* 18 (Winter 1977): 5–35.

Howd, Cloice R. *Industrial Relations in the West Coast Lumber Industry.* Bureau of Labor Statistics Bulletin no. 349. Washington, D.C.: Government Printing Office, 1924.

Howe, Irving, and Lewis Coser. *The American Communist Party: A Critical History (1919–1957).* Boston: Beacon Press, 1957.

Hudson, Roy. "Rooting the Party on the Waterfront." *Party Organizer* 14 (December 1934): 1164–1170.

———. "The Work of the Marine Union." *Party Organizer* 7 (May–June 1934): 26–30.

Hutchinson, John. *The Imperfect Union: A History of Corruption in American Trade Unions.* New York: E. P. Dutton, 1970.

"Indestructible Bridges." *New Republic* 120 (April 18, 1949).

Industrial Workers of the World. *The Lumber Industry and Its Workers.* Chicago: Industrial Workers of the World, n.d.

International Longshoremen's Association, Local 38–79. *The Maritime Crisis: What It Is and What It Isn't.* San Francisco: International Longshoremen's Association, [1937].

Isserman, Maurice. *Which Side Were You On? The American Communist Party During the Second World War.* Middletown, Conn.: Wesleyan University Press, 1982.

Jacobs, Paul. *The State of the Unions.* New York: Atheneum, 1963.

Jensen, Vernon H. *Hiring of Dock Workers and Employment Practices in the Ports of New York, Liverpool, London, Rotterdam, and Marseilles.* Cambridge: Harvard University Press, 1969.

———. *Strife on the Waterfront: The Port of New York Since 1945.* Ithaca: Cornell University Press, 1974.

Johns, Orrick. *Time of Our Lives: The Story of My Father and Myself.* New York: Stackpole, 1937.

Johnson, Malcolm. *Crime on the Labor Front.* New York: McGraw-Hill, 1950.

Josephson, Mathew. "Red Skies over the Water Front." *Colliers* 118 (October 5, 1946): 17, 88–90.

Kagel, Sam. "A Right Wing Dual Union." 1930. Typescript.

Kampelman, Max M. *The Communist Party vs. the CIO: A Study in Power Politics.* New York: Praeger, 1957.

Karsh, Bernard, and Phillips L. Garmen. "The Impact of the Political Left." In *Labor and the New Deal,* edited by Milton Derber and Edwin Young, pp. 77–119. Madison: University of Wisconsin Press, 1961.

Karson, Marc. "Catholic Anti-Socialism." In *Failure of a Dream? Essays in the History of American Socialism,* rev. ed., edited by John H. M. Laslett and Seymour Martin Lipset, pp. 82–102. Berkeley and Los Angeles: University of California Press, 1984.

Keeran, Roger. *The Communist Party and the Auto Workers Union.* Bloomington: Indiana University Press, 1980.

Keitel, Robert S. "The Merger of the International Union of Mine, Mill and Smelter Workers into the United Steelworkers of America." *Labor History* 15 (Winter 1974): 36–43.

Kendall, Patricia L., and Katherine M. Wolf. "The Two Purposes of Deviant Case Analysis." In *The Language of Social Research: A Reader in the Methodology of Social Research,* edited by Paul F. Lazarsfeld and Morris Rosenberg, pp. 167–170. Glencoe, Ill.: Free Press, 1955.

Kerr, Clark, and Lloyd Fisher. "Conflict on the Waterfront." *Atlantic Monthly* 184 (September 1949): 17–23.

———. "Multiple Employer Bargaining: The S.F. Experience." In *Insights into Labor Issues,* edited by Richard A. Lester and Joseph Shister, pp. 25–61. New York: Macmillan, 1948.

Kerr, Clark, and Abraham J. Siegel. "The Interindustry Propensity to

Strike—An International Comparison." In *Labor and Management in Industrial Society*, edited by Clark Kerr, pp. 105–147. Garden City, N.Y.: Doubleday, 1964.

Klehr, Harvey. *The Heyday of American Communism: The Depression Decade*. New York: Basic Books, 1984.

Kolko, Gabriel. *The Triumph of Conservatism: A Reinterpretation of American History, 1900–1916*. New York: Free Press, 1963.

Kruijt, Dirk, and Menno Vellinga. "On Strike and Strike Propensity." *The Netherlands Journal of Sociology* 12 (December 1976): 137–151.

Kwoka, John E., Jr. "Monopoly, Plant, and Union Effects on Worker Wages." *Industrial and Labor Relations Review* 36 (January 1983): 251–257.

Lambert, T. Allen. "Generations and Change: Toward a Theory of Generations as a Force in Historical Process." *Youth & Society* 4 (September 1972): 21–45.

Lampman, Robert J. "The Rise and Fall of the Maritime Federation of the Pacific, 1935–1941." In *Proceedings of the Twenty-Fifth Annual Convention of the Pacific Coast Economic Association*, pp. 64–67. Corvallis, Ore.: Pacific Coast Economic Association, 1950.

Lamson, Robert. "The 1951 New York Wildcat Dock Strike: Some Consequences of Union Structure for Management-Labor Relations." *Southwestern Social Science Quarterly* 34 (March 1954): 28–38.

Lang, Frederick J. *Maritime: A Historical Sketch and a Workers' Program*. New York: Pioneer Publishers, 1943.

Lannon, Al. *The Maritime Workers and the Imperialist War*. New York: Communist Party, USA, 1939.

LaPiere, Richard T. "The General Strike in San Francisco: A Study of the Revolutionary Pattern." *Sociology and Social Research* 19 (March–April 1935): 355–363.

Larrowe, Charles P. *Harry Bridges: The Rise and Fall of Radical Labor in the United States*. 2d ed. Westport, Conn.: Lawrence Hill, 1977.

———. *Maritime Labor Relations on the Great Lakes*. East Lansing: Labor and Industrial Relations Center, Michigan State University, 1959.

———. *Shape-Up and Hiring Hall: A Comparison of Hiring Methods and Labor Relations on the New York and Seattle Waterfronts*. Berkeley and Los Angeles: University of California Press, 1955.

Lash, Scott. *The Militant Worker: Class and Radicalism in France and America*. London: Heinemann, 1984.

Laski, Harold. *Trade Unions in a New Society*. New York: Viking Press, 1949.

Laslett, John H. M. "Giving Superman a Human Face: American Communism and the Automobile Workers in the 1930s." *Reviews in American History* 9 (March 1981): 112–117.

———. "Socialism and the American Labor Movement: Some New Reflections." *Labor History* 8 (Spring 1967): 136–155.

———. "Why Is There Not More of a Socialist Movement in the United States?" *Reviews in American History* 5 (June 1977): 262–268.

Laslett, John H. M., and Seymour M. Lipset, eds. *Failure of a Dream? Essays in the History of American Socialism*. Rev. ed. Berkeley and Los Angeles: University of California Press, 1984.

Leggett, John C. *Class, Race, and Labor: Working-Class Consciousness in Detroit*. Oxford: Oxford University Press, 1968.

Leinenweber, Charles. "The Class and Ethnic Bases of New York City Socialism, 1904–1915." *Labor History* 22 (Winter 1981): 31–56.

Lembcke, Jerry, and William M. Tatam. *One Union in Wood: A Political History of the International Woodworkers of America*. New York: International Publishers, 1984.

Levenstein, Harvey A. *Communism, Anti-Communism, and the CIO*. Westport, Conn.: Greenwood Press, 1981.

———. "Economism, Anti-Economism, and the History of the Communist Party." *Political Power and Social Theory* 4 (1984): 289–295.

Levinson, David A. "Left-Wing Labor and the Taft-Hartley Act." *Labor Law Journal* 1 (November 1950): 1079–1094.

Levinson, Edward. "Waterfront East and West." *New Republic* 96 (September 14, 1938): 151–153.

Levinson, Harold M. *Determining Forces in Collective Bargaining*. New York: Wiley, 1966.

———. "Unionism, Concentration, and Wage Changes: Toward a Unified Theory." *Industrial and Labor Relations Review* 20 (January 1967): 198–205.

Lichtenstein, Nelson. "Auto Worker Militancy and the Structure of Factory Life, 1937–1955." *Journal of American History* 67 (September 1980): 335–353.

———. "Defending the No-Strike Pledge: CIO Politics During World War II." *Radical America* 9 (July–August 1975): 49–75.

Liebes, Richard A. "Longshore Labor Relations on the Pacific Coast, 1934–1942." Ph.D. dissertation, University of California, Berkeley, 1943.

Lipset, Seymour Martin. *Political Man: The Social Bases of Politics*. Garden City, N.Y.: Anchor Books, 1963.

———. "Radicalism or Reformism: The Sources of Working-Class Politics." *American Political Science Review* 77 (March 1983): 1–18.

———. "Why No Socialism in the United States?" In *Radicalism in the Contemporary Age,* vol. 1 of *Sources of Contemporary Radicalism,* edited by Seweryn Bialer and Sophia Sluzar, pp. 31–149. Boulder: Westview Press, 1977.

Lipset, Seymour Martin, Martin A. Trow, and James S. Coleman. *Union Democracy: The Internal Politics of the International Typographical Union.* New York: Free Press, 1956.

Lipsitz, George. *Class and Culture in Cold War America: "A Rainbow at Midnight."* South Hadley, Mass.: J. F. Bergin, 1982.

"Longshore Labor Conditions in the United States—Part I." *Monthly Labor Review* 31 (October 1930): 1–20.

Lowi, Theodore J. "Why Is There No Socialism in the United States? A Federal Analysis." *International Political Science Review* 5, no. 4 (1984): 369–380.

Lucy, George E. "Group Employer-Employee Industrial Relations in the San Francisco Maritime Industry, 1888–1947." Ph.D. dissertation, St. Louis University, 1948.

Lynd, Staughton. "The Possibility of Radicalism in the Early 1930s: The Case of Steel." *Radical America* 6 (November–December 1972): 37–64.

Mabon, David W. "The West Coast Waterfront and Sympathy Strikes of 1934." Ph.D. dissertation, University of California, Berkeley, 1966.

McAdam, Doug. "Tactical Innovation and the Pace of Insurgency." *American Sociological Review* 48 (December 1983): 735–754.

McDonnell, Lawrence T. "'You Are Too Sentimental': Problems and Suggestions for a New Labor History." *Journal of Social History* 17 (Summer 1984): 629–654.

Mann, Michael. *Consciousness and Action Among the Western Working Class.* London: Macmillan, 1977.

Mannheim, Karl. "The Problem of Generations." In *The New Pilgrims: Youth Protest in Transition,* edited by Philip G. Altbach and Robert S. Laufer, pp. 101–138. New York: David McKay, 1972.

Marony, James C. "The International Longshoremen's Association in the Gulf States During the Progressive Era." *Southern Studies* 16, no. 2 (1977): 225–232.

Marx, Karl. "American Pauperism and the Working Class." In *On America and the Civil War,* vol. 2 of *The Karl Marx Library,* edited by Saul K. Padover, pp. 7–8. New York: McGraw-Hill, 1972.

———. "The Possibility of Non-Violent Revolution." In *The Marx-Engels Reader,* 2d ed., edited by Robert C. Tucker, pp. 522–524. New York: W. W. Norton, 1978.

Matles, James J., and James Higgins. *Them and Us: Struggles of a Rank and File Union.* Boston: Beacon Press, 1974.

Mears, Eliot Grinnell. *Maritime Trade of the Western United States.* Stanford: Stanford University Press, 1935.

Mettee, Grace. "Zero Hour on the Coast." *The Nation* 139 (July 25, 1934): 102.

Michels, Robert. *Political Parties: A Sociological Study of the Oligarchical Tendencies of Modern Democracy.* New York: Free Press, 1962.

Miller, Raymond Charles. "The Dockworker Subculture and Some Problems in Cross-Cultural and Cross-Time Generalizations." *Comparative Studies in Society and History* 11 (June 1969): 302–314.

Mills, C. Wright. *The Sociological Imagination.* New York: Oxford University Press, 1954.

Mills, Herb. "The San Francisco Waterfront: The Social Consequences of Industrial Modernization." *Urban Life* 5 (July 1976): 221–250.

Mills, Herb, and David Wellman. "Contractually Sanctioned Job Action and Workers' Control: The Case of San Francisco Longshoremen." *Labor History* 28 (Spring 1987): 167–195.

Milton, David. "Class Struggle American Style." *Political Power and Social Theory* 4 (1984): 263–269.

Mintz, Beth, and Michael Schwartz. *The Power Structure of American Business.* Chicago: University of Chicago Press, 1985.

Montgomery, David. *The Fall of the House of Labor: The Workplace, the State, and American Labor Activism, 1865–1925.* Cambridge: Cambridge University Press, 1987.

———. "Spontaneity and Organization: Some Comments." *Radical America* 7 (November–December 1973): 70–80.

———. *Workers' Control in America: Studies in the History of Work, Technology, and Labor Struggles.* Cambridge: Cambridge University Press, 1979.

Moody's Manual of Investments. American and Foreign Industrial Securities. New York: Moody's Investors Service, 1931.

Moore, Wilbert. "Sociological Aspects of American Socialist Theory and Practice." In *Socialism and American Life,* edited by Donald Drew Egbert and Stow Persons, vol. 1, pp. 523–556. Princeton: Princeton University Press, 1952.

Morris, Aldon D. *The Origins of the Civil Rights Movement: Black Communities Organizing for Change.* New York: Free Press, 1984.

Morris, George. *A Tale of Two Waterfronts.* New York, 1953.

National Adjustment Commission. *Longshore Labor: An Investigation in Hours, Earnings, Labor Cost, and Output in the Longshore Indus-*

try in the Port of New York. New York: National Adjustment Commission, 1920.

Nelli, Humbert. "The Italian Padrone System in the United States." *Labor History* 5 (Spring 1964): 153–167.

Nelson, [Joseph] Bruce. "Maritime Unionism and Working-Class Consciousness in the 1930s." Ph.D. dissertation, University of California, Berkeley, 1982.

———. "'Pentecost' on the Pacific: Maritime Workers and Working-Class Consciousness in the 1930s." *Political Power and Social Theory* 4 (1984): 141–182.

———. "Unions and the Popular Front: The West Coast Waterfront in the 1930s." *International Labor and Working-Class History* 30 (Fall 1986): 59–78.

Nelson, Joel I., and Robert Grams. "Union Militancy and Occupational Communities." *Industrial Relations* 17 (October 1978): 342–346.

Nelson, Steve, James R. Barrett, and Rob Ruck. *Steve Nelson: American Radical.* Pittsburgh: University of Pittsburgh Press, 1981.

Neuberger, Richard L. "Bad-Man Bridges." *Forum* 101 (April 1939): 195–199.

———. "Labor's Overlords." *American Magazine* 125 (March 1938): 16ff.

New York. *Record of the Public Hearings Held by Governor Thomas E. Dewey on the Recommendations of the New York State Crime Commission for Remedying Conditions on the Waterfront of the Port of New York.* June 8, 9, 1953.

Northrup, Herbert R. "The New Orleans Longshoremen." *Political Science Quarterly* 57 (December 1942): 526–544.

O'Brien, F. S. "The 'Communist-Dominated' Unions in the United States Since 1950." *Labor History* 9 (Spring 1968): 184–209.

O'Connor, Harvey. *Revolution in Seattle: A Memoir.* New York: Monthly Review Press, 1964.

O'Connor, James. *The Fiscal Crisis of the State.* New York: St. Martin's Press, 1973.

Ogg, Elizabeth. *Longshoremen and Their Homes.* New York: Greenwich, 1939.

Olson, Mancur, Jr. *The Logic of Collective Action: Public Goods and the Theory of Groups.* Cambridge: Harvard University Press, 1965.

Overholt, William. "Sources of Radicalism and Revolution: A Survey of the Literature." In *Radicalism in the Contemporary Age,* vol. 1 of *Sources of Contemporary Radicalism,* edited by Seweryn Bialer and Sophia Sluzar, pp. 293–335. Boulder: Westview Press, 1977.

Ozanne, Robert W. "The Effects of Communist Leadership on American Trade Unions." Ph.D. dissertation, University of Wisconsin, 1954.

Pacific American Shipowners. *White Paper: West Coast Maritime Strike.* San Francisco: Waterfront Employers' Association of California, 1948.

Palmer, Donald, Roger Friedland, and Jitendra V. Singh. "The Ties That Bind: Organizational and Class Bases of Stability in a Corporate Interlock Network." *American Sociological Review* 51 (December 1986): 781–796.

Palmer, Dwight L. "Pacific Coast Maritime Labor." Ph.D. dissertation, Stanford University, 1935.

Parker, Carlton H. *The Casual Laborer and Other Essays.* Seattle: University of Washington Press, 1972. Originally published in 1920.

Pelling, Henry. *American Labor.* Chicago: University of Chicago Press, 1960.

Perlman, Selig. *A Theory of the Labor Movement.* New York: Augustus M. Kelley, 1949. Originally published in 1928.

Perry, Louis B., and Richard S. Perry. *A History of the Los Angeles Labor Movement, 1911–1941.* Berkeley and Los Angeles: University of California Press, 1963.

Petras, James, and Maurice Zeitlin. "Miners and Agrarian Radicalism." *American Sociological Review* 32 (August 1967): 578–586.

Phillips, Almarin. "A Theory of Interfirm Organization." In *Interorganizational Relations,* edited by William M. Evan, pp. 17–26. Philadelphia: University of Pennsylvania Press, 1978.

Pilcher, William W. *The Portland Longshoremen: A Dispersed Urban Community.* New York: Holt, Rinehart & Winston, 1972.

Piven, Frances Fox, and Richard A. Cloward. *Poor People's Movements: Why They Succeed, How They Fail.* New York: Vintage Books, 1979.

Preis, Art. *Labor's Giant Step: Twenty Years of the CIO.* New York: Pathfinder Press, 1964.

Preston, William, Jr. *Aliens and Dissenters: Federal Suppression of Radicals, 1903–1933.* Cambridge: Harvard University Press, 1963.

Prickett, James R. "Anti-Communism and Labor History." *Industrial Relations* 13 (October 1974): 219–227.

———. "Communism and Factionalism in the United Automobile Workers, 1939–1947." *Science & Society* 32 (Summer 1968): 257–277.

———. "Communists and the Communist Issue in the American Labor Movement, 1920–1950." Ph.D. dissertation, University of California, Los Angeles, 1975.

———. "New Perspectives on American Communism and the Labor Movement." *Political Power and Social Theory* 4 (1984): 3–36.

————. "Some Aspects of the Communist Controversy in the CIO." *Science & Society* 33 (Summer–Fall 1969): 299–321.

Przeworski, Adam. "Proletariat into a Class: The Process of Class Formation from Karl Kautsky's *The Class Struggle* to Recent Controversies." *Politics & Society* 7, no. 4 (1977): 343–401.

Quin, Mike [Paul Ryan]. *The Big Strike.* New York: International Publishers, 1979. Originally published in 1949.

Radius, Walter A. *United States Shipping in Transpacific Trade, 1922–1938.* Stanford: Stanford University Press, 1944.

Radosh, Ronald. "The Corporate Ideology of American Labor Leaders from Gompers to Hillman." *Studies on the Left* 6 (November–December 1966): 66–88.

Randolph, Robert E. "History of the International Longshoremen's and Warehousemen's Union." M.A. thesis, University of California, Berkeley, 1952.

Rank and File Committee (New York ILA). *This Is Our Story.* New York, 1945.

Ratcliff, Richard E. "Introduction." *Research in Social Movements, Conflicts, and Change* 6 (1984): ix–xv.

Ratcliff, Richard E., and David Jaffe. "Capitalists vs. Unions: An Analysis of Anti-Union Political Mobilization Among Business Leaders." *Research in Social Movements, Conflicts, and Change* 4 (1981): 95–121.

Record, Jane Cassels. "The Rise and Fall of a Maritime Union." *Industrial and Labor Relations Review* 10 (October 1956): 81–92.

Resner, Herbert. "The Law in Action During the San Francisco Longshore and Maritime Strike of 1934." Works Progress Administration Project, Alameda County, California, 1936. Typescript.

Rosenbaum, Edward. "The Expulsion of the International Longshoremen's Association from the American Federation of Labor." Ph.D. dissertation, University of Wisconsin, 1954.

Rosenblatt, Maurice. "Joe Ryan and His Kingdom." *The Nation* 161 (November 24, 1945): 548–550.

————. "The Scandal of the Waterfront." *The Nation* 161 (November 17, 1945): 516–519.

Ross, Arthur Max. *Trade Union Wage Policy.* Berkeley and Los Angeles: University of California Press, 1948.

Ross, Philip. "Distribution of Power Within the ILWU and the ILA." *Monthly Labor Review* 91 (January 1968): 1–7.

Rubin, Lester. *The Negro in the Longshore Industry.* Philadelphia: Industrial Research Unit, The Wharton School, University of Pennsylvania, 1974.

Rueschemeyer, Dietrich. "Theoretical Generalization and Historical Particularity in the Comparative Sociology of Reinhard Bendix." In *Vision and Method in Historical Sociology,* edited by Theda Skocpol, pp. 129–169. Cambridge: Cambridge University Press, 1984.

Russell, Maud. *Men Along the Shore.* New York: Brussel & Brussel, 1966.

Sabel, Charles F. *Work and Politics: The Division of Labor in Industry.* Cambridge: Cambridge University Press, 1982.

Saposs, David J. *Communism in American Unions.* New York: McGraw-Hill, 1959.

———. *Left Wing Unionism.* New York: International Publishers, 1926.

Schatz, Ronald. *The Electrical Workers: A History of Labor at General Electric and Westinghouse, 1923–1960.* Urbana: University of Illinois Press, 1983.

Schneider, Betty V. H., and Abraham Siegel. *Industrial Relations in the Pacific Coast Longshore Industry.* Berkeley: Institute of Industrial Relations, University of California, 1956.

Schneiderman, William. *The Pacific Coast Maritime Strike.* San Francisco: Western Worker Publishers, 1937.

Schulberg, Budd. "Joe Docks, Forgotten Man of the Waterfront." *New York Times Magazine,* December 28, 1952, pp. 28–30.

Schwartz, Harvey. "Harry Bridges and the Scholars: Looking at History's Verdict." *California History* 59 (Spring 1980): 66–78.

———. "A Union Combats Racism: The ILWU's Japanese-American 'Stockton Incident' of 1945." *Southern California Quarterly* 62 (Summer 1980): 161–176.

———. "Union Expansion and Labor Solidarity: Longshoremen, Warehousemen, and Teamsters, 1933–1937." *New Labor Review* 2 (Fall 1978): 6–21.

Segal, Martin. "Union Wage Impact and Market Structure." *Quarterly Journal of Economics* 78 (February 1964): 96–114.

Seidman, Joel. *American Labor from Defense to Reconversion.* Chicago: University of Chicago Press, 1953.

Selznick, Philip. *The Organizational Weapon: A Study of Bolshevik Strategy and Tactics.* Glencoe, Ill.: Free Press, 1960.

Sewell, William, Jr. "Classes and Their Historical Formation: Critical Reflections on E. P. Thompson's Theory of Working-Class Formation." In *E. P. Thompson: Critical Debates,* edited by Harvey J. Kaye and Keith McClelland. Oxford: Basil Blackwell, forthcoming.

Shalev, Michael, and Walter Korpi. "Working Class Mobilization and American Exceptionalism." *Economic and Industrial Democracy* 1 (February 1980): 31–61.

Shannon, David A. *The Decline of American Communism: A History of the Communist Party of the United States Since 1945.* New York: Harcourt, Brace, 1959.

Shannon, William V. *The American Irish.* London: Macmillan, 1966.

Shields, Art. "The San Pedro Strike." *Industrial Pioneer* 1 (June 1923): 14–18.

Shorter, Edward, and Charles Tilly. *Strikes in France, 1830–1968.* Cambridge: Cambridge University Press, 1974.

Simon, Hal. "The Rank and File Strike of the New York Longshoremen." *Political Affairs* 24 (December 1945): 1088–1096.

Smith, Darrell Hevenor, and Paul V. Betters. *The United States Shipping Board: Its History, Activities, and Organization.* Washington, D.C.: Brookings Institution, 1931.

Sombart, Werner. *Why Is There No Socialism in the United States?* Edited by C. T. Husbands; translated by Patricia M. Hocking and C. T. Husbands. White Plains, N.Y.: International Arts and Sciences Press, 1976. Originally published in 1906.

Sparks, N. *The Struggle of the Marine Workers.* New York: International Pamphlets, 1930.

Spira, Henry. "The Unambiguity of Labor History." In *Autocracy and Insurgency in Organized Labor,* edited by Burton Hall, pp. 249–254. New Brunswick, N.J.: Transaction Books, 1972.

Squires, Benjamin M. "Associations of Harbor Boat Owners and Employees in the Port of New York." *Monthly Labor Review* 7 (August 1918): 45–62.

———. "The Strike of the Longshoremen at the Port of New York." *Monthly Labor Review* 9 (December 1919): 95–115.

Starobin, Joseph R. *American Communism in Crisis, 1943–1957.* Berkeley and Los Angeles: University of California Press, 1972.

Stepan-Norris, Judith. "The War Labor Board: The Political Conformity and Bureaucratization of Organized Labor." In *How Mighty a Force? Studies of Workers' Consciousness and Organization in the United States,* edited by Maurice Zeitlin, pp. 198–230. Los Angeles: Institute of Industrial Relations, University of California, 1983.

Stephens, John D. *The Transition from Capitalism to Socialism.* Urbana: University of Illinois Press, 1979.

Swados, Felice. "Waterfront." *New Republic* 93 (February 2, 1938): 362.

Szymanski, Albert. *The Capitalist State and the Politics of Class.* Cambridge, Mass.: Winthrop, 1977.

Taft, Philip. *Corruption and Racketeering in the Labor Movement.* Bulletin no. 38. Ithaca: New York State School of Industrial and Labor Relations, Cornell University, 1970.

————. "Ideologies and Industrial Conflict." In *Industrial Conflict*, edited by Arthur Kornhauser, Robert Dubin, and Arthur M. Ross, pp. 257–265. New York: McGraw-Hill, 1954.

————. "Theories of the Labor Movement." In *Interpreting the Labor Movement*, Industrial Relations Research Association, Publication no. 9, pp. 1–38. Champaign, Ill.: Industrial Relations Research Association, 1952.

Taylor, Paul S., and Norman Leon Gold. "San Francisco and the General Strike." *Survey Graphic* 23 (September 1934): 405–411.

Thomas, C. *West Coast Longshoremen and the "Bridges Plan."* 1943. Pamphlet.

Thompson, David E. "The ILWU as a Force for Interracial Unity in Hawaii." *Social Processes in Hawaii* 15 (1951): 32–43.

Thompson, E. P. *The Making of the English Working Class*. New York: Vintage Books, 1963.

Tilly, Charles. *From Mobilization to Revolution*. Reading, Mass.: Addison-Wesley, 1978.

Trimble, Peter. "Thought Control on the Waterfront." *The Nation* 173 (July 14, 1951): 27–29.

United States Bureau of the Census. *Population 1910. Thirteenth Census of the United States*. Vol. 4. Washington, D.C.: Government Printing Office, 1914.

————. *Population 1920. Fourteenth Census of the United States*. Vol. 4. Washington, D.C.: Government Printing Office, 1923.

United States Congress. Senate. Committee on the Judiciary. Hearings Before the Subcommittee to Investigate the Administration of the Internal Security Act and Other Internal Security Laws. *Scope of Soviet Activity in the United States, Communism on the Waterfront*. 84th Cong., 2d sess., June 21 and July 12, 1956. Pt. 30.

United States Congress. Senate. Subcommittee of the Committee on Education and Labor. *Hearings on Violations of Free Speech and Rights of Labor*. 76th Cong., 2d sess., December 16, 18, 1939.

————. *Hearings on Violations of Free Speech and Rights of Labor*. 78th Cong., 1st sess., 1943. S. Rept. 398, pt. 1.

United States Congress. Senate. Subcommittee on War Mobilization of the Committee on Military Affairs. *Mobilization of Shipping Resources*. 78th Cong., 1st sess., October 7, 1943. S. Rept. 3.

United States Department of Commerce, Bureau of Foreign and Domestic Commerce. *Statistical Abstract of the United States, 1932*. Washington, D.C.: Government Printing Office, 1932.

United States Department of Labor. *Official Report of Proceedings Before the Immigration and Naturalization Service of the Department of*

Labor. Docket no. 55073/217. In the Matter of Harry Bridges, Deportation Hearing. 1939. Typescript (trial transcript), International Longshoremen's and Warehousemen's Union Library, San Francisco.

United States Department of Labor, Bureau of Labor Statistics. *Handbook of Labor Statistics.* 1947 ed. Bulletin no. 916. Washington, D.C.: Government Printing Office, 1948.

United States District Court, Northern District of California, Southern Division. Case no. 32117-H. *United States vs. Harry Renton Bridges, Henry Schmidt, and J. R. Robertson.* 1950. Typescript (trial transcript), International Longshoremen's and Warehousemen's Union Library, San Francisco.

United States Office of the Federal Coordinator of Transportation. *Hours, Wages, and Working Conditions in Domestic Water Transportation.* Vol. 1. Washington, D.C.: Government Printing Office, 1936.

United States Shipping Board, Bureau of Research, Maritime Records Division. *United States Water Borne Traffic by Port of Origin and Destination and Principal Commodities.* Washington, D.C.: Government Printing Office, 1930.

Useem, Michael. "Business and Politics in the United States and United Kingdom: The Origins of Heightened Political Activity of Large Corporations During the 1970s and Early 1980s." *Theory and Society* 12 (March 1983): 281–300.

Vecoli, Rudolph J. "Contadini in Chicago: A Critique of the Uprooted." In *Many Pasts: Readings in American Social History, 1865–the Present,* edited by Herbert G. Gutman and Gregory S. Kealy, vol. 2, pp. 164–194. Englewood Cliffs, N.J.: Prentice-Hall, 1973.

Vorse, Mary Heaton. "The Pirates Nest of New York." *Harpers Magazine* 204 (April 1952): 27–35.

Waltzer, Kenneth. "The New History of American Communism." *Reviews in American History* 11 (June 1983): 259–267.

Ward, Estolv. *Harry Bridges on Trial.* New York: Modern Age Books, 1940.

Waring, William Davis. "Harry Renton Bridges and the International Longshoremen's and Warehousemen's Union." M.A. thesis, University of Washington, 1966.

Weber, Max. *Economy and Society.* Edited by Guenther Roth and Claus Wittich. Berkeley and Los Angeles: University of California Press, 1968.

———. *The Methodology of the Social Sciences.* New York: Free Press, 1949.

Weinstein, James. *The Corporate Ideal in the Liberal State: 1900–1918.* Boston: Beacon Press, 1968.

Weintraub, Hyman. "The I.W.W. in California, 1905–1931." M.A. thesis, University of California, Los Angeles, 1947.

Weir, Stanley. "American Labor on the Defensive: A 1940s Odyssey." *Radical America* 9 (July–August 1975): 163–185.

———. "The ILWU: A Case Study in Bureaucracy." In *Autocracy and Insurgency in Organized Labor,* edited by Burton Hall, pp. 80–92. New Brunswick, N.J.: Transaction Books, 1972.

———. *Informal Workers' Control: The West Coast Longshoremen.* Reprint series no. 247. Urbana-Champaign: Institute of Industrial Relations, University of Illinois, 1975.

———. "U.S.A.: The Labor Revolt." In *American Society Inc.: Studies of the Social Structure and Political Economy of the United States,* 2d ed., edited by Maurice Zeitlin, pp. 487–524. Chicago: Rand McNally, 1977.

West, James. "Communists in World War II." *Political Affairs* 48 (September–October 1969): 91–103.

Wilentz, Sean. "Against Exceptionalism: Class Consciousness and the American Labor Movement, 1790–1920." *International Labor and Working-Class History* 26 (Fall 1984): 1–24.

Williams, William Appleman. *The Contours of American History.* Chicago: Quadrangle Books, 1966.

Winstead, Ralph. "Enter a Logger: An I.W.W. Reply to the Four L's." *Survey* 44 (July 3, 1920): 474–477.

Zalburg, Sanford. *A Spark Is Struck: Jack Hall and the ILWU in Hawaii.* Honolulu: University of Hawaii Press, 1979.

Zeitlin, Maurice. "On Classes, Class Conflict, and the State: An Introductory Note." In *Classes, Class Conflict, and the State: Empirical Studies in Class Analysis,* edited by Maurice Zeitlin, pp. 1–37. Cambridge, Mass.: Winthrop, 1980.

———. "Political Generations in the Cuban Working Class." *American Journal of Sociology* 71 (March 1966): 493–508.

———. *Revolutionary Politics and the Cuban Working Class.* Princeton: Princeton University Press, 1967.

Zieger, Robert H. *American Workers, American Unions, 1920–1985.* Baltimore: Johns Hopkins University Press, 1986.

Zolberg, Aristide R. "How Many Exceptionalisms?" In *Working-Class Formation: Nineteenth-Century Patterns in Western Europe and the United States,* edited by Ira Katznelson and Aristide R. Zolberg, pp. 397–455. Princeton: Princeton University Press, 1986.

Archival Sources

Army Service Forces. Papers. Record Group 160. National Archives, Washington, D.C.

Beck, Broussais. Papers on Industrial Espionage. Suzzallo Library, University of Washington, Seattle.

Bell, Daniel. Papers. Tamiment Institute, New York University.

Brandwen, Maxwell. Papers. Record Group 248. National Archives, Washington, D.C.

Browder, Earl. Papers. University Research Library, University of California, Los Angeles. Microfilm.

Industrial Workers of the World. Papers. Archives of Labor and Urban Affairs, Wayne State University, Detroit, Michigan.

International Longshoremen's and Warehousemen's Union. Papers. International Longshoremen's and Warehousemen's Union Library, San Francisco.

Murnane, Francis. Papers. Oregon Historical Society, Portland, Oregon.

Northwest Waterfront Employers Union. Papers. International Longshoremen's and Warehousemen's Union Library, San Francisco.

Pacific Maritime Association. Papers. Pacific Maritime Association, San Francisco.

United States Maritime Commission. Papers. Record Group 157. National Archives, Washington, D.C.

United States Shipping Board. Papers. Record Group 32. National Archives, Washington, D.C.

War Production Board. Papers. Record Group 179. National Archives, Washington, D.C.

War Shipping Administration. Papers. Record Group 248. National Archives, Washington, D.C.

Waterfront Employers' Association. Papers. Pacific Maritime Association, San Francisco.

Xavier Institute of Industrial Relations. Papers. Xavier Institute of Industrial Relations, New York.

Oral Histories

Bailey, Bill. Interview with author. San Francisco, September 15, 1981. Tape recording.

Baylin, Meyer. Interview with author. Mill Valley, California, January 23, 1984. Tape recording.

Berenson, Mitchell. Interview with author. Chappaqua, New York, May 8, 1986.

Brown, Archie. Interviews with author. San Francisco, September 12, 1981, and September 7, 1982. Tape recordings.

Bulcke, Germain. Interview with author. San Francisco, September 4, 1981. Tape recording.

Carey, Reverend Philip. Interview with author. New York, October 6, 1981. Tape recording.

Connolly, Tom. Interview with author. New York, October 18, 1981. Tape recording.

Craycraft, Rosco. Interview with author. Seattle, Washington, December 16, 1981. Tape recording.

Darcy, Sam. Interview with author. Fort Lauderdale, Florida, May 10, 1986. Tape recording.

Dwyer, Johnnie. Interview with Debra Bernhardt. November 21, 1980. Immigrant Labor History Collection, Tamiment Institute, New York University. Tape recording.

Franklin, Odell. Interview with author. Berkeley, California, January 23, 1984. Tape recording.

Hagen, Bill, and Larry Sullivan. Interview with author. New York, October 1981.

Hagen, Oscar. Interview with author. San Pedro, California, June 2, 1982. Tape recording.

Halling, Bjourne. Interview with Herb Mills and David Wellman. Grass Valley, California, October 16 and 17, 1979. Transcript.

Harer, Asher. Interview with author. San Francisco, May 25, 1982. Tape recording.

Jones, Ben B. Interview with author. Mill Valley, California, January 26, 1984.

Langley, Al. Interview with author. San Pedro, California, February 4, 1982. Tape recording.

Longhi, Vincent "Jim." Interview with author. New York, May 7, 1986. Tape recording.

Madell, Sam. Interviews with author. New York, October 6, 1981, and May 6, 1986. Tape recordings.

Mevert, Elmer. Interview with author. San Pedro, California, June 2, 1982. Tape recording.

Mills, Herb. Interview with author. San Francisco, September 4, 1981.

Morris, George. Interview with author. Los Angeles, September 2, 1980. Tape recording.

Mowrey, Jack. Interview with author. Portland, Oregon, December 21, 1981. Tape recording.

Nau, Fred. Interview with Herb Mills and David Wellman. Sausalito, California, November 15, 1979. Tape recording.

Osborne, Seldon. Interview with author. San Francisco, September 11, 1981. Tape recording.

Plant, Thomas G. Interview with Corinne L. Gilb. 1956. Oral History Collection, Social Science Library, University of California, Berkeley. Transcript.

Richardson, Fred. Interview with author. Seattle, Washington, December 18, 1981. Tape recording.

St. Sure, Paul J. Interview with Corinne L. Gilb. 1957. Oral History Collection, Social Science Library, University of California, Berkeley. Transcript.

Schmidt, Henry. Interview with author. Sonoma, California, January 25, 1984. Tape recording.

Stack, Walter. Interview with author. San Francisco, May 28, 1982. Tape recording.

Ware, Paul. Interview with author. Palm Desert, California, January 23, 1982. Tape recording.

Weir, Stanley. Interview with author. San Pedro, California, April 22, 1981. Tape recording.

Werner, Joe. Interviews with author. Portland, Oregon, December 14, 1981, and July 15, 1985. Tape recordings.

Williams, Cleophas. Interview with author. Oakland, California, January 25, 1984. Tape recording.

Yoneda, Karl. Interview with author. San Francisco, January 26, 1984. Tape recording.

Index

Compositor: G & S Typesetters, Inc.
Printer: Braun-Brumfield, Inc.
Binder: Braun-Brumfield, Inc.
Text: 11/13 Sabon
Display: Sabon